PITMAN EDUCATION SERIES
Rychard Fink, GENERAL EDITOR

ACQUISITION OF TYPEWRITING SKILLS
Leonard J. West

ELEMENTARY CURRICULUM: A BOOK OF READINGS
Edited by Robert E. Chasnoff

GROUPING IN THE ELEMENTARY SCHOOL
Edited by Anne Morgenstern

INTELLECTUAL FOUNDATIONS OF AMERICAN EDUCATION
Edited by Harold J. Carter

NEW PERSPECTIVES IN READING INSTRUCTION
Edited by Albert J. Mazurkiewicz

PATTERNS OF POWER: SOCIAL FOUNDATIONS OF EDUCATION
Edited by Thomas Linton and Jack Nelson

SEVEN STORIES FOR GROWTH
Daniel Sugarman and Rolaine Hochstein

TEACHER-PUPIL PLANNING FOR BETTER CLASSROOM LEARNING
Yvonne Waskin and Louise Parrish

TEACHING HISTORY AND THE SOCIAL STUDIES IN SECONDARY SCHOOLS
Gerald Leinwand and Daniel Feins

TEACHING OCCUPATIONAL SKILLS

Louis Cenci *Executive Secretary*

Advisory Board for Vocational and Extension Education
New York City Board of Education

&

Gilbert G. Weaver *Formerly Director*

of Industrial Teacher Training
New York State Department of Education

TEACHING OCCUPATIONAL SKILLS

SECOND EDITION, REVISED AND EXPANDED

Originally published as

APPLIED TEACHING TECHNIQUES

Pitman Publishing Corporation

New York   Toronto   London   Tel Aviv

Copyright © 1960, 1968 by Pitman Publishing Corporation
All Rights Reserved
Library of Congress Catalog Number: 67-12325

Manufactured in the United States of America
2.987654321

(*Originally published as* APPLIED TEACHING TECHNIQUES)

Contents

	Introduction	3
1	How People Learn	7
2	Analyzing Occupations for Teachable Content	17
3	Understanding the Learner	31
4	Projecting and Planning Instruction	42
5	Questioning as an Aid to Communication	69
6	Presenting the Instructional Unit	81
7	Teaching the Group and Instructing the Individual	97
8	Sample Lesson for Study and Critique	107
9	Visual Aids	123
10	Projections and Other Teaching Aids	133
11	Testing as a Means of Evaluation	151
12	Instruction Sheets as Aids to Learning	179
13	Rating Student Performance and Progress	212
14	The Teacher's Role in Guidance	227
15	Other Roles and Responsibilities of Teachers	241
	Bibliography	259
	Index	261

TEACHING OCCUPATIONAL SKILLS

Introduction

Teaching Occupational Skills is a revision of *Applied Teaching Techniques* and reflects the dramatic changes that have taken place in vocational education since the passage of the Vocational Education Act of 1963. The term "occupational education" is becoming more and more popular; in fact, it has replaced the term "vocational education" in many states. The field of occupational training has mushroomed beyond the secondary school into community and junior colleges and into such programs as Manpower Development and Training and the various antipoverty programs. Programs at the secondary school level have been broadened to include occupational training at the less-than-skilled level, and the three-year, four-period sequence of training is no longer found in all schools.

Occupational preparation still starts at the secondary level, however, and regardless of time and structure still requires effective teaching. Occupational education at the secondary level, offered in the unit trade school, the multi-trade school, the comprehensive high school, or in the area center, is the second step in a continuum of occupational training and retraining. It is an integral part of the concept of a lifetime of learning. The first step in the continuum, of course, is in the industrial arts which are being offered in the earlier grades.

Teachers of occupational skills must do more than teach occupational skills, techniques, and processes. They should be valuable resource personnel for vocational guidance and should have continuous contact with the world of work as it changes and new skills and new jobs evolve. The teacher as well as the student must continually learn. While learning to be an effective teacher takes years of training and experience, *Teaching Occupational Skills* can help new teachers avoid wasting time and energy in this training. It can help new teachers organize their work and overcome many frustrations that result from lack of experience. Although this text cannot describe every situation encountered in the teaching environment, it attempts to include techniques, methods, and teaching skills, with explanations and examples as a basis for further development.

Teaching Occupational Skills has been written for teachers of occupational skills at all levels, ranging from industrial arts in secondary schools to the community colleges. Although different age groups will require different levels of presentation, the basic skills of effective and creative teaching are quite similiar and require only a change of emphasis.

There are three areas in which effective teachers must be competent: occupational or subject mastery, teaching skill, and teaching personality.

Teachers are considered to be experts in their fields and should have a high degree of skill and competency in the occupational and subject areas they are to teach. It is assumed that potential teachers have acquired a mastery of their fields before entering the teaching profession. This is a practical book written for the person who wants to know how to teach his occupational skills and information in the best possible way. It is based on a firm belief that teaching is an art. Successful teaching is not accidental—it is a dynamic process that requires conscious effort by the teacher. It is based on the following teacher activities:

1. Careful occupational analysis by the teacher of all the skills and information of the subject.
2. Organization of that material into the best possible learning order.
3. Planning of each lesson, as well as the work of the whole term or course.
4. The utilization of all the aids of learning and all the methods of teaching for effective variety.
5. Development of a democratic atmosphere conducive to a high degree of morale and teacher-learner rapport, based on a feeling of mutual respect, responsibility, and confidence.
6. Achievement of maximum communication between teacher and learner.

Few professions involve personal relationships to the extent that teaching does. Teachers must recognize the worth and the potential of each individual and, through insight and understanding, develop the spirit of cooperation that is so important to learning. Teachers of occupational subjects have a rare opportunity to develop this relationship through which good future craftsmen and citizens are produced.

In recognizing the importance of developing students' abilities and of helping them in their aspirations, teachers of occupational skills should be concerned with the most effective methods of teaching occupational skills and, in addition, with teaching learners how to learn. It is when people learn how to learn that they develop and become truly successful. There are three major paths for students in occupational courses to follow: They may enter employment after graduating or leaving school; they may continue training in apprenticeship or other types of programs; or they may go on to higher education. Teachers should attempt to structure their courses to include preparation for all of these three possibilities. The most satisfying rewards that teachers enjoy come from the successes and progress of students whom they have helped to prepare for life's experiences.

The material in this book is based on sound and accepted psychological principles of learning. Although many principles of psychology are recognized and discussed, no attempt has been made to elaborate upon them. A course in educational psychology is recommended as a means of enhancing the value of this textbook, as well as broadening the student teacher's background. The authors wish to point out that the same is true of other areas in teacher training. Teachers should never stop learning.

The transfer of occupational skills and information from one generation to another is a vital function of any educational program. It is to teachers at all levels of occupational and technical instruction that this book is presented.

How People Learn

When a mother holds her baby's hands while the baby attempts his first faltering steps, she is teaching. When a father shows his son how to grip a baseball bat correctly, he is teaching. When you took your first job and someone "showed you the ropes" and "broke you in," that was teaching. When you take your first teaching job and another teacher instructs you in the procedures of the school, that, too, is teaching. In its simplest form, teaching is helping others to learn. In all the examples cited the teaching was on a nonprofessional basis. It is like the friendly advice to take an aspirin when you do not feel well, or the assistance one might receive from a well-meaning friend in drawing up a legal document.

The teaching was, in all these cases, spontaneous, unplanned, and often included inaccurate as well as accurate facts. To the professional teacher, then, teaching is not only helping others to learn, but it includes planning and organizing, using accepted methods, and capitalizing on recognized principles of learning and teaching. We learn much in life which is valuable, and we also learn other things which add little to our growth and progess. Teaching, as referred to in this text, implies the instruction of essential skills, related information, and attitudes necessary to the student for his success in the occupational area of his choice, as well as in worthy citizenship.

Successful teaching calls for imagination, creativity, and ingenuity on the part of the instructor in the application of his professional training. Teaching is a dynamic art: It must meet the needs of the times, keep up with change, and very often must anticipate future requirements. The alert, interested teacher is always a learner. Today's vocational teacher is not only a technician, but also a highly skilled and trained professional person who should seek continually to improve his methods, his material, and his profession. In this process of growing, learning, and experimenting, the teacher should have one guiding criterion: "Is the student benefiting from my own improvement?"

A machine can be repaired, altered, or replaced. It can be stored for future use, painted, or discarded. It is inanimate, has no soul, and knows no emotion. It will never vote, earn a living, or raise a family, and its only claim to fame may be that it makes more pieces at less cost than another machine. That is not true of a person.

The time we spend with a student can never be regained or recaptured. It is irrevocably gone, and the only good we can do is limited by the time we are with that student. The responsibility placed on the teacher to do the most he can for his students in the best way possible is an enormous one. There is no accurate gauge for measuring the extent of the good, bad, or indifferent influences which a teacher has on his students. Shop teaching has as its primary goal the training of youth for gainful employment, with character training as a concomitant goal.

In the industrial arts area, the student is not trained for a specific trade but rather is shown the requirements and opportunities of various vocations, plus the consumer education values which are part of that program. The industrial arts experience is often a guidance factor in the choice of trade training at a later date. Its other great value lies in the educative process of dignifying labor for the benefit of all society. Progress and industrial growth in America were accomplished through hard work and a willingness to labor for the things we need and want. Teachers of industrial arts must be aware of these facts if they hope to be successful representatives of their profession. It probably has become apparent that teaching is many-sided. Our first definition of education, "Helping others to learn," will hold, however, for the things we will talk about in the following pages.

Our primary problem in vocational education is the teaching of an occupation consisting of many manual skills. We are concerned with teaching concrete facts and skills in most cases, along with the theory and information necessary for the mastery of a trade or technical area. If education is the transfer of man's accumulated knowledge through the years from generation to generation, then it is the particular duty of the trade and technical teacher to transfer the hand skills, machine skills, and new electrical and electronic skills to new generations without a loss of craftsmanship or a sacrifice of high-quality work. We may be living in the age of automation or the age of electronics or the atom age—it makes no difference what historians call it—but all man's efforts still spring from his mind and utilization of his hands. Trade and technical training stands in the forefront of man's educational needs. We must learn *how* to teach willing and sometimes clumsy hands to perform new skills peculiar to our occupation, and at the same time to train the mind to direct those hands. Our problem is how to teach these many skills.

Teaching and learning have often been compared to the two sides of the same piece of cloth. In other words, the things that make for good teaching make for good learning. By the same token, those things which help the learner learn should become the tools of teaching.

We have already stated that the learner is the most important factor in teaching from the standpoint of the ultimate aim and accomplishment of the teacher's effort. Let us therefore consider three important principles of learning.

PRINCIPLES OF LEARNING

There are three main principles of learning. They are that people learn best (1) by doing, (2) when there is a need for learning, and (3) when new things are presented in terms of the old.

Although these statements seem self-evident, they need further discussion and explanation since they involve many broad implications for the professional teacher. The theory of learning by doing is not new. It was understood by the educational pioneers of ancient times such as John Comenius, Johann Pestalozzi, Johann Basedow, and Philipp von Fellenburg. The Swedish Sloyd System was also characteristic of this same idea. The theory of training the hand as well as the mind is referred to in Rousseau's *Emile*. This book relates the story of a boy's training and education. The ancient Romans also believed in "doing the thing to be done," because they believed in learning by doing.

The phrase quoted above is the key to learning by doing. It implies that the student must take part in the learning and teaching process. The student not only listens and absorbs, but takes an active part in the lesson as well. To the trade and shop teacher, this means that he does not stop at telling or showing how to do the thing being taught, but having satisfied himself that the learner is ready, encourages and permits the learner to do it. It goes beyond the skills of the trade; it includes all learning. If we are teaching trade mathematics, the student must do a sufficient number of problems to master the subject. If we are teaching trade science, the teacher must find ways and means of having his students apply that science. To hear about something is good; to see the thing is better; to do the thing is best of all. "We learn by doing" means that the student must do something about the thing that is taught, if he is going to learn it well.

The next essential point is that we learn when there is a need for learning. Man is a curious creature; he also has a mind which is capable of thought and discrimination. Youth, especially, always asks "why." This is probably one of youth's greatest assets. Therefore, we should never become annoyed or impatient with the question, "Why, teacher?" We want to know *why* we are doing things. We want reasons, explanations, connections, and correlations. The teacher must recognize this and be prepared to make the best possible use of the student's natural inquisitiveness, or be prepared to create curiosity and need.

The range of needs for knowing is great. The need might be an immediate one, such as needing to learn one step in order to go on to the next one, or it may be a more distant need, such as earning a diploma or obtaining employment. It may be intrinsic or extrinsic and stimulated by the teacher. The teacher should always include good, sound reasons for learning a skill or operation. If there are no reasons, or only weak reasons, then perhaps the teacher should re-evaluate his material and revise it, omitting the nonessentials.

A carpenter can build a house only as well and as rapidly as his tools and knowledge permit him. He cannot use tools he does not own or knowledge he does not possess. A student can only learn with the equipment he has. His equipment consists of a certain amount of manual dexterity, previous education, limited experience, and whatever natural aptitudes and abilities he may possess. Some boys are more nimble with their hands than others, or have profited more from previous schooling; others are apt and quick, some slow and plodding. Some have had part-time work experiences or travel experiences which have taught them much. Environmental and cultural influences are often important factors. It is up to the teacher to know each of his

Learning by doing becomes truly meaningful when student involvement is realistic. In this illustration, brick masonry students are working on a new faculty home.

student's mental and physical assets and liabilities. He must ascertain their reading and mathematics abilities as well as their mechanical abilities.

The teacher would do well to become acquainted with the guidance and health personnel of his school, as they are a source of help and information. He should observe the dexterity of his students before concluding that the biggest boy is the strongest or the smallest boy the most nimble. Health authorities tell us that all the body organs in teen-agers do not mature at the same rates of speed: A boy of sixteen might be a fine ball player, yet clumsy in shop until he trains his muscles to new uses.

The teacher must also get acquainted with the intellectual level of his class. He must neither talk above nor below their level. He must speak their language so that they can easily understand the things being taught. The teacher can, by using analogy, comparison, example, and association and by applying to practical uses and to things already known, use the past experiences of his students to teach the new ones. By rearranging what students already know, the skillful teacher can lead his students to new heights of learning. The teacher is a builder:

He takes the pliable material in the form of a new student and teaches him the refinements, the skills, and the knowledge that are needed for a place in our society. The teacher adds to the student's education, being careful to start at the student's level. There is little sense in assuming what we think the student should know. To be effective, and economical in the long run, we must deal in terms of what the student already knows in order to teach him what he should know.

We have discussed some of the ways in which the student learns. The question which now confronts us is: "Just how does the student learn?" The learning process is the result of a student using his mind to acquire facts, ideas, skills, and principles which are new to him. How does he acquire these things?

A person communicates by means of his five senses. Some senses, of course, are more important than others. In order to show the relationship, we might list the senses and assign percentile values to each. Psychologists differ as to the precise proportions, but generally agree as to the relative order of importance.

THE IMPORTANCE OF THE FIVE SENSES IN LEARNING

Learning occurs through one or more of the five senses. It has been estimated that 75 percent of all learning occurs through the sense of sight, 13 percent through the sense of hearing, 6 percent through the sense of touch, 3 percent through the sense of smell, and 3 percent through the sense of taste. The implications of these figures for the vocational teacher are many. For one thing, the nature of the trade or job, or an operation within the trade or job, well involve one of the lesser-rated senses far more than the figures indicate. In trade teaching, the sense of touch certainly is utilized far more than the 6 percent would indicate. Remember that the values are comparative and serve as a basis for discussion. The teacher must be most expert in:

1. Utilizing those senses that are most important to the student in relation to the specific lesson at hand.
2. Stimulating these senses as often as possible for retention in learning.
3. Utilizing a combination of as many of the senses as possible.

We have all experienced hearing a sentence or word that recalled a song; a phrase that recalled a poem; a familiar scene that recalled an event; a touch that recalled a material; a smell that recalled a process; or a taste that was characteristic of a good or a poor product. When the teacher stimulates a special sense in relation to an operation or other teaching point, he is giving the student an additional key to learning and recalling.

There are practical ways in which the teacher can apply the skills of teaching to sense appeal:

Sight. The teacher may draw, sketch, diagram, demonstrate, show, write; use tools, equipment, and materials. The teacher must be prepared to jobs; use books and have students read, label, color; visit industry and observe industrial processes and machinery.

Hearing. The teacher must speak well, clearly, simply, distinctly, pleasantly, audibly, with change of tone and pitch. He must become skilled in the art of explaining.

Touch. The teacher should see to it that students feel, weigh, handle, and use tools, equipment, and materials. The teacher must be prepared to point out the important factors in the feel of a material or in distinguishing a tool by touch.

Smell. The teacher must associate characteristic odors with trades, processes, and materials, such as the odor of burnt insulation, wood, varnish, oils, plastics, cooking, smoke of welding galvanized material.

Taste. The teacher also must associate characteristic tastes with trades, processes, and materials. In the food trades, taste is of far greater importance than in other trades. However, industrial fumes and by-products of trade processes often give off vapors which leave characteristic acrid tastes.

The teacher must be sure in his shop teaching that all can see, hear, and have adequate opportunity to work with and get the feel of the thing being taught. The senses are used not only in performing operations but, as every tradesman knows, they are used in detecting danger signs. A hot bearing, a grinding gear, a smell of smoldering material, the burnt look, the bitter taste in the air are often warnings of impending breakdown. The teacher can use this approach also in his lessons. The use of more than one sense in teaching is called the multiple sense appeal. Senses are the avenues of communication between teacher and pupil. The teacher should strive to improve constantly his means of communication with his students.

The student uses his mind and his senses in diverse ways in order to learn. Students learn by:

Action. Participating, doing, applying what they have learned by acting upon it. The student may do the job, draw the diagram, practice the skill, perform an experiment.

Observation. Students watch as the teacher performs skillfully the operations of the trade or the techniques of the job. The more observant the student, the more he will learn. The more the teacher stimulates thinking as the students observe, the more they will learn.

Imitation. It is the following of instruction in a step-by-step fashion. Figuratively, it is taking the student by the hand, if necessary, until the student masters the skill or thing that has been taught.

Memory and recall. Students learn by recalling past learning, past experience, and things they have seen, heard about, or done.

Imagination. The ability to picture mentally, visualize, and have abstract conceptions helps students learn. This is often difficult to do, and the teacher must aid the process with sketches, drawings, and explanations.

Reasoning. The ability to reason helps the student solve problems. It enables him to come to conclusions and make comparisons. The teacher should make every effort to help his students to reason why and how jobs or operations are performed.

Repetition. Practice may not make perfect, but it is a very valuable tool of learning. Repetition of the thing learned makes the learning more permanent, leads to greater skill in the operations of an occupation, and by that proficiency instills confidence in the student and enables him to progress.

Because the learner learns in these ways, it is incumbent upon the teacher to become expert in his performance, correct in his information, and accurate in his judgment. He must be attentive also to details which he might otherwise feel are not important, such as dress, speech patterns, personal conduct, and personal ethics.

The teacher should be not only an inspiration to his students but also a person to emulate. He should continuously require of his students an increasingly higher standard of performance and quality of work. Negligence in these factors will turn repetition into busywork, observation into daydreaming, and an otherwise eager mind into one of indolence and disinterest.

Instructors should realize that students at the secondary level of education have been exposed to years of schooling. Nevertheless, it often behooves instructors to constantly stimulate or motivate students to learn. Every opportunity and method to motivate students should be grasped. Devices used range from the display of good student work to the use of charts showing individual student progress in graph form. The teacher should use any device which he deems necessary and most effective in keeping his students interested. The principles of learning and teaching apply to a course, a unit of the course, or to a lesson. Students can and should be encouraged to learn as much as they possibly can.

It would be wonderful if we could turn back the clock and with our present experience become youngsters again. If we could relive our days in high school and sit on the other side of the desk—if we could go back to those times when we were students—we would surely have much about which to advise the teacher. We cannot do that, so let us do the next best thing: try to understand the learner, understand his problems, and realize his possibilities and limitations. We should stimulate him, guide him, and help him utilize all his faculties. This will lead to more effective teaching.

Summary

"Learning starts with what the learner knows, not with what the teacher knows."

Teaching is essentially helping others to learn. We are as teachers, however, professional people who make the best use of the psychological principles of learning as well as the accepted experiences of leaders of education over the years. As professional teachers, we should realize the grave responsibility teaching imposes upon us, especially since our students are, for the most part, teen-agers. Learning is work; it is our task to make it as pleasant and as meaningful as possible.

We must recognize the part other branches of education play in the total process of learning. The teacher must be aware of the influence he wields over his students. He must learn and remember the principles of learning, the importance of the five senses in learning, and the ways in which the student learns. He must constantly seek the best and most effective means of teaching an occupation, be it industrial or technical in nature.

Questions and Projects

1. Teaching is difficult work and requires time for planning and preparing. Why is it considered economical, nevertheless, to plan?
2. Make a list of the traits or characteristics which a person should develop in order to become a good teacher.
3. Develop a list of reasons why teachers in different subject areas should learn something about each other's work.
4. Discuss the statement, "Teaching and learning principles are like two sides of the same piece of cloth."

5. List as many operations, skills, or processes of an occupation as you can which involve the special use of one or more of the senses.
6. Recall and briefly describe several learning situations in your experience which utilized the principles of learning discussed in this chapter.
7. Which skills of an occupation might best be learned by each of the following: action, repetition, observation, imitation, memory and recall, imagination, and reasoning?
8. Why is it wise for anyone, especially teachers, to be constant learners?

Analyzing Occupations for Teachable Content

Few teachers of occupational and technical skills are really aware of the tremendous amount of information they possess about their individual specialty. The skilled craftsman or technician performs the operations of his occupation almost automatically. He seldom gives much thought to either the manual skill or the underlying theory involved in his work. There are two good reasons for this situation. In the first place, he is so familiar with the manual skills of the occupation that his hands move without conscious direction; second, he has no need to explain his actions to anyone—his main concern is in getting the job done.

To illustrate the point, let us consider a conversation which is familiar to most teachers of occupational subjects. A teacher of many years' experience was talking to a group of new teachers. He was recalling his experiences as an instructor in order to help the new teachers get the proper start. He said, "I remember the first day I faced a class. I had made many mental notes on what I was going to teach. In addition, I had written a list of topics I expected to discuss. Well, I talked for almost an hour and a half. I must have done an outstanding job that day because I taught the entire occupation in one class session." The new teachers looked at each other and then burst out laughing. Something similar had happened to each of them.

There is a dual problem which all teachers must face and solve. Teachers must know how to teach and what to teach. The only way to determine what to teach is to make a careful and exhaustive analysis of the occupational area to be taught. In a majority of vocational teacher training programs, a course in occupational analysis is a required subject. It is not the purpose of this text to delve deeply into the subject of analysis. However, we must discuss the analysis technique in order to use the methods to be explained in the succeeding section of this book. To help the reader comprehend and derive the most benefit from the text, the authors suggest that you relate the recommended material and devices to real situations in your specific area of interest.

It is a basic requirement for successful and effective teaching that the program be planned. Intelligent and analytical forethought can avoid waste of time, effort, and material on the part of the students, and also discouragement for the instructor. Advance planning should be applied to:

1. The scope of the course.
2. The required work for the school term and year.
3. The weekly schedule.
4. The content of each unit of instruction.
5. The individual lesson plan.

Preliminary planning calls for the skillful application of analysis of occupational content and student needs, as well as application of sound teaching principles.

AIMS AND OBJECTIVES OF OCCUPATIONAL ANALYSIS

To chart a course well, we must know what we hope to accomplish. Occupational analysis should not be done haphazardly, but should be organized according to a clear definition of aims and objectives based on certain sound educational procedures. Analyzing an occupation has as its goal the development of a complete course of study for the purpose of teaching the occupation in its entirety. Casual learning of an occupation takes place when a person works in an unorganized program in various areas of a given occupation. This is the way some craftsmen and technicians "pick up" the occupational skills. This kind of informal training is at best haphazard and often leaves large gaps in the acquisition of the manual skills, particularly in the related information of the occupation.

The professional instructor, by formalizing his course of instruction through the medium of careful occupational analysis, seeks to include all the necessary skills and information needed for success in the occupation. Few skilled craftsmen and technicians are aware of the fact that teaching their crafts is one of the best ways of learning more about them. Making a thorough analysis will greatly benefit the instructor. Once the analysis is made as completely as possible, the instructor will have a vast store of organized material to use when called upon to teach the content of any special phase of it.

HOW TO ANALYZE AN OCCUPATIONAL SKILL

How can an occupation be analyzed for its teachable content? There are many ways in which this can be done. Basically, all occupations involve certain manual skills and certain informational or theoretical knowledge. An effective approach to the development of the teachable content is to list some of the innumerable things that must be taught concerning the subject matter. Some of the things which apply to most occupations are listed below. It is entirely possible that each instructor will discover other items peculiar to his vocation which have not been included in the following list. He should add additional material to make the analysis more comprehensive.

1. The jobs of the occupation.
2. The hand tools.
3. The machinery.
4. The equipment.
5. The materials.
6. The products and services.
7. Occupational technology and information.

a. Mathematics.
b. Science.
c. Codes, rules, laws, occupational practices.
d. Drawings, blueprint reading, schematic diagrams.

It can readily be seen that all occupations include the use and application of the things listed, although the importance attached to each will vary from one occupation to another. A listing of all materials, equipment, machinery, hand tools, and so on of the occupation will give the instructor a basis for developing teaching material. Next, he must answer the question: What must be taught about each of these things? For example, a woodworking teacher would certainly list the jack plane among his hand tools. The following information could be taught about this simple tool:

1. How to use the plane.
2. How to store and maintain it.
3. The parts and their functions.
4. How to sharpen a plane iron.

Each of these four points may be taught by including the many details involved. The following lists of items represent the *partial* results of occupational analysis in a few areas. It is evident that each of these things should be included in a course of instruction. An *exhaustive analysis* is necessary, however, to develop the complete content to be taught in any occupation.

A. *Woodworking*

Hand Tools	Claw hammer	Chalk line
	Folding rule	Jack plane
	Crosscut saw	Block plane
	Rip saw	Adze
	Square	Nail puller
	Level	Framing square
	Chisel	Oilstone
Power Tools	Skilsaw	Electric planer
	Electric drill	Saber saw
Machinery	Band saw	Jig saw
	Table saw	Lathe
	Drill press	Planer
	Disc sander	Belt sander
Material	Pine	Oak
	Mahogany	Walnut
	Gumwood	Teak
	Fir	Plywood
	Hot glue	Water glue
	Varnish	Shellac
	Nails	Sandpaper

Analyzing Occupations for Teachable Content

Equipment	Saw horses	Stepladders
	Straight ladders	Scaffolds
	Carpenter clamps	Wood vises
	Workbenches	Miter box
Occupational Information	Linear measurement	Calculating angles
	Square foot measurement	Selecting lumber
	Board foot measurement	Story of lumber
	Job opportunities	Compensation
	Layout of patterns	Building rules

B. Pipefitting

Hand Tools	Stillson wrench	Snake
	Hacksaw	Tape rule
	Reamer	Claw hammer
	Cold chisel	Ball peen hammer
	Chain wrench	Monkey wrench
Power Tools	Pipe threader	Power reamer
	Hydraulic bender	Power saw
Materials	Ropes	Galvanized pipe
	Brass pipe	Copper pipe
	Black iron pipe	Threading compound
	Lead pipe	Lead bars
	Oakum	Red lead
	Pipe hangers	Fittings
Occupational Information	Linear measurement	Angular measurement
	Types of heating systems	Types of fittings
	Calculation of heat loss	Galvanic action of dissimilar metals
	Calculation of bend allowances	

C. Electrical Installation

Hand Tools	Cutting pliers	Diagonal pliers
	Folding rule	Pollynose pliers
	Claw hammer	Screwdrivers
	Electrician's knife	Stillson wrench
	Open end wrenches	Box wrenches
	Hacksaw	Long nose pliers
Power Tools	Threading machine	Hydraulic bender
Equipment	Hydraulic lugger	Power winch
	Power saw	Lathe
Material	Types of wire	Friction tape
	Rigid conduit	Plastic tape
	Electrical metallic tubing	Wiremold
	Armored cable	Romex
	Parkway cable	Straps
	Metal mold	Fittings
Occupational Information	National Electric Code	Local codes
	Estimating material	Ohm's Law
	Types of circuits	Dwelling requirements

TEACHING OCCUPATIONAL SKILLS

Voltage drop
Number of wires in conduit
Current carrying capacities of wires
Wages and conditions

Principles of electrical devices:

The incandescent lamp
The transformer
The fluorescent lamp
The electromagnet

D. Machinist

Hand Tools	Micrometer	Ball peen hammer
	Scale	Drill gauge
	Center punch	Outside calipers
	Dividers	Inside calipers
	Scriber	Compass
Machinery	Grindstones	Drill press
	Power saw	Wire brush, flexible shaft
	Electric drill	
	Milling machines	Lathes
	Boring machine	Shaper
Materials	Brass	Iron
	Steel	Aluminum
	Copper	Flat bar
	Angle iron	Cold rolled steel
Occupational Information	Layout work	Reading the micrometer
	Reading blueprints	Converting fractions to decimals
	Types of steel	Characteristics of various metals
	Drill sizes	Trade drawing
	Indexing	Cutters
	Job opportunities	The tool and die maker

It may tend to simplify the making of an analysis if the various divisions of the occupation to be taught are listed. These divisions vary, as they depend on the nature of the particular field of work being analyzed. These variations of divisions are indicated in the following examples:

1. Division on the basis of machines used, as in Machine Shop
   - Lathe
   - Milling machine
   - Shaper
   - Boring mill
   - Drill press

2. Divisions based on the basic processes used, as in Printing
   - Composing
   - Presswork
   - Linotype
   - Proofreading
   - Estimating

3. Divisions based on construction units, as in Carpentry
   - Rough framing
   - Outside trim
   - Inside trim
   - Roofing
   - Stair building
   - Siding

4. Divisions based on materials used, as in Plumbing
   - Lead (for wiping)
   - Cast iron pipe
   - Wrought iron
   - Copper pipe
   - Chromium (fixtures)

5. Divisions based on services rendered, as in Cosmetology
   - Haircutting
   - Manicuring
   - Permanent waving
   - Massaging
   - Shampooing
   - Hair dying

6. Divisions may be varied and include a number of the classifications in the above cases. The electrical field may be used as an example. The divisions in the field could be developed this way:
   - House wiring
   - Low voltage signal wiring
   - Telephony and telegraphy
   - AC motors
   - DC motors
   - Transformers

7. Divisions in Industrial Arts based on the fields of activities, include:
   - Wood
   - Metal
   - Plastics
   - Leather
   - Electricity
   - Ceramics

8. Divisions of material in the related subjects are rather consistent and similar for all occupations:
   - Related mathematics
   - Related drawing and art
   - Related science
   - Occupational information
   - Occupational opportunities
   - Codes and laws

These divisions are somewhat arbitrary and incomplete; however, they serve to demonstrate further how teachable content may be derived by the technique of analysis. It is probable that the breaking down of an occupation into its main divisions will aid in the listing of all the tools, materials, machines, skills, and related information which constitute a master analysis.

Sources of Reference for Occupational Analysis

Although the person making an analysis may have had excellent training and experience, it is highly advisable to use considerable reference material for suggestions and to avoid omissions. The following list will serve as a general guide for sources of supplementary references:

- Job experience
- Trade texts
- Magazines
- Newspapers
- Occupational monographs
- Manufacturers' catalogs
- Industry literature
- Union job requirements

Handbooks	U.S. Department of Labor
Code books	U.S. Government Printing Office
Physics texts	Civil Service examinations
Math texts	Blueprints, schematics, etc.
Chemistry texts	Service manuals

How to Use the Analysis

It is from the master list that the instructor will develop lessons that serve as vehicles for teaching. He will also devise the jobs that serve as vehicles for learning by the students. It is interesting to note that practically the same techniques can be used in organizing subject matter for almost any type of teaching material regardless of subject, whether vocational or academic.

The following definitions are given as a means of clarification:

The Lesson. A single complete unit of teaching (or learning) whereby the instructor attempts to teach the skills or information of a subject.

The Job. A unit of the occupation consisting of a series of occupational skills utilized in the successful completion of the task.

The Operation. A single skill needed for the successful completion of the job.

The instructor uses the lesson to teach the student the skills and information about a tool, piece of equipment, or material. The student will apply the newly learned skills or information on a job which requires the application of these skills and information. Both lesson and job are, however, the result of the instructor's work and can readily be developed from the occupational analysis. Let us consider a job in carpentry as an example.

Job	*Skills*	*Information*
Hanging a door	Cut the door to size	Measure the opening
	Plane the edges	Measure and square
	Sand the edges	off the door
	Set the hinges	Check the floor level
	Install the stops	Lay out the hinges

Some of the skills were probably learned in previous lessons and jobs. Sawing and planing certainly would have been learned by this time. The new skills might well be planing the end grain of wood or using the chisel to set hinges. New information needed might be checking the floor for being level and the free opening of the door, as well as laying out the hinge locations. The lesson which would normally precede the performance of this job would be a demonstration lesson in which the teacher would teach his students how to hang the door. The skills and information noted would then become teaching points in the lesson. If an instructor feels that certain skills or information are too complex or important to become part of such a lesson, he must make the decision to develop a lesson devoted to those specific things.

It is important for the instructor to thoroughly understand what he must teach. Instructors in occupational subjects are responsible for teaching the actual occupational techniques which are current practice. There can be no make-believe—real tools, equipment, materials, machinery, and practices must be used. Teachers of occupations do not simply tell about jobs; they require their students to do the jobs. The shop experience should be as realistic as possible; therefore, the instructor must make an inventory of his occupation, which has been previously referred to as an occupational analysis. All teachers should realize that their analysis should not be allowed to become static. They should keep abreast of new developments in their areas of specialty, and introduce the new information and techniques in their teaching, as well as drop obsolete practices.

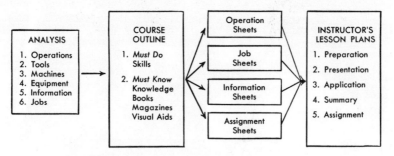

The Breakdown of an Occupation

Step 1. Break down the occupation or subject into its most suitable divisions or categories.

Step 2. Break down each division into the component parts that are best suited to the subdivision.

Step 3. Break down each subdivision into teaching points by listing operational skills and operational information. List steps and skills.

Step 4. Select suitable jobs that will include skills and operations to be found in the various subdivisions.

TEACHING OCCUPATIONAL SKILLS

Step 5. Develop a selected list of related information topics (mathematics, science, drawing, etc.) that must be taught to supplement the manual skills for intelligent performance and thorough understanding of the job.

The first big step is to break down the occupation as indicated above. The next step is to organize the results of the analysis.

Organizing Teaching Content from Occupational Analysis

Step 1. Organize the operational or manual skills and jobs into a sequential arrangement in which the skills and jobs become increasingly difficult.

Step 2. Arrange the related information units to complement the learning of skills, processes, and jobs.

Step 3. Develop instructional aids such as job sheets, information sheets, operation sheets, assignment sheets, project sheets, experiment sheets, and other work sheets to round out the use of occupational or subject analysis.

Step 4. Develop lesson plans for effective teaching of the operation and information units.

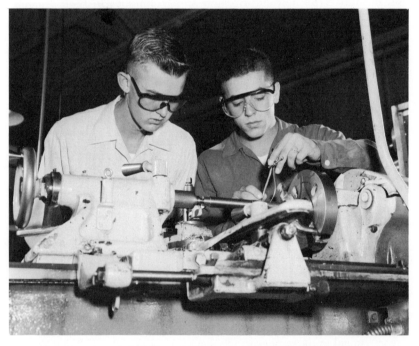

In analyzing occupational skills, a teacher must identify the hazards involved in specific jobs and provide for safety precautions.

ORGANIZING TEACHABLE CONTENT

The following three basic principles should be observed in organizing teaching content: (1) present material from the simple to the complex, (2) present material step by step, (3) present material in the best learning sequence.

A trade analysis, or inventory as it is often called, is really a list of things to be taught about an occupation or subject and is arranged step-by-step in sequence of difficulty. The keynote to successful use of the list is careful organization. There are certain principles that apply to good organization of which the teacher must be constantly aware:

1. He must develop and follow aims and objectives that are clearly understood.
2. He must recognize those things that the analysis indicates the student should learn.
3. He must know and understand fully the implications of several principles of teaching which apply to organization:
    a. Material should be presented from the simple to the complex.
    b. Material should be presented step-by-step.
    c. Skill and informational material should be presented in the best learning sequence.
4. The instructor must be aware of the resources and devices for learning and put them to use.
5. The instructor must be aware of and implement the principles of learning and teaching.

A major problem confronting a new teacher is organizing the content of his occupation for teaching purposes. He must develop new concepts and reorient his thinking in terms of his students' learning requirements. Quite often, the sequence of performance, as the craftsman does it, cannot be applied in the school situation without some modification. There are many considerations which influence occupational instruction. The age of the learner, safety of tools and machinery, sequence according to the psychology of learning, physical limitations of supplies, and, very often, job opportunities in the community will all tend to influence the development of a course of study. It is imperative, therefore, to organize the teachable content for effective learning.

The instructor will become a far better teacher if he has a broad and enriched course of study. Since he will have more than enough to teach, he will gain the flexibility needed to deal with individual differences and various course requirements. Teachers are often called upon to develop courses for apprentice training or perhaps courses in evening trade extension programs. Very often, special needs must be met within the occupational group. Courses for supervisors, unit courses dealing with advanced theory or skills, or new methods in the occupation are requested. If a teacher has made a comprehensive occupational analysis, it will be easy for him to formulate courses to meet these varied demands.

Competent teachers are well organized. They know what must be taught and always have plenty of jobs to assign to their students. They wisely plan enough variety to make the occupation interesting and complete. Teaching involves many things, and new teachers soon discover that they must play various roles. The many functions include showing the way, clarifying a principle, explaining an operation, and interpreting written material. In order to do these things well, the instructor must himself understand the many skills required of him as an expert craftsman before he can teach others. He will soon realize how jobs and operations differ. He will recognize the factors which determine the simplicity or complexity of a job, such as:

1. Accuracy required in the finished job or product.
2. Speed with which the job must be done.
3. Number of operations or steps required to complete the job.
4. Degree of trade judgment required.
5. Calculations needed for the job.
6. Number, size, and complexity of tools required for the job.
7. Material, quantity, and cost.
8. Technical information required, such as blueprint reading and related science and mathematics.
9. Machinery required.
10. Safety precautions which must be observed.
11. Familiarity and dexterity required for the job.

Instructors will very often develop jobs which are on the borderline of acceptability when measured by the above criteria. They may be too complex or require an undue amount of time. Questionable jobs may be included, but the instructor must plan to do the more difficult operations or to prepare the more difficult parts himself. As the learner gains confidence and skill, the teacher will need to do less and the student or learner will do more. The best practice is to accept jobs that are within the ability of the students at the time the work is requested. The instructor must be careful that he does not supersede instruction with production. Furthermore, the shop should not become a repair department for doing jobs with questionable educational value.

As the instructor applies the principles of analysis, he will become aware of a desirable sequence of training. The problem of what to teach will be solved, and a sequence will be suggested which is best for the learner and in keeping with the aims and objectives of the course.

Summary

"Course content should be based on an analytical approach."

The new instructor faces a twofold problem. He must learn *how* to teach as well as *what* to teach. Although this is primarily a text dealing with the subject of how to teach, it is essential for the new instructor to have some insight into the means of analyzing his occupational area for its teachable content. The methods presented in this book will be more meaningful if discussed in terms of the actual course content consisting of skills and related information.

Any occupation, or for that matter any subject, can be analyzed by breaking down the area under consideration into its component parts. In the occupational areas this can be done by listing all the machines, equipment, hand tools, power tools, jobs, services, and related information, such as occupational science, drawing, mathematics, charts, codes, rules, and occupational guidance peculiar to the subject. The instructor can then complete each of the categories which apply to his area of specialization. He can develop lessons and jobs about each of the skills, machines, or related information which will be the instruments of teaching and learning.

Instructors must be aware of the aims of the course they teach. They must learn to understand the implications of the needs of each group. The material taught in any occupational area must be real, up-to-date, and worthwhile. Instructors should constantly revise the course content. Old and obsolete material should be dropped and new material added. Shop and classroom teaching experience will serve as a valuable guide in revising and making adjustments in the sequence of teaching certain subject matter. Instructors must constantly weigh occupational needs against student readiness and student needs. Very often the sequence which is followed in the occupation is not the best sequence for the learner. Alert instructors will quickly perceive these differences and make the necessary changes.

It can be said without reservation that instructors cannot be too meticulous in making an analysis. Most new instructors tend to teach too much at one time. It is far better to develop more teaching material than is actually needed than to be short of content. Having more than enough material is a desirable goal. What may seem to be an excess will actually be needed when the instructor develops special jobs and projects for the slow learner or the fast learner. He will rely on the extra material when called upon to set up special courses for apprentices, advanced theory classes, and other specialized training.

One of the marks of outstanding teachers is the way they are organized. Competent teachers are well organized and have developed a meaningful, worthwhile course of study in a sequence which assures continuity and understanding on the part of the student. Good organization does not preclude the addition of valuable material suggested by students or by needs which reveal themselves as the course unfolds. A good occupational or subject analysis will help any teacher become well organized.

Questions and Projects

1. What is the main purpose of a subject or occupational analysis?
2. How does the teacher profit from making an analysis?
3. Why is it undesirable to develop a uniform set of divisions or categories for all occupations?
4. One of the best ways to learn a subject or occupation is by teaching it. How does an analysis help accomplish this learning?
5. List at least five sources of information in your subject or occupational area which will help you make an analysis for teachable content.
6. Develop a set of standards or criteria which will help you determine whether or not material is obsolete, or should be included.
7. Make a complete occupational analysis of one of the following divisions:
    a. Hand tools   c. Machinery
    b. Power tools   d. Materials
8. Develop a list of things which must be taught about each of the items in the analysis you have developed in answering question 7. Some key words are *use, care, maintenance, storage,* and *cost.*
9. Apply the three principles of good organization to the list, and rearrange the material for a good sequence of learning and teaching.
10. Now that the list is as complete as possible and arranged in the best order, develop lesson aims or titles and jobs which you can use in your teaching.

Understanding the Learner

It has been pointed out from time to time that the teacher plays many roles. He is at one time a leader, another time a salesman, another time a demonstrator, and so on. In addition to role-playing, the good teacher must know how to handle different situations as they arise. Sometimes he must solve group problems and, more often, he must solve individual problems. At all times the teacher must be understanding. To deal successfully with the many problems which arise with students, the teacher must recognize the fact that individuals differ. There are many characteristics that people have in common. One consistent characteristic is that each person is an individual in his own right and, depending on many factors, will be more or less different from his neighbor.

It is essential to be an expert in the knowledge and performance of the occupational area one teaches, but expertness alone will not guarantee successful and effective teaching. Part of the job involves guiding the student so that he can take his place in the job situation and learn to cooperate with others. To reach each student requires that the teacher learn the factors which are responsible for individual differences. By learning these factors and then understanding their basis, teachers can help each student develop his potential.

Classes are never truly homogeneous. We describe a class as being homogeneous when all the students have approximately the same characteristics, particularly as regards mental ability. A heterogeneous class is a group of individuals with different characteristics. Individuals in such a class represent a wide range of ability, intelligence, age, and aptitude. The words homogeneous and heterogeneous have been defined here because they are important and applicable when we consider the composition of most classes. Classes are never truly homogeneous, however, because no class is ever composed of exactly the same type of students. Even within a homogeneous class, there are differences. The main difference in most cases between homogeneous and heterogeneous classes is that the range of differences in the former has been narrowed.

IN WHAT WAYS DO INDIVIDUALS DIFFER?

Individuals differ in many, many ways. For our purpose we can discuss five broad areas of differences: mental, physical, environmental, cultural, and emotional.

We are interested in the relationships of these areas to the task of teaching occupational skills, habits, and attitudes. We must be interested because success in teaching is impossible without healthy relationships between teacher and student. Appreciation of the principles of good teacher-student relationships will help develop rapport.

Mental Differences

Mental differences take into account the mental ability of students as related to the commonly used tests and other measuring devices for determining intelligence. The term I.Q. is a very familiar one and is often used to determine the mental maturity of a person. It is a statistical term and, although important, should not be taken as the ultimate evidence of potential accomplishment. If the knowledge of a student's I.Q. causes a teacher to form a preconceived, stereotyped picture of that person, then it is better not to refer to the I.Q. There are too many factors which influence the I.Q. results to accept them as anything but general.

The I.Q. value is obtained by dividing the mental age (obtained by using an intelligence test) by the chronological age. A person with a chronological age of 14 and a mental age of 14 would have an I.Q. of 100. A standard text on educational psychology will deal at greater length with this subject, but it should be understood that some of the factors which enter into the score on the intelligence test are national background, language differences, and reading comprehension. Deficiencies in any one of these areas will have an effect on the test score, thereby producing a questionable I.Q. rating.

People differ in rate of learning. Some are quick and some are plodding. Some students will be able to organize their work better than others; some will have difficulty with abstract things, while others will be able to visualize and see the abstract more easily. Some people have a vivid imagination, others have a poor imagination; some students can concentrate for longer periods of time than others. Some of the mental abilities which bear directly on the learning of occupational skills are mathematics, reading, and problem-solving. Teachers should determine the desirable level of competency to be acquired in these areas. They should neither teach at a level which is too high, thereby precluding success, nor should they teach at so low a level that students will lose interest through boredom.

There are two important factors to consider. In the first place, the teacher should consult the cumulative records to determine the individual's performance in mathematics and reading. Second, he should devise a good pre-test to help him determine the mental level of the individual. He must evaluate his findings in terms of the level of success necessary in the occupational area involved. Student competency in the subareas of mental accomplishment will often be of assistance to the teacher or guidance counselor in helping the student to find his best place in the subdivisions of the occupational area.

One of the prime requisites for success is success. That is, the teacher must find a way to help his students achieve some degree of success in their work. To do this he must work within the framework of the student's ability. When he explains a problem, his use of words must be within the range of the student's understanding. His instructional material must take into account the slow, average, and fast learners. He must aim for the average but also arrange special help for the slow learner, and provide extra jobs, projects, and problems for the fast learner. Each student must be challenged to constantly expand his skill and knowledge, as well as to develop a thirst for knowledge beyond the minimum.

Physical Differences

Classes of students to whom occupational skills are taught usually range from the junior high school level through the senior high school, the junior college, and community college. This span coincides with the years of adolescence for the majority of boys and girls. It is the period in the life of youth when mental and physical changes accompany the emergence into adulthood from childhood. In this development process, the adolescent encounters many contradictions. He is apt to be clumsy at a time when most people will expect him to be graceful. He will expend a great deal of energy which must be restrained and confined in many situations. He may have the frame of a six-footer, but his internal organs may not have grown in like ratio. Size is no indication of strength, and teachers will often have a group of sixteen-year-olds, for example, who will range widely in height.

Adolescents are quite sensitive and aware of their growth. The teacher should avoid disparaging remarks or comments which might seem harmless but which disturb the sensitive boy or girl. Some young people can take such teasing and others cannot. Although teachers are not advised to become protective, they should become tolerant and understanding. The little fellow may be adopted as a "mascot" or be "picked on" because of his size, while the oversized boy may develop into a bully or a protector. The teacher can do much to help direct these activities into healthy channels and by his attitude make the adolescent period more tolerable. Tasks involving lifting, carrying, and heavy work should be closely supervised. The biggest boy may not be the strongest boy. The boy who plays football may find that new muscles must be trained in order to acquire success in developing occupational skills. Physiological growth is uneven. The heart grows in size quite rapidly during the adolescent period and many bone, blood vessel, and glandular changes take place. Sexual changes become apparent, and teachers should help their students to adjust themselves. Habits of cleanliness and hygiene should be stressed by developing a system of clean-up periods.

Teachers should look at the health records of their students and check on those students with specific deficiencies. Some of the more common difficulties are poor eyesight, hearing deficiencies, slight heart conditions, asthma, hernia, and other physiological defects. Teachers must insist that students avoid aggravating any physical deficiency they might have. When giving a demonstration, he should arrange the group in such a way that the taller students stand behind the

Performing actual occupational skills helps a student to determine his abilities and aspirations. Pictured here is a graphic arts class.

shorter students. He might form teams on the basis of equalizing the work, so that the individuals learn to assist each other and accept each other's strengths and weaknesses.

Environmental Differences

It has been said that people are products of their biological and cultural heritage. Biological heritage can influence the mental and physical endowment of an individual, but the environmental and cultural factors will influence the development of that heritage. A poor home environment will make the struggle for success more difficult, whereas a good home will usually make success more easy; of course, neither of these statements can be held to be absolute in the light of other factors which may exist. After all, many people have surmounted great environmental handicaps to become highly successful. Environmental handicaps do not preclude success, but they do make it more difficult. By the same token, a good environment alone cannot insure success.

Since teachers must recognize the influence of environment, they should become familiar with the backgrounds of their students.

Some students have their own little workshops or use their own bedrooms in which to work or study. Others must share cramped living quarters with brothers and sisters so that privacy for study and work is almost impossible. Students from underprivileged areas will find it inconvenient to join clubs, go on field trips, or buy extra things. Consequently, these students will find it difficult to develop enthusiasm for some projects. Teachers must be alert to these differences so that provision can be made to help the youngster. Perhaps a part-time job will give the boy or girl the financial assistance needed to develop a certain amount of independence. Many young people will act and react in terms of their environmental experiences and background, which may be quite different from that of the teacher.

The struggle for status by adolescents is serious to them, and the effects of environment are important. In the larger sense, environment extends beyond the home and neighborhood of the student. It includes the medium of communication and the problems of society and the impact they have on teen-agers. Teachers are constantly competing for the attention and the minds of students, and the competition is real and diversified. Today, teen-agers are the object of sales campaigns, educational drives, draft requirements, and the demands of peer groups. They are pulled in many directions and, because they are teen-agers, may become highly elated or greatly discouraged. Very often the conduct or interest displayed by a student in a school situation is the reflection of these many environmental influences. Teachers must be able to recognize and allow for these differences so that proper evaluation may be made and proper measures may be applied.

Cultural Differences

Cultural differences are closely akin to environmental differences. In fact, environment might be said to be part of the cultural background. Cultural values and behavior values are learned. The desire to learn might be more highly valued within some social groups than others. The value of skilled labor differs in terms of the economic level of the group. In our culture, the democratic idea of getting ahead, or attaining economic and social prestige, is highly prized. Our schools are the motivating instrument of this idea of upward mobility. Teachers are bound to be influenced by cultural patterns and, when asking students to conform to accepted patterns, will find that they must modify some of their own. This can be done without losing face or lowering any standards.

It has been said many times that America is great because we have adapted the best of many cultures to the needs of our society. Teachers must be aware of this situation and duly respect the cultural differences. If changes must be made and growth stimulated, teachers must work within the framework of the student's heritage. Ethnic background, the level of society in which he lives, and the values of his social group will determine his cultural heritage. His social attitudes must be respected before they can be changed, if change is necessary. The attitude of a student is usually the result of his environmental influences.

Emotional Differences

The adolescent period, with its many and sudden changes influenced by the physical growth which takes place during that time, is also a time of great emotional stress. Some adolescents can control their emotions better than others, while some will use the school situation as an outlet for their emotions. At such times the teacher may become a sympathetic confidant. It is essential for the teacher to realize his role in the school environment, and to understand that the emotional stability of the group is very often the reflection of his own emotional stability. Shouting will beget shouting; temper will provoke temper. It is incumbent upon the teacher to act as an adult and to keep control of his emotions in dealing with his students.

Students will respond to fairness and firmness and, most important of all, they will respond to a consistent pattern of teacher behavior. This situation calls for true insight and understanding on the part of the teacher. If the teacher will consider a school as a place to teach, accept each individual as being a person of worth and value, and in turn dignify that concept by sincerity, his teaching efforts will become more pleasant and effective.

Teachers must realize that, although the students are in their adolescent years, they are developing personalities of their own in terms of their heritage and background. They deserve sympathetic and understanding relationships with their teachers and will return as much respect as they receive. An ideal teaching situation is a quiet, well-organized classroom or shop in which the teacher gets to know each student, helps each student to learn, and develops the best in each student. A touch of humor from time to time is very desirable.

The introduction of variety in his teaching and a program which will develop interest and cause students to be conscious of progress, cannot help but enhance the teacher's reputation and self-satisfaction.

It is the teacher's responsibility to learn the different characteristics of each of his pupils. He should learn and appraise their symptoms of conduct in order to prevent, whenever possible, outbreaks of temper or other unsociable actions. Many classroom and shop incidents could be avoided if teachers would realize that the students are adolescents and not adults. Teachers should act as adults and not take minor infractions as personal affronts, but as traits to be corrected. Students seldom come to school as mature, well-rounded, well-controlled individuals. They come as growing, energetic, free young people going through the process of maturation. It is the school's function to accept these students and mold them into socially desirable citizens. The teacher who thinks that his only job is to teach his subject does not fully comprehend his function as a teacher. True, people in the teaching profession are vitally concerned with teaching skills and knowledge of specific areas, but as teachers, in the full sense of the word, they must understand that they are also molding human character. They are helping boys to become men and girls to become women. From time to time we encounter young people who are disturbed, emotionally unstable, neurotic, and ill in other ways. However, they are in the minority, and teachers must exercise extreme care in jumping to conclusions when labeling them "problem children." Discipline problems in the school are often magnified beyond proper proportions, or are actually created, because teachers are not aware of the true needs of adolescents. It is true, however, that as a teacher gains experience, his work becomes better organized, his confidence increases, and his problems of discipline decrease.

HANDLING INDIVIDUAL DIFFERENCES

No teacher is expected to assume the role of a psychologist in treating differences. He is expected to recognize them and to accept them as characteristic of people in general. His task is to develop students by channeling their energies into constructive and worthwhile activities in the shop and classroom, as well as by urging them to take part in other school programs. He must be skilled enough to recognize when a student is working at his limit or under his potential. He must provide each student with an opportunity to strengthen his weaknesses and improve his talents. He can do this by wise administrative procedures as well as by methodology.

Team formation, previously mentioned, is an important aspect of the problem. The teacher provides freedom with responsibility in allowing students to choose partners, and then follows up by observing the relationships between partners. He must remember the precept that people learn by imitation, observation, and emulation. In short, the teacher is the example for the class to follow. He sets the standard and he develops the pattern. His class will be as neat or as slovenly as he is. Students will be as loud or as reserved as he is; they will obey the rules if he does; and they will achieve a standard of workmanship commensurate with his demands, if the demands are at all reasonable.

There are two major implications in the recognition of individual differences. One is the understanding of the fact, and the other is the professional attempt to do something about it. It is not enough to acknowledge the differences. Teachers must attempt to reach all the students in their classes. It is here that variety in teaching methods becomes imperative. Variety has been described as being very important for the teacher in retaining the attention of his class. It has been stated that change is stimulating. If one method does not succeed with a student, another one will. For example, the best-composed instruction sheet may be too difficult for a student with a reading handicap, whereas a good visual aid may serve to impart the instruction. A well-planned demonstration of a principle may not be understood by some members of a class, whereas a film will clarify the situation. A teacher's explanation may seem to be lost on some members of the class, whereas a youngster who has grasped the explanation can often, in his own words, get the idea across to his classmates. Some can "do" but find it hard to "tell how." Some can answer essay questions well; others do better on objective-type tests; some draw well; others draw only passably.

The judicious teacher will ask his students to help him in developing such a tool as a visual aid in order to stimulate thought. He may ask the boy who draws well to do the lettering, and the boy who is a good craftsman to mount the material. Everyone will have had a share in the completed task, and everyone will have learned that through cooperative endeavor almost anything can be accomplished.

It must be remembered that there are levels of work within any occupational area, and that the student who enters the field will find his own level. The teacher can teach his best and do all he can to bring each student up to the highest level of accomplishment, but he is limited by the individual student in terms of capability. How much the student does with his training may depend on other factors, but teachers should be able to feel that they have taught their subject effectively and that they have helped to develop the characters and personalities of their students. Every adolescent needs a sense of belonging; therefore, the teacher should take steps to mold his class into a cohesive, cooperative group. When he does, he will be on the way in establishing high group morale and performance.

Summary

"Understanding human beings is a teacher's greatest asset."

All individuals are different in one way or another. Each individual has worth and value, and each has something to offer. It is the teacher's responsibility to learn the differences in individuals and to accept these differences in a tolerant way. Teachers must understand that cultural and biological heritages influence a person's behavior. He must work with the abilities the student has and constantly strive to upgrade and improve the student's efforts.

A teacher must recognize the psychological needs of the students, as well as their material needs. He must realize that students are to be taught subjects, but he must not become a strictly subject-centered teacher.

In order to influence people, a teacher must first understand them. He must implement this understanding by providing school experiences that will reach all the members of his class. His attention must be equally divided among those who need it. Jobs, projects, experiments, and other work experiences must be devised to satisfy the slow and the bright, as well as the average student.

His class organization and management program must allow for physical differences among students. Teams and tasks must be devised with these differences in mind. Teachers can help students through the difficult stage of adolescence by being sympathetic and understanding. In addition, they should utilize school activities outside the shop area to expand the opportunities of all their students.

Questions and Projects

1. Refer to a standard text on educational psychology to define the following terms:

a. Environment
   b. Culture
   c. Physiological
   d. Emotion
   e. Intelligence
   f. Mental health
   g. Morale
   h. Peer group
   i. Reading level
   j. Adolescence
2. Describe in simple terms how environmental influences might affect a student's performance on:
   a. Written I.Q. tests
   b. Reading tests
   c. Practical performance tests
3. List five influences existing in our society which act as restraints for teachers in trying to get a student's attention.
4. Listed below are statements based on generalities and stereotyped notions. Each contains a fallacy. Note the fallacy for each one.
   a. John is a tall, husky boy; let him do the heavy work.
   b. Jimmy is small and thin; he must be quick and nimble.
   c. Ann will learn to drive easily, she is so light on her feet.
   d. Roger's father is a very smart man. I am sure Roger will have no trouble in shop.
   e. The only way to make an impression on this class is to shout at them.
   f. I expect the same finished job from each one of you.
   g. There is only one reason why your work is never done on time and that is laziness.
   h. I don't see why you have not copied it correctly. I wrote it on the blackboard, didn't I?
   i. Anthony is so clumsy that I don't think he will ever become a mechanic.
   j. You are not a child any more; you are a big boy. Why don't you start acting like a man?
5. Make a list of student differences of which a teacher should be aware, and also plan for their consideration in preparing a demonstration.
6. Note some organizational devices that you can introduce in the shop area to promote student interest in and respect for:
   a. Good grooming
   b. Personal hygiene
   c. Neatness
   d. Accepted dress
   e. Good conduct
7. Show how a teacher can provide for developing a tolerance and respect for differences in:
   a. Cultural customs
   b. Ideas
   c. Nationalities
   d. Social levels
   e. Vocational interests

Projecting and Planning Instruction

The teacher who analyzes an occupational area will quickly realize that teachable content falls into two general categories:

1. Manual skills of the occupation.
2. Information and technology of the occupation.

Although the two categories are correlated and are often included in a lesson, the main content will usually deal primarily with either a physical skill or a mental skill.

TYPES OF LESSONS

The type of lesson will depend on the objective of the lesson. To help teachers of occupational subjects organize lessons for better unity and simplicity of communication, two main types of lessons have been identified as follows:

1. *Operation type of lesson.* A lesson in which the main focus is on the teaching of physical occupational skills.
2. *Information type of lesson.* A lesson in which the main focus is on the teaching of technology, theoretical background, and various related information.

Each detail, point of information, safety note, or skill that must be taught in a given lesson is called a teaching point. A planned lesson might be considered as a collection of essential and pertinent teaching points that must be included for successful communication and learning.

The operation lesson is a type of instructional unit that must be developed for all skill training. For example, a woodworking teacher might develop an operation lesson on how to sand a finished surface. In doing so, he would demonstrate to the class the proper way to wrap the sandpaper around a wood block. That would be a teaching point.

The industrial arts instructor might teach an operation lesson by demonstrating to his class the proper method of scribing around a template on a sheet of plastic before cutting. A teaching point would be to remind the students that the template must be held rigidly in the same position while scribing.

A technical school instructor might teach his class the proper method of setting up a machine for hardness testing. In this case a teaching point would be to center the material being tested. To further simplify and clarify the intent of any operation lesson, the teacher should ask himself this question: "Am I going to teach the students how to do something?" If the answer is yes, then the lesson will be an operation lesson.

The teacher can ask himself another question: "Is the intent of this lesson to explain and tell about something?" If the answer is affirmative, then the lesson will be an information type of lesson. In this type of lesson, the teacher instructs his students in the theory and basic fundamentals of the area being taught. It is by means of an information lesson that the industrial arts teacher explains the composition of the plastics with which his class will work. It is by the same means that the college instructor explains the principles of the hardness tester.

The area covered by the information lesson seems to be broader than that covered by the operation lesson because so many subtopics

TEACHING OCCUPATIONAL SKILLS

can be included. Grouped under the heading of related trade information lessons are such other topics as occupational information, related mathematics, science, use of various code books and handbooks, as well as the related physics of the area. When the teacher begins to develop the teachable content of his subject, he will see that the list of operation lessons will also grow quite long.

Source Material for Operation Lessons

1. Hand skills of the occupational area or field.
2. Measuring or laying out as applied in the occupation.
3. Safety applications of the occupation.

Source Material for Information Lessons

1. Mathematics
2. Physics
3. Chemistry
4. Electricity
5. Circuitry
6. Drawing
7. Blueprint reading
8. Safety rules
9. Principles
9. Principles
10. Uses of devices
11. Types of devices
12. Labor laws
13. Codes and rules
14. Guidance-occupational information
15. Health regulations
16. Reviews

Meaning of a Lesson

What is a lesson? It is necessary that we define it as a basis for further use. A lesson is a single complete unit of learning. A good learning situation is not composed of disjointed, fragmentary pieces of information or demonstrations. Learning is stimulated and aided when the teacher can present a coherent and sequential series of lessons, each of which is clear-cut in aim.

Important Characteristics of a Lesson

The lesson must be a unit of learning. What is to be learned should be made apparent to the students in the title of the lesson. It should be clear to the teacher also when he develops his aim for the lesson.

Each lesson should contain something new. Exclusive of review lessons or some other lesson of the same general type, a lesson should contain something old for connective tissue and something new for progress in learning the subject.

The lesson should be reasonable in scope. It should be balanced, interesting, and neither too simple nor too complex.

The lesson should be adapted to the needs of the students. The material should be within the capabilities of the learners. It should be consistent with the needs of the students in keeping with the purpose of the course and the progress of the group. It should not be based on any favored idea or whim of the teacher. It should not be given simply because it is dictated by a rigid teaching timetable.

The lesson should have a clear-cut beginning, a presentation, and an end. The language of the teacher should enable the student to follow the teacher when he begins, to comprehend the presentation of the lesson, and to absorb the material with a feeling of understanding and accomplishment. Students should never be left "up-in-the-air" over a lesson.

The lesson should require a measurable standard of achievement. Perhaps one of the most vital aspects of a teacher's work is in setting standards of achievement. A lesson should contain that element. High standards of performance should start at the beginning and continue throughout the lesson.

TEACHER PLANNING

The best kind of teaching is based on good planning, a well-disciplined class, and good presentation. Good planning is based on a series of steps which were first devised along the lines of preparation, comparison, and application. These are known as the Herbartian steps. Johann Herbart was an educational philosopher who was interested in teacher training. He was the first to formalize the basic steps of teaching.

The steps have undergone changes through the years which have improved and modernized his concept of a formal procedure in teaching. Herbart's contribution was not to formalize teaching but to introduce the idea of organized teaching. It is this concept of organizing a teaching program, or a unit called a lesson, that is so important.

Many professions have drawn upon the teaching profession for instructional techniques, and we teachers can do well to look to other occupations for suggestions and help in teaching. For example, in organizing a lesson we might look to the successful speaker. Some of the techniques used are:

1. Get everyone's attention.
2. Introduce the main idea.
3. Develop the idea.
4. Make it important to the listener.
5. Sum up the main points.

Generally, experienced teachers do these very things. Just as a speaker makes notes and the architect a drawing or a blueprint, the teacher draws up a plan. Although individual plans vary, the most common pattern is that of the developmental type of plan. It simply means developing a logical method of presentation.

Main Parts of a Lesson

1. Topic	4. Motivation	7. Summary
2. Aim	5. Presentation	8. Assignment
3. Preparation	6. Application	9. Reference

Throughout the lesson the teacher should check learning and test for progress by asking questions, stimulating participation, and inviting discussion. It is also wise to note at the foot of the plan any references used in developing the lesson. List texts, catalogs, and authorities relative to the lesson which may in turn be relayed to the students for further study.

A complete understanding of the function of each part of the plan is essential to the teacher. What he is doing must be clear to him before it can become clear and understandable to his students.

Divisions of the Lesson Plan

1. <u>Topic.</u> Topic refers to the general area of which the specific lesson is a part. It might be the ignition system in an automobile, the fundamentals of electricity, joining pipe in plumbing, wood finishing in industrial arts, composition in printing, or lathework in the machine shop. These are general areas which involve many individual lessons.

2. <u>Aim.</u> The aim is more specific. It is the actual, immediate purpose or goal of the lesson. It is the label on the unit lesson. It is the thing to be taught and the thing to be learned. The aim when written on the board serves to retain student attention and promote understanding of the unit being presented.

    a. *Operation Lessons*

      1. How to set the points of a distributor.
      2. How to cut a thread on a lathe.
      3. How to make a pigtail splice.
      4. How to sharpen a plane iron.

    b. *Information Lessons*

      1. How the distributor operates.
      2. What is meant by the pitch of a screw thread?

3. Code requirements for good splices.
4. Types of planes.

3. <u>Teacher preparation</u>. It is here that the teacher lists supplies, tools, material, and equipment which he will need for the lesson. His preparation might include charts, tables, diagrams, books, and material for demonstrations. Student preparation should also be noted; it might consist of a reading assignment, a previous job or experiment, or bringing in notebooks, graph paper, and drawing equipment. A field trip might even be the desirable preparation.

4. <u>Motivation</u>. Motivation means to stimulate something or someone. Motivation is one of the prime tasks of teaching. Motivation should be constant and should not stop at any given point. In order to organize a lesson unit, however, we use motivation for the special purpose of arousing interest in the lesson to be given. It is used at the beginning of the lesson as a means of introducing the material, stimulating interest, arousing curiosity, and developing the specific aim. Motivation is more than a mere statement of the lesson—it should show the need for the lesson and serve as the connecting link between the present lesson and previous work.

5. <u>Presentation</u>. This is the part of the lesson in which the thing to be learned is presented. If an information lesson is being taught, it will consist of explanations. If an operation lesson is being taught, it will consist of a demonstration of procedures. It should be based on the principles of learning and teaching which we have previously discussed. Presentation should proceed, step-by-step, simple-to-complex, with teaching points interspersed in the proper sequence. The teacher should think out the procedure or explanation beforehand and then develop it, including key questions.

6. <u>Application</u>. Practicing the thing to be learned is the keynote of successful learning and teaching in the fields of trade shopwork, industrial arts, or technical subjects. The application part of the lesson makes use of this principle by providing an opportunity for the student to do something about the thing learned. Application might be the taking of notes or the copying of a diagram. It might be the performance of an operation just learned by a few students or the completion of an experiment to prove the principle just taught. Application is the involvement of the class in the lesson being taught by the use of various means, such as sending students to the board or having them copy notes and diagrams in their notebooks.

7. <u>Summary</u>. The summary should terminate the formal instruction. The teacher, by means of the summary, brings together and

emphasizes the main points made during the lesson presentation. He crystallizes the aim and highlights the presentation.

8. <u>Assignment</u>. The assignment phase of a lesson may be considered as a continuation of the application. Assignments provide a meaningful further application of the thing just learned. It is an aid to retention. It differs from application, as it may consist of preparation for the next lesson. It may be done at home or in the shop or laboratory. It can consist of performing a job, working on a project, reference reading, doing problems, or visiting a business establishment or manufacturing plant.

9. <u>Reference</u>. The teacher is, in many instances, the expert and source of authority. As a skilled and trained person the teacher sets the standard and is responsible for methods, drawings, notes, explanations, and other material included in his lessons.

The wise teacher will keep a record of his sources of materials by listing next to his references the names of texts, booklets, trade manuals, and other authoritative sources of material for future reference. These notations will form a source of ready reference for the student or person who wishes to pursue a subject further. It is a sound practice to follow and will help the teacher to broaden his knowledge and improve his teaching.

LESSON PLANNING

A teaching plan is an outline of the lesson. It should be easy to follow and should contain the key phrases and notes which will serve as a guide for the instructor. The plan is not to be used as a text. It should be placed in a convenient position to permit casual reference to it from time to time. The teacher should not attempt to memorize the plan as an actor might memorize a script. He should know what he is going to teach as a result of having developed the lesson before class. The plan is simply his record or guide of the lesson with the material arranged in a logical order for reference during teaching in the shop, classroom, or laboratory. A typical lesson plan format is shown on page 49.

Note the heading given to this particular work sheet. Insertion of the teacher's name serves to identify the author of the plan and to establish ownership, whereas the number will help to index the plans if numerous ones are developed. An efficient way to index lesson materials is to number them with a whole number and a decimal; for example, Lesson No. 1.0 or 12.0. This arrangement will permit you to

| Teacher's Name | Lesson No. |

Topic:

Aim:

Preparation: *Teacher's* *Student's*

Motivation:

Presentation:

Application:

Summary:

Assignment:

References:

— Check and Test —

add lessons later, thus eliminating the necessity of changing all the numbers.

The sequence might read Lesson 1.00, 1.01; then Lesson 2.00, Lesson 2.01, Lesson 2.02; and then Lesson 3.00 and so forth. You will note that the words "Check" and "Test" are listed in a vertical position. The reason is simple: No teacher should reach the end of a lesson before checking to see whether or not his students are learning. Checking should be a continuous procedure to promote complete understanding and avoid confusion.

Flexibility

A lesson plan should be designed with a degree of flexibility. A rigid, inflexible plan is as bad as a sketchy plan. In either extreme, the plan may inhibit good teaching. Teachers should be prepared to seize every opportunity for teaching when natural or spontaneous interest is aroused. When planning is too rigid, a teacher finds it somewhat difficult to depart slightly from the plan. This lack of flexibility may cause him to lose many opportunities to do an effective teaching job. When emergencies arise, such as the failure of a mechanical teaching aid, the teacher must be prepared to depart from his planned program in order to control the group and to use the time effectively.

Improved Plan

A teaching plan can grow and improve. When a teacher finds that a certain method, explanation, teaching aid, or other device is particularly successful, he should note that fact. If questions recur in the teaching of a lesson which tend to be confusing, then those phases should be omitted or avoided. On the other hand, a student may offer points of value. In such an instance the teacher should be receptive and include the offered suggestion in an improved plan.

Writing the Plan

In writing a plan you might find it easier not to follow the order of the suggested lesson plan. If you choose, the sequence might be as follows:

1. <u>Note the topic or general area,</u> such as "Use of Hand Tools," "Measuring Instruments," "Radio Transformers," "Working with Copper," "Tests for Strength of Materials," "The Fuel System of a Car," "The Drill Press," and so forth.

2. <u>Write the aim</u>. Remember this is specific; it is single-purpose, and should be clear enough to meet the criteria for lesson units. A clear aim in the teacher's mind will result in good teaching and clear understanding in the student's mind.

3. <u>Develop the presentation after your aim is clear and established</u>. Develop your presentation in outline form, step-by-step, numbering the steps. The numbers will help you find your place as you glance at your plan from time to time. Apply the principles of step-by-step, simple to complex, and best sequence possible. State your teaching points in key phrases. Long sentences will be difficult to follow while teaching a group. Include key questions and safety precautions which are necessary. Also include simple sketches and diagrams which you intend to use. Remember you will be handling a group, writing on the board, answering a question, framing a question, or correcting a student. While you are performing an operation, with all your activity it will be quite easy to forget temporarily an important point or to forget a key section of a chalkboard sketch.

4. <u>Determine the application you want students to make of the point being taught</u>. Decide on the best method for learning the particular lesson. The student participation may be taking notes, reading and explaining text material, drawing a diagram, coloring main parts of a drawing or labeling them. It might include solving problems, either mathematical or mechanical. For variety, instructors should use prepared worksheets and other instructional sheets to relieve students of the monotony of copying notes from the board. Operation-type lessons should always provide for student demonstrations of skills taught.

5. <u>Decide on the preparation to be made.</u> At this point you are ready to list those things needed for student preparation. Students might need certain tools, handbooks, charts, colored pencils, or graph paper. They may be requested to report on a reading assignment or to visit a store, a showroom, or a supply house. Whatever it may be, you should note it on your plan. You also should list what you as the teacher will need. You should list the tools, materials, visual aids, laboratory equipment, texts, instruction sheets, and other teaching aids needed for a successful lesson presentation.

6. <u>Decide on the motivation you will use.</u> Which method, aid, personal appeal, story, question, film, or other device will best introduce the lesson, create interest, point out need, or otherwise stimulate your students to think, concentrate, and learn. We can give value to the lesson by showing its practical applications as well as its personal value to the student. Teachers can create interest by appealing to certain drives common to everyone. Almost all people are:

a. Curious. People want to see, hear about, and know about different things.
b. Gregarious. People as a rule want to feel they belong. They want to be a part of a group. The teacher should motivate his class by developing group morale and spirit.
c. Competitive. Most people will take up a challenge, or seek to surpass another person or group. Nothing is done so well that it cannot be done better. <u>Therefore, it is wise to create competition</u>.
d. Willing to learn an easier way. Perhaps this can be better stated by saying that many people are comfort seekers. Very often, the promise of a better and easier way to do something will motivate people to learn.
e. Success seekers. A little success is a motivating factor and can often change a disinterested person into one eager to learn.

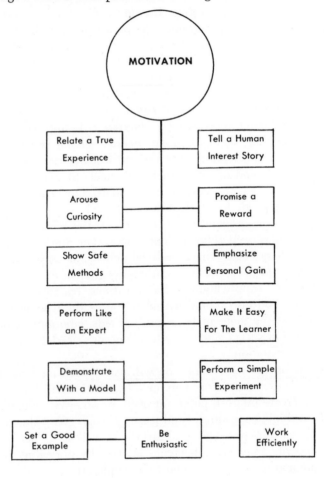

f. *Ambitious.* The opportunity for better jobs and greater earnings acts as a motivating factor in many cases.

Another responsibility of the teacher is to decide the stimuli to be used in making his appeal. Of course motivation does not end here, but it is a continuing process designed to keep interest at a constantly high level. When planning a lesson it is important to provide for motivation and then to determine how best to motivate.

7. <u>Assignment</u>. The final step in developing your plan is a decision on the kind of assignment to give. This is not always easy. A meaningless assignment consisting of busywork results in little benefit to the student. It should be something of real value which is necessary to better understanding and experience. At this point all references used in developing the lesson should be noted. Also, list books, authors, pages, or other information which will help the student locate the sources quickly and easily.

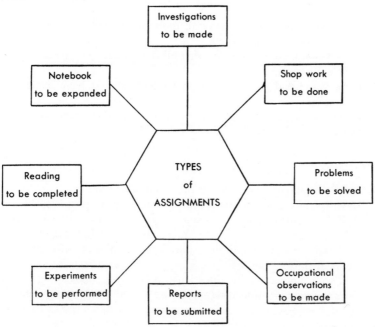

A CHECKLIST FOR LESSON PLANNING

The following questions when answered in the affirmative will indicate that a lesson plan has met the desirable established standards.

Topic

1. Is the topic related to the general area of the course?
2. Does the topic relate to a division of the occupational analysis?
3. Has the topic been fully developed?

Aim

1. Does the lesson have a single-purpose aim?
2. Is the aim in keeping with the topic?
3. Does the aim lend itself to a clear, simple lesson title?
4. Can the aim be achieved within the lesson period?
5. Does the aim indicate the type of lesson?
6. Does the lesson aim fit in with the continuity of the preceding lesson?
7. Will the aim be readily understood when written on the chalkboard?

Preparation

1. Have you listed all the material, tools, equipment, and teaching aids you will need for the lesson?
2. Have you checked to be sure that all these things are available and in sufficient quantity?
3. Have you listed materials which students should have available for the lesson?
4. Have you listed the special equipment needed such as electrical extension cords, protectors, and colored chalk?

Motivation

1. Have you planned for a means of getting attention?
2. Have you made use of any stimuli which motivate people to learn?
3. Will the motivation help develop a clearly understood lesson aim?
4. Will the motivation emphasize the significance of the lesson?
5. Will the motivation introduce the lesson and bring the group to a common starting point?
6. Will your motivation be educational rather than entertaining?
7. Does the motivation lead naturally and smoothly into the presentation?

Presentation

1. Has the presentation been developed in a step-by-step sequence?
2. Does the presentation include key sketches and diagrams?
3. Are key questions included?
4. Have necessary safety precautions been included?
5. Has each lesson point been noted in the form of key phrases or short, simple sentences?

6. Have appropriate reminders been included for use of aids at the proper time?
7. Has sufficient detail been included to satisfy the needs of the learner?
8. Have the techniques of explaining and showing been utilized?
9. Has provision been made for individual differences?

Application

1. Have you developed the best possible means for the group to put the new knowledge to use during the lesson?
2. Have you decided the number of students to be utilized if you plan to have student participation?
3. Have you clearly indicated what material should be copied into the notebook, if you use this device?
4. Have you considered the use of some prepared instructional material?
5. Have you considered the use of the chalkboard?
6. Have you provided for student chalkboard work?
7. Have you tried to develop some new and novel way of student application of the lesson?
8. Have you estimated the time required for application of the new material?
9. Will your students spend the greater part of their time learning and applying new information rather than taking unnecessary notes and making complicated and irrelevant sketches?

Summary

1. Have you planned a summary which will bring out the highlights of the lesson?
2. Have you considered having the students develop the summary?
3. Will you supplement the students' summation?
4. Have you listed the essential points of the lesson?
5. Have you considered carefully whether an oral or chalkboard summary is best for the lesson given?

Assignment

1. Have you thought of the assignment as a continuation of the application of the lesson?
2. Does the assignment put newly learned material to use?
3. Dose the assignment have real value to the learner?
4. Have you provided for an explanation of the assignment so that all the students will know what to do?
5. Is the assignment reasonable in length, scope, and achievement?

References

1. Have sources of authority for your material been noted?

2. Have you listed further sources of information relative to the lesson for students' use?
3. Does your reference give text, chapter, and page, if necessary?
4. Have you provided for use of references by the students to broaden their knowledge of occupational material and other texts?

General

1. Does your plan show evidence of careful analysis of the unit to be taught?
2. Has the information or operation to be taught been analyzed completely enough so that another teacher could work from the plan and do a creditable job?
3. Have you anticipated questions, problems, or other common shop incidents which might arise during the lesson?
4. Does the completed plan present a neat, professional appearance?
5. Is there space on the plan for revisions?
6. Have you remembered to include definitions of new and difficult terms?
7. Have you tried to introduce variety into your teaching of the lesson?
8. Have you identified the plan by course and index number for future use?
9. Have you prepared any problem sheets, work sheets, or other instructional material which would enhance the lesson?
10. Do you plan to use some of the lesson material for a quiz or test?
11. Does overall inspection of the plan reveal a developmental approach utilizing the principles of learning and good organization?
12. Does the plan meet the needs of the students?

OPERATION VERSUS INFORMATION LESSON

It is very important that a teacher decide whether to teach an operation lesson or an information lesson first. In most cases he will find that the operation lesson should precede the information lesson. It is easier to explain the electromagnets in a bell after a boy has seen the bell and wired it than it is to discuss it before he has ever used a bell. An explanation of types of enamel will mean more to a student after he has fired several pieces of work. The purpose of oil rings is easier to understand after he has used the rings in a piston job.

This does not mean that an information lesson may never be given before an operation lesson. The aim of the lesson is the determining factor. An information lesson might well be used to introduce a new area of learning. It might be used as a means of motivating the learning. The teacher must keep in mind that students learn more easily and better the things they have seen, worked with, or things with which they are familiar.

A good lesson plan makes use of the accepted practices of modern teaching methods. As a teacher develops a series of plans it should become apparent that the utilization of variety in presentation and application is very advantageous from the standpoint of his knowledge of how students learn. He should remember the importance of such factors as observation, recall, past experience, action, imagination, reasoning, and repetition. At the same time he should avoid rote learning. Students should be taught to associate and reason rather than to memorize and recite. A student can be taught to memorize Ohm's Law, yet not understand its implications in wiring a circuit. He might memorize Boyle's Law of Gases, yet not understand a thing about its application. A test of a good lesson plan is whether or not another

A teacher should carefully check his lesson plan before giving a demonstration. All necessary tools, equipment, and other aids should be available to ensure a smooth, sequential presentation.

A TYPICAL OPERATION-TYPE LESSON PLAN

Topic: Hydraulic Brakes
Aim: How to Make a Minor Adjustment on Foot Hydraulic Brakes.
Preparation:

Teacher	Students
1. Have car equipped with hydraulic brakes on lift.	1. Have read assignment on Bendix brakes.
2. Have one front wheel removed. (Leave drum on.)	2. Have studied principles of brakes.
3. Brake spoon, scraper, screwdriver, feeler gauge, G.M. chart (brakes).	3. Told to have notebooks, compass and straightedge.

Motivation:
1. Why must brakes be adjusted?
2. How often must brakes be adjusted?
3. Bring out the point that brakes should be designed for quick, easy adjustment.
4. Hang G.M. Chart. What points of adjustment are shown here?

Presentation:
1. Refer to chart. Name parts.
2. Point out contour of brake lining to drum.
3. Bring out the nine points of adjustment.
4. Develop simple diagram on B.B.

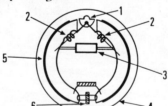

(1) Major adjustment
(2) Return springs
(3) Wheel cylinder
(4) Drum
(5) Shoe
(6) Minor adjustment

5. Ask students to name terms and to label parts.
6. When should all points be checked and adjusted?
7. Have wheels turned so group can see inside face of wheel.

8. Group class around wheel. (Be sure all can see and hear.)
9. Check that all are in safe positions.
10. Clear dirt away. Remove grommet on minor adjustment.
11. Adjust wheel brake. Explain each step.
12. Repeat operation more slowly. Point out danger of scraped knuckles, etc.

Application:
1. Have several students perform one or more steps in the operation.
2. Have students check clearance.
3. Question students as work progresses.

Summary:
1. Clean area of work. Carefully store parts.
2. Why make minor adjustments first?
3. Why check all points?
4. Why is it important to replace grommet?
5. Review rest of operation.
6. Why check jack? Why use metal horse?
7. What care should be exercised in using hand tools?

Assignment:
1. Student teams work on car, one team on each wheel.
2. Copy diagram into notebooks.
3. Answer questions in notebook.
   a. What difference will be found in height of foot pedal after adjustment?
   b. How do the threads of lug nuts differ between left and right-hand side?
   c. Why should master cylinder be checked after brake adjustment?

References:
1. G.M. Chart of Bendix Hydraulic Brake System.
2. Motor's Manual, pgs. 656-678.

teacher can take that plan and do a creditable job of teaching the lesson. It should be noted that the sample plans shown on succeeding pages have the following characteristics:

1. Are written in outline form.
2. Have a clear aim and purpose.
3. Are easy to read, not crowded.
4. Consist of motivating factors.
5. Include essential points and details.
6. Contain key phrases.
7. Provide for student participation.
8. Indicate key questions.
9. Summarize clearly.
10. Use a variety of teaching aids and techniques.
11. Include an assignment.

The careful, complete planning requisite for successful teaching is based on sound reasons. Every teacher can think of benefits which have accrued to him as a result of planning. Here are some of those reasons for planning:

1. Thinking done before teaching a lesson is unhurried thinking.
2. A plan insures a good sequence.
3. Learning to plan a lesson will develop competency in planning anything.
4. A plan is a visual presentation of the teacher's thinking and helps him to check his effectiveness.
5. Plans prevent forgetting of essential material.
6. A plan serves as a good record of what has been taught.
7. A plan provides a basis for improvement.
8. To learn to plan is to learn to organize, and an organized teacher is a good teacher.

There are factors in teaching which cannot be ignored when developing a lesson plan. The teacher is sometimes restricted by the physical facilities of his shop or laboratory, or he may not have sufficient material or equipment to present the lesson as he would prefer. The availability of time is also an important factor. In some cases two short lessons may be necessary in lieu of one long lesson.

A CHECKLIST FOR LESSON EVALUATION

The effectiveness of a lesson may be measured by the following checklist. Check each item as accurately and objectively as possible, in one of the three columns, as an aid in self-evaluation and improvement.

Projecting and Planning Instruction

	Good	Fair	Poor
1. A clearly stated aim			
2. A single-purpose title			
3. An effective motivation			
4. Sufficient preparation of lesson material			
5. Explanation of new words and terms			
6. Proper use of blackboard			
7. Patience and resourcefulness in explaining			
8. Good use of teaching aids			
9. Liberal use of questions for checking			
10. Variety of means for sustaining interest			
11. Step-by-step presentation			
12. Provision for student participation			
13. Sticking to the aim			
14. Relation of material to actual use			
15. Relation of material to other subjects			
16. Proper safety instruction			
17. Evidence of flexibility in handling lesson			
18. Good, clear, specific summary			
19. Reasonable, valuable, understandable assignment			
20. Enthusiastic performance by teacher			
21. Preparation of room (light, heat, air, etc.)			
22. Evidences of good order and conduct			
23. Expeditious handling of attendance, etc.			
24. Satisfactory student responses			
25. Good timing from beginning to end			

Range of Content

Do not cover too much in a lesson plan. It is far better to teach two lessons well than to try to teach too much in one. The teacher who attempts to teach too much will experience disappointing results. He will have to review more frequently; he will have to repeat the lesson

SAMPLE LESSON PLAN: PLUMBING

Occupational Division: Cast Iron Pipe

Lesson Title: How to Yarn a Joint.

Preparation:

Students	Teacher
1. Shop aprons, safety goggles, rulers.	1. 4 pieces of cast iron pipe —2 hub and 2 spigot. 2. Oakum. 3. Yarning irons, long, short and stub. Ball peen hammer.

Introduction:
1. Joints in cast iron pipe must be watertight and gas tight.
2. Why? (To prevent sewage and sewer gas leaks.)
3. Public health starts with sanitation systems.
4. How can we seal such a large joint?

Procedure:
1. Roll and twist several length of oakum into about ¾" diameter.
2. Point out that some manufacturers sell oakum already twisted.
3. Why should mechanics learn this skill anyway?
4. Set up 2 lengths, vertically—hub end up.
5. Place spigot end into hub.
6. Center pipes for even spacing all around. Why?
7. Have student check spacing with ruler. Put safety goggles on.
8. Pack oakum into joint loosely. Tamp in with long yarner.
9. Why is long yarner offset?
10. Lay in several layers and tamp. Why are several needed?
11. Use short yarner to pack oakum firmly.
12. Select student to tamp oakum to within ¾" of hub top.
13. Stress danger of chips of steel from hammer or iron.
14. Drive oakum down with stub yarner to 1" below hub.
15. Check spacing with students.
16. Check vertical plane and alignment of pipes.

Application:
1. Have several students take turns in yarning second joint.
2. Check on spacing.

Summary:
1. Why should caulking be done carefully?
2. Name tools one at a time. Write their names on blackboard.
3. Why must spacing be even all around?

    4. How do we prepare oakum?
    5. Why use the long iron first?
    6. How much oakum do we use before using the stub iron?
    7. Why wear safety goggles?

Assignment:
    1. Teams ready for yarning will obtain material and complete one joint. Have instructor check.
    2. Sketch line method of alignment of horizontal joints as shown in *Lead Work for Modern Plumbing,* pages 105, 106.

References:
   Lead Work for Modern Plumbing, Lead Industries Association. *Plumbing* by Miller; Van Nostrand Co., pp. 71-76.

SAMPLE LESSON PLAN: CAFETERIA AND TEA ROOM MANAGEMENT

Lesson No._____

Topic: Table Settings

Aim: How to Set a Table for Dinner

Preparation:

Students	Teacher
1. Read Chap. 11, *Everyday Foods* by Harris and Lacey.	1. Prepare table with table cloth only. 2. Prepare one complete setting on tray. 3. Overhead projector and slides. No. 1 through No. 6 dinner settings.

Motivation:
   1. Mealtime should be enjoyable and leisurely.
   2. What helps contribute to a pleasant dinner?
   3. How can table appearance help make dinner pleasant?
   4. Show color transparency of correct table setting for four persons. Point out importance of appearance in food trades.
   5. Bring out the importance of neatness, uniformity, practice and usage.

Presentation:
   1. Explain demonstration to follow.
   2. Start setting with dinner plate. Center plate in "cover".
   3. Explain term "cover". Allow 20 to 24" for each cover.
   4. Place silver. Work outside in. Show slide 2.
   5. Place soup spoon. How does it differ from tea spoon?

6. Place tea spoon.
7. Place knife. Blade toward plate.
8. Place silver on left of plate; fork, then salad fork.
9. Place water glass. Right side at tip of knife. Why?
10. Place bread and butter plate, tip of fork.
11. Show slide 3.
12. Place napkin. Why at left?
13. Place soup cup and plate, cup and saucer to right of knife.
14. Show slide 4.
15. Show slide 5. Complete dinner setting, bring out color harmony.
16. Show slide 6. Complete dinner setting, bring out silver, china harmony.

Application:
1. Have students take turns setting other three places.
2. Others to observe and offer assistance.
3. Make a simple sketch of setting for one in notebook.

Summary:
1. Why use correct table settings? (Social, business, atmosphere.)
2. What is meant by the term "cover"?
3. Why place dinner plate first?
4. Why place silver outside in?
5. How should silver and china harmonize?
6. Why are colors important?

Assignment:
Study diagrams pp. 115, 116 in *Everyday Foods,* Harris and Lacey. Make a carefully drawn sketch of table setting according to Fig. 33, p. 116, same text.

References:
Everyday Foods by Harris and Lacey.

SAMPLE LESSON PLAN: TECHNICAL ELECTRICITY

Course Unit:
Shunt Motors.

Lesson Title:
How to Vary the Speed of a Shunt Motor by Varying Resistance in the Shunt Field.

PRESENTATION

Motivation:
1. Explain needs of industry to run motors at various but constant speeds.
2. Give examples—paper mills, etc.
3. Technicians must learn how to make adjustments.

Procedure:
1. Explain equipment set-up for demonstration.
2. Discuss connections.
3. Have student draw schematic diagram of connections on the chalkboard. (See Figure.)

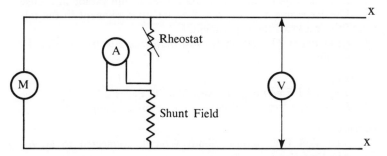

4. Have students check schematic against actual equipment connections. Question students on connections.
5. *Be sure all students are clear of equipment.*
6. Start motor and adjust to rated speed.
7. Have student check speed with tachometer; place reading on the chalkboard.
8. Have student place voltmeter reading on the chalkboard.
9. Have student place ammeter reading on the chalkboard.
10. All students will calculate shunt field resistance.
11. Adjust rheostat in shunt field to increase resistance in successive steps.
12. Check speed with tachometer after each adjustment.
13. Decrease resistance in three steps; read speed after each adjustment.
14. *CAUTION.* Explain why shunt field should never be disconnected: Excessive speed will damage motor. Explain residual field left in field poles due to retentivity of the steel in the poles.

Application:
1. All students to work in notebooks. Copy schematic on the chalkboard.
2. Using demonstration motor at rated load, predict a desired speed, then calculate R, necessary to add or subtract from shunt to obtain this speed.
3. Have several students:
    a. Adjust field to calculated value.
    b. Measure field current.
    c. Measure field resistance.
    d. Check notebook calculations against readings.

Summary:
1. How can the speed of a shunt motor be increased using a rheostat in the shunt field? (Add R.)
2. How can the speed be decreased? (Subtract R.)
3. Why should the shunt field never be left open?
4. What are some uses for shunt wound motors?

Assignment:
1. Plot the data obtained from the three adjustments of the rheostat.
2. List and explain three important uses of this motor in industry.
3. Use Experiment Sheet, No. 8 to set up equipment in the laboratory. Plot results of the experiment.
4. Read Pages 237-249 in Dawes, *Industrial Electricity*, Vol. 1 for next session.

References:
1. *Industrial Electricity*, Dawes, Vol. 1, Pages 231-236.
2. *Industrial Electricity*, Nadon and Gelmine, Chapter 6.

Preparation:
1. 110 Volt D.C. motor, Shunt Wound, connected to approximately rated load.
2. 110 Volt D.C. Voltmeter. (Large Face)
3. 110 Volt D.C. Ammeter. (Large Face)
4. Shaft Tachometer.
5. Rheostat.

Notes:

individually more often; and he may find that equipment is misused because of improper or insufficient instruction.

Further instruction on lesson plans will be treated in succeeding chapters as it applies to the immediate situation. Teachers are expected to plan their lessons and to keep a file of their lesson plans. If they follow this practice they will have an invaluable reference file for the development of future teaching material. As the course grows richer in content and the teacher grows more experienced, teaching becomes more satisfying, problems decline, and learning improves.

Summary

"Plan your work—then work the plan."

There are two main types or kinds of lessons, the operation and the information lesson. The operation lesson emphasizes the manual, or skill with the hand, while the information lesson emphasizes the mental, or skill with the mind.

When a manual or mental skill is too minor for the development of a complete lesson, it is called a teaching point. Many teaching points are included in a lesson. In general, an information lesson concerns the teaching of mental processes, trade or technical information, theory and principles, mathematics and science—all of which are exclusive of using the hands to build or create something.

Lessons must be planned for successful teaching. A form should be followed which will provide continuity in teaching and utilize the principles of teaching and learning which have been discussed. The developmental lesson plan offers a blueprint for teaching whether it be an idea, a theory, a principle, or a manual skill. Each part has a specific purpose, although the whole is a coherent unit. The lesson plan when written does not necessarily have to follow the suggested outline. The parts may be developed by first establishing the topic, then the area, the presentation, and so on.

A plan should be a flexible instrument and should be revised and improved each succeeding time it is used. Plans should be filed and indexed for future reference, thereby avoiding waste of time. The professional teacher considers lesson planning a most essential part of his activities.

Questions and Projects

1. Make a list of five operation type of lesson titles and five information type of lesson titles. The title should clearly indicate the aim of each lesson.
2. Write a presentation of an operation commonly performed in your occupation.
3. Write a presentation of an information lesson related to your occupation.
4. Write a specific lesson aim. Then develop and explain three different ways of motivating the aim.
5. State an advantage for each of the following techniques which are recommended for lesson plan writing:
    a. Key phrases
    b. Key questions
    c. Key sketches
    d. Outline form
    e. Use of 1-2-3 order
6. Make a list of approximately ten means of providing for student application of a lesson, any of which could be used in lesson planning.
7. State a specific lesson aim and then develop a work sheet for distribution to the students for their application of the lesson.
8. Make a list of lesson assignments which would be of particular value in your occupational area.
9. Write a complete lesson plan for:
    a. An operation type of lesson.
    b. An information type of lesson.

Questioning as an Aid to Communication

One of the three important principles of learning already discussed was that people learn the new in terms of the old. The same principle has been stated another way: Experience is the basis for learning. These statements imply that we can learn if we can rearrange the old facts and things we know and coordinate them with new ideas. The professional teacher tries to capitalize on this theory by using students' past experiences as a basis for developing new thoughts, ideas, and concepts. New terms must be defined and new ideas explained because a good deal of the material is outside the experience of the student. Most teachers are conscientious about learning the backgrounds of students in order to do this. This approach is based on the desire to help the student learn new things as easily and completely as possible.

Although this method is necessary, effective, and extensively used, there is yet another method which may, in many cases, be superior. Rather than explaining in terms of the student's past experience, teachers should develop the skill of asking students questions that will stimulate thinking and elicit responses that will lead to the proper answer to a problem. The best learning is that which is the result of self-analysis and individual activity. In short, teachers should develop a speech pattern in which the interrogative sentence is as important and as frequently used, if not more so, than the declarative statement.

Skill in the art of questioning is the basis of high-level, effective teaching. It means competence in forming questions, experience in timing questions, and knowing whom to question. The purposes of questioning have assumed new and broader dimensions.

WHY QUESTION?

Teachers have many reasons for questioning. The following reasons are some of the more important ones:

1. To provoke and stimulate thought.
2. To give the student the opportunity to express himself.
3. To act as a springboard for further discussion and participation.
4. To serve as a guide to reasoning.
5. To help the teacher determine his progress.
6. To aid the teacher in checking his students' progress.
7. To assist the student in determining his own progress.
8. To arouse curiosity, thereby motivating further interest.
9. To cause a student to use previous knowledge in learning new things.
10. To attract attention and encourage participation on the part of all the students.

Other values that arise from skillful questioning will become apparent as the topic is developed further. For example, the oral question is often the forerunner of a written question. It will pay the teacher to be alert to all responses so as to make possible further use of the question in quizzes and examinations.

All of the preceding explanations have been reasons why teachers should make use of questions. The next "why" to be discussed is: What questions to ask and of whom should they be asked? Teachers must exercise discretion when asking questions. Every time a teacher asks a question, he must decide why that particular question is being asked and which student will be called upon to answer it. Some of the reasons listed above should help in making the decision.

Questions are helpful in attracting the attention of a student.

TYPES OF QUESTIONS

The types of questions that teachers ask may be divided into two main categories. They are the *memory question* and the *thought-provoking question*. Each has a very definite function and value.

The Memory Question

The memory question is used when the teacher wants his students to recall information or when he wants to emphasize facts, drill for retention of facts, summarize main points, and obtain some measure of achievement. Answers to memory type of questions are characterized by the following:

1. They usually require a short answer.
2. They sometimes promote guessing.
3. They often have but one correct answer.
4. They usually require little reflection or thought.
5. They are often based on memory rather than knowledge and understanding.

Examples of memory type of questions are easy to recognize:

1. How many volts are in a dry cell?
2. What is the name of the thinner used for shellac?
3. What is the abrasive tool used to polish steel?
4. What plastic is used for airplane domes?
5. What tool is used to cut flatbar?
6. What gas is generated by gasoline engines?
7. What is the name of the process used to join brass pipes?
8. How many inches to the meter?
9. What is the formula for converting centigrade to fahrenheit?
10. What is the name of the movable part of a slide rule?

The Thought-Provoking Question

The thought-provoking question differs from the memory question in that it calls for knowledge and understanding. Although some memory is involved, the student must be able to explain, think about the subject, and produce a logical, correct answer. Guessing is held to a minimum, and real learning—the result of concentration and thought— will result. Thought-provoking questions call for problem-solving: They challenge the student's effort more than the memory question and command greater attention and reflection. They stimulate further activity calling for judgment, analysis, organization, comparison, understanding, insight, and logical thinking. Very often a problem which the teacher finds difficult to teach can be clarified by having students answer thought-provoking questions about it. Some examples are:

1. How does plastic electrical tape compare with friction tape as an insulator?
2. Why is wool a warmer material than cotton?
3. Why are the acrylic plastics said to have memories?
4. What is the principle of the Rockwell Hardness Tester?
5. What is the purpose of the flux on a welding rod?
6. What are the advantages of a Pittsburgh joint?
7. What are three important safety rules to be observed when using a grindstone?
8. Why does an eight-cylinder engine run smoother than a four-cylinder engine?
9. How can a right triangle help in laying out a foundation?
10. Why have building codes been developed?

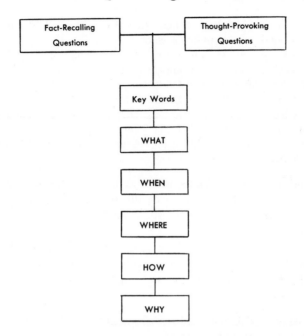

HOW TO QUESTION

Good questioning techniques start with good grammar and language that is familiar to the student. Furthermore, questions should be simple, carefully framed, easy to follow, and readily understood. They should be clear in intent to the learner. If a question is vague, the answer will be vague and without meaning. The very intent of the questioning will thereby be defeated. The result will be wasted time, confusion, and digression. Never be indefinite about what you expect from the student. Remind yourself of the specific aim of your questions. Avoid, as a rule, any question that will invite a general, personal opinion or attitude. The answers you receive may not satisfy or fit in with the work at hand. You can do little about an improper or undesirable response that was opinion and served only to provoke laughter or digression. Frame your question in such a manner so as to insure the answer you want, at least within the context of what you are teaching. Here are some examples that may not only evoke an incorrect response, but may also open the door to "wise-guy" remarks:

1. How would you finish this table? "I wouldn't."
2. What happens when you pour lotion on the scalp? "It runs down the customer's face."
3. How do you draw this diagram? "I copy it from the book."

4. How do you think we can bend this piece of lucite? "Put it in a vise." (And break a good piece of stock.)
5. What would you say about this picture? "I do not like it." (Actually the teacher wanted to prompt a discussion on lighting effects.)
6. Tell what you know about fluorescent lighting. "All of it?"
7. What can you tell us about the drill press? "It drills holes in steel."
8. For what can the slide rule be used? "For making straight lines."
9. When do you use Boyle's Law? "Never—I don't even know the man."
10. Why do you think we are using leather for this belt? "As long as you ask it that way, I would rather use beads."

It should be quite obvious that vague questions do not call for definite answers. Although some of the questions and answers given might seem to be facetious, you will encounter them many times in the classroom.

Never suggest the answer in asking the question; to do so is to destroy the intent of questioning, as well as to deceive the student into thinking he knows the material or is making progress. Compare the following examples.

1. The name of this tool is a hack . . . what?
   What is the name of this tool?
2. Are there 36 or 46 inches to a yard?
   How many inches are there in a yard?
3. Is a transformer used on AC?
   On what type of current can a transformer be used?
4. Should we use a wood, parallel clamp, or a steel "C" clamp to glue the wood joint?
   What is the proper type of clamp to use when gluing wood together?

Notice that in many instances the leading question is stated in poor English.

Questions should include only one idea. Double questions are difficult to follow and complicate thinking unnecessarily. Use your own words—do not follow the wording of a text or any other printed material. Always be specific. Some examples of double questions follow:

1. How and why does a carburetor work?
2. What is the difference between glass tile and ceramic tile, and where are they used?
3. What are worm gears, spur gears, and where are they used?

Of course, any good teacher whose subject or occupational area includes those terms can develop not two but three or four questions in each of these cases involving comparisons, advantages, and principles.

Questions should be asked in a normal, conversational tone of voice as part of the lesson. They should appear to be part of a continuous, sequential presentation of the new work. Teachers should weave questions into the fabric of their teaching so as to produce a natural, easy pattern. Students should expect to be questioned, as well as to be subject to any other legitimate teaching method. Subsequently they will develop habits of study and concentration that prepare them to answer questions intelligently and correctly. Questions add variety to the lesson and set a high standard of teaching which students will recognize and respect.

TECHNIQUES OF QUESTIONING

Questions are only as effective as the manner in which they are used. The entire purpose of questioning is often defeated by teachers who have not learned how or when to use the method. Questions improperly used can be detrimental to learning. Successful use of questions depends on these techniques:

1. *Address the question to the class, hesitate, then call on a specific student.* The intent of questioning is to provoke thought; therefore, this technique stimulates the whole class. This will not occur if a specific student's name is called first. There will be a tendency for the others to rest and "let George do it." Everyone will, by formulating an answer, profit by the thinking involved, and will be in a position to check on the answer given, perhaps even add to the response.
2. *Scatter questions over the entire class.* Avoid any consistent, regular procedure of questioning such as by row, alphabetical order, across the front of the room, or across the back. Again, it must be emphasized that any device is incorrect which tends to remove the class from the thinking process, leaving only the one person to answer. Scattering questions will prevent mental loafing. Some teachers scatter questions by shuffling class cards as they question. Actually, the skilled teacher need not resort to such a teaching aid. However, the new teacher may find such an aid helpful during the early part of his career.
3. *Allow a reasonable interval of time for answering.* Realize that time is needed to formulate an answer. Do not cut a student short but give him time, especially if he needs encouragement. By the same

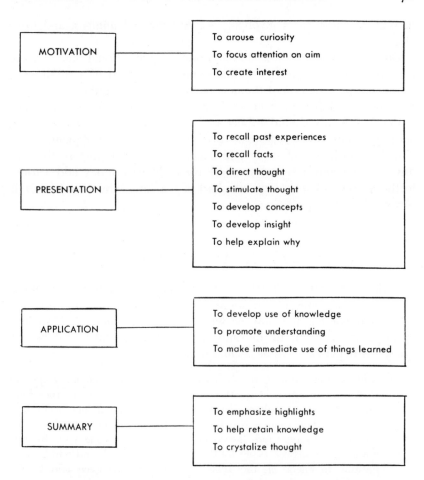

token, do not allow too much time. Wasting time is unfair to the other students. It is embarrassing to a student to grope for an answer in front of his peers. Questioning techniques should never include any factors which will prove embarrassing or cause a student to appear ridiculous to others. In fact, such a procedure is a reason why many students will not respond when a teacher asks questions.

4. *Pose questions within the ability of the student to whom the question is addressed.* There is no point in asking a difficult question of a student who is incapable of answering. On the other hand, it is just as wasteful to ask simple questions of a more capable student. Such easy questions will appear to be pointless and inane to the bright student.

5. *Ask questions of the inattentive.* Many a teacher has entered into conflict with his students because he put the student "on the spot"

due to a minor transgression. For example, a teacher notices that a student is gazing out the window, obviously in a reverie. Rather than make a major issue of such conduct, an experienced teacher will phrase a question for the class and then direct it to the dreamer. The malefactor, if that is what he is, is brought to attention and returned to the learning situation. The teacher, by looking away when the student "comes to," can give the student an opportunity to save face.

6. *Require students to give complete answers.* Do not answer for them by adding to their answers in order to make them complete. In addition, do not repeat answers. Both techniques are to be avoided. After a while, students will listen to the teacher rather than to the student who answers. If a student has trouble, resulting in an incomplete answer, then ask another student to lend assistance. If a student answers in a low tone, ask a student on the opposite side of the room to repeat the answer. If he cannot repeat it, request the first student to answer in a louder tone.

7. *Encourage students to ask questions.* Do not discourage questions on the part of students. Keep them relevant, demand good English, and help students formulate their questions. It is good practice to have other students answer the questions. A good question by a student serves as an indication of his curiosity and interest in the subject, as well as of the talents he possesses.

8. *Do not permit frequent group responses.* Loss of class control often starts with this practice. The answer is often unintelligible and errors are hard to pick up, much less to determine who made them. Individual answers are to be preferred.

9. *Do not ask questions which can be answered by guessing.* A guessed answer, even if correct, is of no diagnostic value to the teacher and is of questionable learning value to the student. It promotes bad study habits and poor learning habits, solves nothing, wastes time, and proves only that some students are good guessers.

10. *Learn to use the key words of questioning.* They are: *how, why, which, where, what,* and *when.*

WHEN TO QUESTION

The time to question is whenever a question can do more good than a mere statement. When is that? It is when you, the teacher, feel that the answer is within the ability of the student and when he will learn better by thinking out the answer than by your giving it to him. Good questions are usually planned. Key questions must be planned. Other questions may and will become spontaneous when questioning becomes part of the teacher's regular style. Questions can be used at the start

TEACHING OCCUPATIONAL SKILLS

of a lesson to create interest and arouse curiosity; they may be used in the development of a thought or concept; they may be used when presenting a principle and demonstrating a skill; they may be used to check the progress of a lesson; or they may be used to summarize a lesson.

Uses of Questioning

1. To spark a discussion.
2. To obtain attention.
3. To review.
4. To drill.
5. To determine what students know.
6. To check students' study habits.
7. To bring out the aim of a lesson.
8. To reaffirm the aim of a lesson.
9. To help solve problems.
10. To obtain explanations.
11. To check facts.
12. To determine individual differences.
13. To develop concepts.
14. To stimulate participation.

Techniques of Questioning

1. Be brief and clear.
2. Be specific.
3. Frame questions according to the students' needs.
4. Frame questions in the students' language, using good English.
5. Use questions that are consistent with students' abilities.
6. Use questions that call upon the students' past experiences.
7. Call on students in an irregular fashion.
8. Call on the inattentive student.
9. Call on students in the rear of the classroom as well as those in the front row.
10. Avoid questions that can be answered wtih a simple "yes" or "no."
11. Avoid questions that will waste time.
12. Avoid questions that suggest the answer.
13. Avoid questions that do not have a worthwhile purpose.
14. Do not answer questions from lazy students, but ask them counter-questions.
15. Ask questions courteously; expect the same in return.
16. Ask questions informally.
17. Ask questions relevant to the lesson.
18. Ask questions in a logical sequence.

19. Enter grades for students' answers after class.
20. Recognize volunteers.

Summary

"Good teaching is a matter of drawing out rather than a matter of putting in."

Teachers should use questions as much as they use statements in their teaching. Questions pry deeply and make use of the student's knowledge and past experience to help him learn new things. When the student's learning is the result of using his own store of knowledge and ability to think, the results are more penetrating and more permanent. Questions are of the memory type or the thought-provoking type; both kinds are important when used properly. Teachers should become skillful in the art of questioning because "to question well is to teach well." Learning the technique of questioning, therefore, is a very important phase of a teacher's training. The key words to questioning are *how, why, when, where, which,* and *what.*

Questions can be used in almost all teaching situations and in all parts of the lesson. They should be well stated, clearly understood, and delivered in a natural, informal manner. Key questions should be planned and developed for every lesson. The real art of questioning can be acquired only by practice with an aim for improvement.

Questions and Projects

1. What are five values of questioning?
2. Describe some values of questioning which apply to your teaching situation.
3. Select the aim for an information lesson and make up a series of key questions which would help you develop that aim with your students.
4. Select the lesson aim for an operation type of lesson and develop a series of five key questions which you could use in the presentation of the lesson.
5. Develop a series of questions for a lesson using the key words *how, why, what, where, which,* and *when.*
6. Develop a series of thought-provoking questions around the following phrases:
    a. Compare the uses of . . .
    b. Describe the function of . . .
    c. Describe the principle of . . .
    d. State the advantage of . . .
    e. Explain how . . .

7. Do the same as in question 6, using five other starting phrases.
8. Develop ten memory type of questions that might be used in a review lesson.
9. Describe how you would handle each of the following typical classroom situations:
    a. The chronic hand-waver.
    b. The student who calls out answers.
    c. The student who thinks he knows.
    d. The student who answers in a low tone of voice.
    e. The student who gives incomplete answers.
    f. The student who always asks for help.
    g. The student who asks a stimulating question.

Presenting the Instructional Unit

There is no more effective way to learn an occupational skill than to practice it. The most effective way to teach an occupational skill is to demonstrate it. If teaching is helping others to learn, then teaching occupational skills can be defined as showing the learner "how to do it." One of the two most essential teaching skills is the ability to demonstrate. The other is the ability to explain. Both are vital to the successful teaching of either an operation lesson or an information lesson.

THE DEMONSTRATION

A demonstration is any planned performance by a teacher of an occupational skill, scientific principle, or experiment. A demonstration might be as simple as showing an individual student how to hold a pair of sheet-metal shears correctly, or it might be the performance of an occupational job such as soldering a splice, or it might be showing a group of youngsters the skill of hand sanding. The art of demonstration is not restricted to manual skills alone. A teacher might demonstrate the use of the slide rule, a wheatstone bridge, or a sensitive balance. Let us remember that the two most important means of communication are the organs of sight and hearing. When a teacher demonstrates, he uses both of these senses. Remember also that the sense of sight is used to a great extent in learning and accounts for approximately 75 percent of what we absorb mentally. Hearing accounts for about 13 percent. The demonstration method of teaching has other advantages. A good demonstration is in itself strong motivation. Learners use the power of observation to acquire new knowledge. The demonstration is an attention-getter; it gives the learner something to watch and something to imitate. A good demonstration can be given to groups or individuals. The size of the group depends on the nature of the demonstration. If the physical size of the equipment or materials is small, the group size should be reduced, but if the physical size of the demonstration materials is large the entire group can be taught. The same applies to the complexity of the demonstration. In brief, demonstration teaching is concrete teaching. It deals with real things and tangible objects.

Preparing for a Demonstration

Preparation for a successful demonstration starts during the period of teacher training. It is during the time spent in professional preparation that teachers should cultivate good command of language, the proper use of terms and words, and become aware of the multiple problems of group teaching. One of the principles of teaching which must be remembered is to teach according to a planned sequence. That is, to demonstrate when the demonstration fits in with the activity and can be applied by the majority of the class as soon as possible. Demonstrate as the need arises. Follow demonstrations with information. It is easier to understand something after seeing it work than to attempt a visualization of an abstract description.

Having determined the need for a demonstration, the next thing to do is to plan for the demonstration itself. One of the most difficult things for any expert to do is to realize that the hundreds of skills he performs almost unconsciously must be carefully demonstrated and explained to the learner. It is here that the lesson plan becomes so necessary. Teachers should learn to list the important points of any skill, in outline form, step-by-step. These points should then be included in the presentation of the plan. It is interesting to observe the list of teaching points which must be taught when such a list is developed. A good lesson is all-inclusive, that is, it should include all the important material for learning the specific thing being taught. Only by carefully planning the lesson can a teacher make it inclusive.

Tips for Preparing a Demonstration

1. A good teaching performance demands preparation. Run through the demonstration in order to identify and anticipate difficult steps. A smoother performance will result in a more successful lesson.
2. Obtain all necessary materials, tools, equipment, visual and other teaching aids before the lesson period.
3. Arrange all materials in advance and have them within easy reach.
4. Check all parts, aids, machines, and equipment to be sure they are in working order.
5. Remove all extraneous and digressive material before the lesson is presented.
6. Time your demonstration during the run-through. If it runs to much more than 15 minutes, review the demonstration. It is possible that you have included too much material.
7. Check for student visibility and grouping. Check for proximity to various facilities, such as electrical, gas, and water outlets.
8. Prepare the chalkboard with preliminary headings and sketches. Have colored chalk on hand.

It is necessary that the teacher include pertinent information as the demonstration proceeds. It is most important to remember that when manual skills are being taught, it is necessary to stick to the aim of the lesson and not include "good" but irrelevant material. Anything that will create digression or cause student interest to wander must be avoided.

In presenting the actual demonstration the teacher should be relaxed and confident. His manner should be somewhat informal and friendly. He should try to bolster the students' confidence in their own ability to learn the lesson being demonstrated. Sometimes it is a good idea to go through the demonstration once at normal speed in order to give the learners an overview of the operation, and then repeat it more slowly for the learner's benefit. Be enthusiastic, speak clearly, make your performance both expert and interesting. Check for safety. Keep the group clear of moving parts, flying chips, and other hazards. Check the following list for some ideas:

Suggestions for Improving a Demonstration

1. Give a good performance but don't be theatrical.

2. Explain each step or process as you proceed. Tell the "why" as well as the "how."
3. Make sure students see the demonstration from the angle they will perform it themselves.
4. Follow your lesson plan; stick to the aim.
5. Be sure everyone can see and hear.
6. Prepare key questions beforehand and ask them as you go along.
7. Put yourself in the learner's place as you demonstrate.
8. Observe all safety rules and procedures.
9. Emphasize key points.
10. Implement your demonstration with the proper instructional aids whenever possible.
11. Use the chalkboard for new terms, explanations, listing steps of procedure.
12. Provide for student participation where possible.
13. Demonstrate the correct way only. First impressions are important, therefore make them correct ones.
14. Remember that students learn by example. Let your demonstration be a good example.
15. Try to plan a demonstration which will develop the skill being taught. Remember the principles of presenting new material: from the simple to the complex and one step at a time.
16. Develop a good motivating device to create immediate attention and interest. Develop the aim and give the students a clear picture of what to observe.

An important adjunct to the demonstration lesson is the chalkboard. The question often arises, "What do I do if I don't have the material and equipment for a demonstration?" The next thing to do is illustrate. In fact, an illustration can often be valuable with a demonstration as an accompanying technique. Use pictures, charts, diagrams, and models to support your illustration. Sometimes a series of sketches showing the sequence of steps and the development of a process are a valuable aid. Another technique is to use a good film or filmstrip to depict a skill or scientific principle. The film has an advantage because it is made with all necessary materials, equipment, and tools available. The camera is able to make a "close-up" and every viewer has a front-row seat. It provides a change of pace, and the sound of a different voice provides a break in the ordinary routine. Interest can be heightened by introducing this kind of variety in presenting a demonstration.

Practically all operation types of lessons make use of the demonstration. This is of necessity true because operation lessons are primarily concerned with teaching manual skills and, as it has been pointed out, the best way to teach "how" is to show "how." The other type of lesson is the information lesson. In presenting either lesson the teacher must be able to *explain*.

THE ART OF EXPLAINING

The art of explaining things to others is the distinguishing mark of good teaching. The teacher plays many roles and fulfills many functions. It is the responsibility of every teacher to simplify, clarify, guide, lead, and explain complex things so the learner can learn more easily. The first requisite for skill in explaining is to understand fully the material to be presented. The instructor must understand how to do the operation properly, why it is being done in a specific manner, and also know the related information pertaining to it. It is a good thing for teachers first to learn basic principles well, then to learn the historical evolution of practices and processes, as well as the manual skills and standards of occupational areas.

How to Explain

1. Use simple language. Use the language of the learner.
2. Be patient and resourceful.
3. Make liberal use of analogy, comparison, example, and illustration.
4. Use visual aids as much as possible.
5. Develop a good sequence of simple-to-difficult, step-by-step techniques in explaining.
6. Use students' knowledge as a base on which to build.
7. Explain and define new terms.
8. Use the technique of "show and tell."
9. Point out relationships of parts and processes.
10. Use logic and reasoning in explaining.
11. Develop concepts, history, and uses in explaining.
12. Be sure the group understands the goal of the explanation.
13. Make use of the chalkboard in developing an explanation.
14. Keep eye contact with the class as you explain.
15. Encourage questions as well as ask them.
16. Call attention to highlights.
17. Use a medial summary to strengthen your explanation.

The secret of an easy-to-follow explanation lies in the ability of the teacher to clearly define and understand the aim, the purpose, and the very core of the thing he is attempting to explain. The next step is to simplify it in terms of the learner, then explain the operation, theory, principle, or process in good, plain language. Teachers are expected to have a wide vocabulary and to use proper English. Their primary function is to teach, and this can be done best by using simple language, a friendly mien, and informal presentation, without sacrificing any standards of quality of good speech. In fact, the skillful teacher will introduce new terms, define them as he uses them, and attempt to enlarge his students' vocabularies whenever possible. His first duty is, however, the teaching of the lesson according to the aim which has been selected. It is often easier to explain by demonstrating concurrently with the explanation.

Some Examples of Good Explanations

1. A group of visitors was being shown through a large machine shop. None of them was a machinist. Their guide was one of the shop foremen. Some of the machines were capable of handling shafts 30 inches in diameter and some had beds 12 feet across. To the uninitiated, all the machines were bewildering. The guide explained the function of all the machines this way: "All these machines do essentially the same thing; they remove metal just as the carpenter planes wood. There are two basic ways to shave off metal. One is to move the cutting tool in relation to the work which is held stationary, and the other is to move the work and keep the cutting tool stationary." He then pointed out examples of each type. Although the people in the group did not become machinists, they all understood what the machines were doing as a result of the explanation. The simple explanation given by the guide might well have been used by a teacher as a starting point or introduction to a new group of students.
2. A teacher found that in explaining X-rays to his class it was rather difficult for some students to grasp the concept of rays being absorbed by dense body structures and easily passing through less dense tissue, thereby forming a readable impression on a plate. He added one simple aid when he explained x-rays to subsequent classes. He used a flashlight and a mock-up of cardboard bones and a white poster card representing the sensitized plate. This is an example of an alert teacher combining demonstration, teaching aids, and explanation to get an important concept across to his students.
3. Explanations can be greatly facilitated by developing a sequence of lessons through which a thread of continuity passes and ties all the learning together.

The following sequence of lessons in electricity illustrate item 3 above. The numbers are arbitrary and are used merely to indicate the sequence.

Lesson One: What happens when electricity flows through a conductor?
(The points brought out are heat and magnetic field.)

Key Drawing

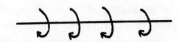

Lesson Two: How electromagnetism is produced.
(The aim is to explain the simple electromagnet. Magnetic field is concentrated.)

Key Drawing

Lesson Three: How a vibrating bell works.
(The aim is to show how electromagnets are put to work.)

Key Drawing

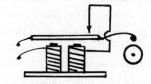

Lesson Four: How the relay works.
(The aim is to teach the principle of the operation of most common relays.)

Key Drawing

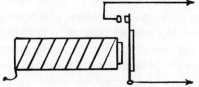

Lesson Five: The principle of the simple bell transformer.
(The aim is to teach the concept of the theory of induction.)

Key Drawing

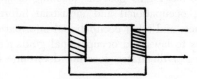

A smoothly planned series of lessons, which build on previous knowledge and lay the groundwork for future learning at the same time, are in themselves an aid to explaining. Some teachers use the same idea in arranging their work on the basis of tools, equipment, materials, jobs, or operations. The analysis of one's teaching area, as well as occupational background, is most essential for the kind of developmental teaching by demonstration and explanation presented in this text.

THE INFORMATION LESSON VERSUS THE OPERATION LESSON

A teacher gave a lesson on how to form a piece of plastic in making a letter-holder. He taught it step-by-step and, in drawing up his lesson plan, included the information he thought necessary for teaching a successful lesson. The plan covered two pages. The lesson ran over the class period, and the students were so busy taking notes that not many observed fully how the material was handled and bent. The steps in the actual operation of making the letter-holder were noted in outline form. Safety notes, such as using asbestos gloves, were also included. This made for a good operation type of lesson. Unfortunately, the teacher also included other points, such as characteristics of acrylic plastics, uses of acrylic plastics, information on the type of bonding cement used with that type of plastic, and the common trade thicknesses of plastic sheets. It might seem at first glance that all the information given was necessary, and it must be conceded that it was. The problem the teacher created in drawing up the plan resulted from a lack of experience on his part. He failed to separate the material which properly belonged to a good information lesson from the few teaching points of information which could have been profitably introduced into the operation lesson. In short, the teacher did not have:

1. A specifically defined aim in his mind.
2. A clear understanding of the two main types of lessons. An information lesson has for its goal the teaching of such things as principles, functions, occupational and industrial information, related mathematics, science, and other occupational information ranging from use of handbooks to laws and occupational guidance. Whether a teacher demonstrates or illustrates does not determine the type of lesson; the intent

and objective of the specific lesson determines the type. Showing and telling, or demonstrating and explaining, are used to best advantage when used together to teach either information or operations.

The information type of lesson seldom includes the teaching of a manual skill. If the skill is incidental to the information, the two types may be combined. Otherwise, reserve the manual skills for an operation type of lesson.

Flexibility

The accurate definition of information and operation types of lessons has but one major purpose: It helps the teacher establish a clear aim and objective for the lesson he prepares and presents. These exacting definitions are not to be taken as an indication of rigidity in teaching. On the contrary, teachers should learn to be flexible. Situations arise in the shop, laboratory, or classroom which are often completely unpredictable, and teachers must be prepared to cope with each problem as it arises.

As an example of flexibility, a teacher may have carefully planned the explanation of a principle. His planning took into account the use of a simple working model. Let us assume that the model failed for some reason to make the explanation clear. The teacher should be flexible enough to try a diagram, sketch, or some other visual technique on the chalkboard to help his students understand the principle. Very often a teacher can have a student who seems to have grasped the point of the explanation act as a teacher and explain the point to the rest of the class.

Enthusiasm and Poise

The discussion of lesson presentation has, up to this point, been concerned with the types of lessons and the mechanics of explaining and demonstrating. Planning and organizing, good methodology, and variety are part of the procedure. There is one other factor that must be taken into consideration. The teacher's style of delivery is just as important as what he is trying to present. He must be enthusiastic, pleasant, patient, and sincere. He must be poised and develop the ability to think on his feet. Flexibility can be a meaningful term only if the teacher is willing to try different approaches, think quickly and clearly, and seize unexpected opportunities to get his planned points across. The presentation of a lesson should be a natural, easy, relaxed performance. The more skilled the teacher, the easier and smoother will be the presentation. A teacher must show how and tell why, sometimes separately in different lessons, or concurrently when the lesson calls for it. He cannot afford to neglect his style of delivery in either instance.

However, there are many fine points of the teaching art which characterize a good teaching performance. They are common to any type of lesson, and the instructor should be familiar with them. The following list presents some of the outstanding characteristics. They do not always appear on a plan, but they should be observed. These characteristics will assert themselves by practice and application as the instructor gains experience.

Characteristics of a Good Teaching Performance

1. Use of good English.
2. Delivery in a pleasant tone of voice.
3. Change of voice with intonations and inflections.
4. Observance of good speaking techniques, posture, and poise.
5. Wearing of appropriate apparel.
6. Display of enthusiasm.
7. Demonstration of occupational skill.
8. Attention to good seating arrangement.
9. Arrangement of good lighting and ventilation.
10. Consideration of students' physical difficulties—hearing, seeing, and so on.
11. Evidences of good practices of shop organization and management.
12. All materials necessary for the lesson, within reach.
13. Distracting or extraneous materials removed.
14. Smooth, skillful presentation of new material.
15. Expert handling of questions and problems.
16. Ability to stick to the aim.
17. Skillful handling of digressions.
18. Adequate use of good questioning techniques.
19. Good group control.
20. Quick and efficient handling of clerical details.
21. Effective use of the chalkboard.
22. Adequate student participation.
23. Display of patience, understanding, and a touch of humor.
24. Ability to talk to students at their level.
25. Setting of a good example to stimulate student improvement.
26. Relaxed, pleasant atmosphere which reflects mutual respect and desire to learn.
27. Pace of the lesson fits the majority of the students.

28. Frequent checking to assure student understanding and learning.
29. Use of example, analogy, comparison, and "for instances" in explaining.
30. Ability of the teacher to think on his feet.
31. Display of tact and patience in avoiding controversy or argument.
32. Freedom of students to ask questions or offer constructive criticism.
33. Successful completion of the lesson within the time allotted.

LECTURING AND TELLING

Good teaching places the emphasis on showing and telling rather than "lecturing." The students whom the junior high, senior high, or community college instructor will meet are interested in learning many new things. Their backgrounds are limited in most cases, therefore the teacher must build upon the students' previous knowledge as he progresses with the work. He must recognize the need for applying the principles of teaching and learning and be aware of individual differences. He should supplement his telling with teaching aids whenever and wherever possible.

The opposite of this type of instruction is the lecture. The lecture is generally utilized by a specialist addressing a group of highly trained and well-informed people who usually know something about the subject. However, under these circumstances, the lecturer should not abandon good organizational techniques in developing his presentation. He may, and usually does, dispense with questioning, demonstrating, and using aids. The types of audiences which can profit from the lecture method of presentation are seldom found in the areas of teaching considered by this text. Lectures are very limited as good teaching devices.

When to Use the Lecture

Despite the shortcomings of the lecture as a teaching method, it has value in secondary education, limited though it may be. Most important among these values are:

1. The lecture may be useful in the development of general interest. Thus a lecture by a shop teacher on his past experiences, how he secured different positions, or the history of tools, processes, and so on, of the occupation, might have value in arousing occupational interest. In the same way, a lecture on various methods of doing a particular job as practiced in industry would perhaps arouse interest and might become the means of stimulating greater student effort.

2. The lecture may be a useful means of giving vocational guidance by informing students of the advantages of a particular vocation.
3. The lecture is useful in providing supplementary information and background on various subjects such as the making of castings, commercial glues, the manufacture of steel, technological advances, and many other topics.
4. The lecture is particularly useful in presenting information about material that is not readily available; for example, a discussion on the production of molded plastics or on the manufacture of synthetic gasoline.

Teachers often give shop talks. In fact, they have occasion to give many so-called "talks" to their students during the school year. Invariably, however, they should accompany their talks with an illustration, example, demonstration, or aid of some kind. Teachers should not take advantage of their position to monopolize discussions or to neglect good teaching techniques and become strictly lecturers.

The shop talk or telling method, as used in informational lesson presentation during the regular class session, has the values described above. It can help maintain interest and even create enthusiasm when properly executed. Teaching of many phases of information can oftentimes be accomplished in this manner. It is an especially valuable device to use during periods of irregular time, such as shortened periods or other unusual circumstances when regular presentations are not possible.

Techniques for Preparing a Shop Talk

In vocational and practical arts courses, the term "shop talk" is applied to the presentation commonly known as a lecture. The following suggestions should help make the shop talk successful:

1. Limit the talk to one major subject.
2. Limit the scope, deciding on the essential points to be covered.
3. Arrange the material in some definite sequence. An outline of the subject briefed on a card enables a teacher to follow the sequence from beginning to end.
4. Provide an interesting opening to compel attention. A brief story is an easy and effective way to begin and should be related to the lesson in the talk.
5. Plan to include illustrations and concrete examples. Pictures, charts, and diagrams help to clarify verbal explanations. Have them ready and in the right order for use.
6. Have a strong conclusion that summarizes the points of the talk and drives them home convincingly.

7. Allow time for students to ask questions. Any exchange of questions will cause students to listen more carefully and to learn more rapidly and accurately.

Techniques for Delivering a Talk

A broad set of rules and principles which may be found in specialized texts has been evolved for public speakers. It will suffice here to highlight those rules and principles of public speaking which seem especially pertinent to teachers. It will be found that close observance of the following points will produce encouraging results.

1. Remove all distractions such as charts, chalkboard drawings, or unusual desk decorations irrelevant to the subject.
2. Stand where every student can see you without having to strain or sit in an uncomfortable position.
3. Face and look directly at your students. Don't neglect any section of the class by not looking at the individuals in that section.
4. Insure proper room temperature and lighting.
5. Present your material in an organized fashion. When a teacher says "Let's see now," or "Where was I?" he is probably unorganized.
6. Learn to speak smoothly and coherently from notes. Avoid reading the whole talk from a manuscript in a dull, uninterrupted manner.
7. Do not assume an unnatural tone of voice or affected pronunciations.
8. Regulate your rate of speaking so that it is neither too fast for student comprehension, nor too slow for student interest.
9. Speak distinctly and with enough volume so that all students may hear. Adjust your voice to the size of the room; speaking loudly in a small room is very irritating.
10. Increase the volume of your voice slightly to express strong feeling or emphasis.
11. Encourage your students to take notes.
12. Change your position occasionally. Don't make a habit of leaning on a chair or sitting on a desk.
13. Change your facial expressions often. Avoid such things as scowling, a look of arrogance with head held high, or talking out of the side of the mouth or looking bored.
14. Have the courage to admit that you do not know the answers to questions when that is the case.

Habits and Mannerisms of Teachers and Public Speakers

Psychologists state that our habits are patterns of conduct we have established by reacting repeatedly to certain stimuli so that our reactions have become virtually unconscious or automatic. Although some habits are useful or beneficial, others that are formed unconsciously

TEACHING OCCUPATIONAL SKILLS

can be very irritating. Each individual has his own peculiarities that people associate with his personality. These personal peculiarities, called mannerisms, influence the impression people form of us. Some of the most common of these distracting mannerisms found among teachers and public speakers are as follows:

1. Chin rubbing.
2. Nose pulling.
3. Ear pulling.
4. Cuff pulling.
5. Pencil waving.
6. Brow wiping.
7. Coin jingling.
8. Palm rubbing.
9. Ceiling gazing.
10. Floor gazing.
11. Fidgeting.
12. Floor pacing.
13. Tie adjusting.
14. Toe balancing.
15. Key chain swinging.
16. Chalk tossing.
17. Eyeglass adjusting.
18. Throat clearing.
19. Paper waving.
20. Hair smoothing.

Are you guilty of any of these mannerisms? Students will watch for your quirks in lieu of concentrating on what you say. Most individuals who stand before a group to speak or teach are entirely oblivious to what they do while standing there. It may never occur to them that what they do while speaking will have a great influence on the listeners. The only one who can correct these mannerisms is the person who tries to become aware of his shortcomings. An occasional offense is not serious. It is the repetition of mannerisms that causes a speaker to be known by his faults rather than by his virtues.

Summary

"The man who can make hard things easy is a real teacher."

There are two main types of lessons in teaching occupational skills: the information lesson and the operation lesson. Although the demonstration seems to be ideally suited for teaching operations and manual skills in general, its use should not be restricted to that type of lesson. A demonstration is a visual means of teaching. It is showing how something is done or how something works. It gives the learner the opportunity to observe and helps him to reason. Teachers can demonstrate principles, applications of mathematics, mechanical and chemical processes, and many other things classified as information.

Good lesson presentation demands liberal use of demonstrations. They should be carefully planned, not only for the material and equipment needed but also for anticipating questions and handling of demonstration equipment. A teacher must develop also the ability to explain. Explaining is communicating, and one of the difficulties encountered in teaching is a lack of facility to convey thoughts, concepts, and ideas to other people. A teacher must use the language level of the learners in his classes. He must use simple yet good English, enunciate clearly, speak loudly enough to be heard, question sufficiently to be sure that the students understand him, and use whatever aids are necessary to convey his ideas.

Teachers must be flexible enough to make adjustments and changes on the spot if the material fails to register with students. They must be versatile enough to use the chalkboard for sketches and to use diagrams to supplement whatever method they may have planned.

New teachers often fall into the habit of lecturing in shop or laboratory rather than telling or showing. The important difference is that lecturing can only be successful when the audience is partially informed and has some background for listening to a specialist elaborate or philosophize on the subject. Secondary school students have so much to learn that successful and effective instruction must utilize telling and showing in lieu of lecturing. Shop talks must be supplemented with simple explanations, use of demonstrations, and the inclusion of appropriate teaching aids. The talk must be planned, be simple, have a specific aim, and in general be an informal, yet well-organized presentation. Shop talks may be delivered to the whole group, several of the group, or even to a team during the follow-up of a lesson presentation.

Questions and Projects

1. Select three principles that must be taught in your occupational area. Develop a simple demonstration for each.
2. Describe by means of sketches and diagrams, accompanied by suitable explanation, three simple devices you could use in explaining three skills or points of related information.
3. Evaluate a recent lesson demonstration you have presented or observed. Refer to these main areas:
    a. Adequacy of advance planning.
    b. Use of teaching aids.
    c. Questioning technique.
    d. Evidence of students' understanding.
4. List two or three formulas, principles, or other related information not commonly referred to in the occupation but which require explanation for complete understanding of the occupation.
5. Develop a sequence of steps utilized in the presentation of an information type of lesson. Include a demonstration in your planning.

6. Develop a similar sequence for an operation type of lesson.
7. What are some of the facets of showmanship which are essential for a successful demonstration?
8. Lectures are like a one-way street. Explain the disadvantages of this concept in occupational instruction.
9. Develop a list of teaching skills and devices which should appear in a specific shop talk.

Teaching the Group and Instructing the Individual

It is often said that the teacher teaches the group and instructs the individual. Nowhere in the teaching profession is this so true as in the teaching of occupational skills. Both individual instruction and group teaching require special skills and understanding. Each presents unique advantages that the teacher must be aware of and be ready to use when needed.

INDIVIDUAL INSTRUCTION

There are certain advantages in individual instruction which the teacher should recognize. He should follow up the majority of his demonstrations and explanations by checking every student. He should give supplementary instruction to each one who needs it, and to those who are ready for additional work. He must help the student achieve his maximum potential. Some of the characteristics of individual instruction are:
1. The pace of the lesson can be more rapid.
2. Less formality is required.
3. One student is easily checked and corrected.
4. The student can ask more questions.
5. Instruction is easily adjusted to one person.
6. There are no problems such as seeing clearly.
7. The student receives the full attention of the teacher.

Less preparation is needed in teaching an individual student than in teaching a group, but many more teachers would be needed if all instruction were on an individual basis. Therefore, group teaching constitutes the major part of all teaching. Group teaching, although it is not the only solution to economic costs and the shortage of teachers, does have important results and values that arise from an interchange of ideas, discussion, and group endeavor. Skillful teachers have found many ways of profiting from the offerings within a class. Students will bring in new ideas, new thoughts, and often up-to-date applications of occupational skills. Workers in all occupational areas find that people seldom work alone. There must be cooperation on the job between individuals from different occupations. Students must learn to work within a group and apply the principles of cooperative conduct.

Most groups are heterogeneous, which poses the problem of determining the teaching level. The range of individual differences is broad, and the teacher in reaching the group can only attempt to reach the majority. At the same time, he must provide for the minority, which consists of the students at both ends of the curve of distribution. In any given class there are those who are faster, those who are slower, and the majority or largest number of the group who represent the so-called average. Within these three general groupings, teachers will find a wide range of individual differences. The following list indicates some of the ways in which individuals differ:

1. Mechanical ability.
2. Mental ability.
3. Physical health, size, and development.
4. Reading ability.
5. Mathematics ability.
6. Interests and goals.
7. Environmental and cultural differences.

It is the teacher's responsibility to recognize the worth of each individual and to discover the student's potentialities, and then to help the individual develop his latent ability. It is just that responsibility which leads to the statement already made that the teacher must teach the group and instruct the individual.

GROUP INSTRUCTION

In discussing group instruction, it might be well to discuss the small class and the large class. The techniques used in both are similar, but the degree to which they are used may vary. If the group is large, more formality is needed; therefore group control becomes more essential. In both instances, whether small or large groups, the teacher steps into another role. It is the role of public speaker. He must gain interest, hold attention, have something of value to present, and get the message across to as many students as possible. In addition, the teacher must constantly check and test the progress he makes as he goes along. Some major factors of group instruction which must be given consideration are:

1. The teaching must be geared to the needs of the majority. It should be in a sequence and tempo which is timed to the progress of the majority of the class.
2. The conditions under which the lesson is given must be well-organized in order that every student can see, hear, and profit from the lesson. If the size of the group indicates that the results may be of doubtful value, then plans should be made to teach the lesson to two small groups. One group can be assigned work while the other receives the instruction. The teacher's performance must be expert with a minimum chance for error or omission. He must plan ways and means of encouraging as many pupils as possible to participate in the lesson. Also, he should check carefully with well-phrased questions to determine the degree of learning that has taken place.
3. The teacher must provide for the fast and the slow learner. Although there are many common characteristics among students, he must be sure to provide the slow learner with appropriate questions and tasks,

and likewise to challenge the faster learner with more difficult questions and explanations when appropriate. Teachers should neither cater to the especially alert student nor neglect the slow learner.
4. The teacher must pay close attention to his own personal qualities. He must develop a sureness, poise, and delivery which will instill confidence in his students. He must be able to speak clearly, using proper speech and proper pronunciation. He should develop a good command of language so that he is able to explain well, define new terms, as well as speak the language of the learner when necessary. The teacher should dress properly. A shop coat or apron is always appropriate dress when teaching an occupational skill, especially in the shop area. The teacher must also develop the skills of demonstrating, questioning, thinking on his feet, and making decisions quickly.
5. The teacher must learn certain techniques of controlling groups such as keeping eye contact and making use of the multiple sense appeal. He should be able to sense fatigue and other symptoms which are the forerunners of confusion, distraction, and loss of group control. He should learn to use the best teaching aids necessary in a given teaching situation.

Group teaching should be followed with individual instruction. A teacher can detect flaws in his presentation when he checks and helps each individual. This typing class is sponsored by the Manpower Development and Training Program.

Although the major part of teaching involves groups, the teacher often finds that certain skills do not lend themselves to group instruction. In that case, he should teach those particular skills on an individual basis or at least to small groups. Those skills that involve the sense of delicate touch or hearing, or an operation that involves a small mechanism or the use of new muscles or new uses for groups of muscles, might require that the teacher repeat a lesson many times. Practice makes perfect, and many mechanical skills can be perfected only in this way. The teacher must determine how best to teach such skills. He must, however, avoid a boring, monotonous method that will turn interest into disinterest. Learning can be repetitive; yet when it is presented in connection with several jobs or projects, the repetition does not become irksome. The repetition of a skill will in turn develop craftsmanship.

The teacher should use the students to improve the shop as well as to improve their learning. This is done in a variety of ways. Advanced students may be rewarded with the opportunity to engage in special projects, following the completion of the regular assignments. Students with special talents can help develop special teaching aids. Many students are creative, and if asked to examine the shop for the purpose of improving it, will oftentimes offer good suggestions. From time to time the products of the individual shops may be valuable in the completion of a general school project. In this way students will not only broaden their skills but also learn the values of cooperation.

The teacher should develop extra jobs for the superior or particularly able students. These need not be advanced jobs only; they may be more jobs of a similar kind on the same learning level. In other words, the instructional material which every teacher should develop should be enriched horizontally as well as vertically. It is up to the teacher to decide whether or not a student should be given extra jobs to perfect or develop a certain skill to a higher level of proficiency. This decision falls upon the teacher. He must be fair and impartial and decide in terms of the best interest of the student. He must also develop jobs, projects, and other instructional material for the slower learner. These should be more detailed, more comprehensive, involve more sketches and diagrams, and require more explanations.

Teachers should equip themselves with various types of textbooks in the professional field. Books on applied psychology will prove of particular value in learning how to handle students. A wide variety of catalogs and trade literature should be included in the teacher's reference library. No single text may fit your particular needs, and no one text will suit every individual. By using many sources of reference material, students improve their learning to a very marked degree, if properly guided.

Using Notebooks in Instruction

The notebook, probably one of the most frequently used teaching aids, is valuable in group teaching because of its versatility. It is ideal for written communication with a group of learners and can also be used in individual instruction. When notebooks are properly used, students are trained to improve their use of written English and their organization of thoughts, ideas, and facts.

Teachers should not abuse notes by assigning them merely as "busywork." On the other hand, students who have been overconditioned in note-taking become automatons and record everything. Many teachers announce to their classes, "You should take notes," which further confuses the situation. They announce that notes are a part of the course requirements and then assume that students know how to take them. If you try this loose approach, you will probably reject the majority of notes submitted. If notes are valuable, they should be dignified by at least giving some instruction on why they are to be taken, how they are to be taken, and what kind of material should be recorded.

It is well to start with why notes are taken. Develop with the class a list of reasons for taking notes, such as:

1. Notes are a record of work done.
2. Notes are a source of study material.
3. Note-taking is an aid to learning.
4. Note-taking assists in retaining material.

It is quite possible that there are other advantages based on individual situations that may be added to this list.

Students should be warned also against excessive note-taking. They should be trained to listen for key words and phrases, such as "This is especially important," "We must learn this," or "It would be well to note this."

Some of the things which lend themselves to good note-keeping are:

1. Sketches and diagrams of job parts, construction drawings, and wiring diagrams.
2. Tables, formulas, charts, lists of advantages or disadvantages of a certain technique or process.
3. Items cut out of magazines, newspapers, trade material, and catalogs.
4. Lists of definitions, glossaries of trade terms, texts, and symbols.

5. Technical information, explanations, and special data or information sheets distributed by the teacher.
6. Lists of materials and their characteristics and uses.

In number 5 above, reference is made to material distributed by the teacher. It is often a good practice to distribute material to be filed in the students' notebooks. It not only injects variety into teaching but it also serves as an expression of cooperation between teacher and students. Such material should be an example of how good notes should appear. The teacher might distribute drawings that must be completed, or drawings that can be colored to identify parts that require labeling. He might distribute charts to be completed or a list of problems to be solved. The notebook serves to utilize the multiple sense appeal. There is definite value in writing, drawing, sketching, and labeling. The notebook is another application of the principle of learning by doing.

It is important in discussing notebooks to warn against over-uniformity. The suggestions made here are for the purpose of helping the student get started in keeping a well-organized set of valuable notes. Students should be encouraged to note not only the teacher's ideas and explanations but also any others that they think are valuable. They should be encouraged to be creative and to develop their own notes and techniques; they should not be restrained by requirements of conformity.

The best form of notebook is a loose-leaf binder, 8½" × 11" in size. Drawings, charts, clippings, tables, and teacher-distributed material usually will fit into a notebook of this size. The loose-leaf feature allows flexibility in use. A good grade of paper should be used, both lined and unlined. The teacher should encourage his class to develop a method of indexing notes. He might develop with the class a set of simple standards for keeping notebooks. For example, the class might proceed along these lines:

1. All books must be loose-leaf.
2. All books must be 8½" x 11" in size.
3. All notes should have standard headings.
4. All notes must be written in ink—drawings in pencil.
5. All notes must observe margins of 1" on both sides.

Other ideas can be developed with the class, yet leave latitude for individual performance. Many students will decide on their own initiative to color their drawings. Others will underline all headings in color. Others will attempt to type their notes. Seldom are notebooks identical in appearance.

Notebooks can be of value to the teacher. He can check his own

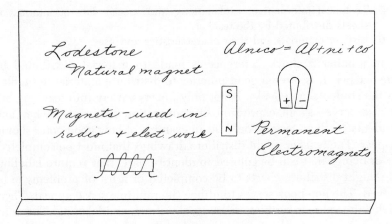

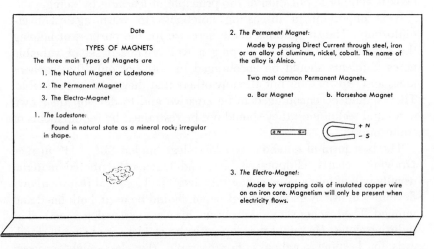

Orderly blackboard work will teach students good habits of organization and facilitate learning. Write the lesson title on the board. Arrange the material in left-to-right order according to the sequence of presentation. Do not crowd the board. If necessary, erase material that students have copied and begin again.

teaching progress as he checks the notebooks. From the notebooks he can identify special talents and qualities which students possess that may become valuable in guiding the students. He can use the better notebooks as motivation to produce quality work. They can be displayed and the owners identified. They can serve as examples worthy of imitation for other students. Students should be encouraged continually to keep notebooks on their own initiative. If the notebooks are properly organized, they constitute a record of a student's work in a given course.

Notebooks may be used as a source of evaluation for grades. Teachers must be objective in grading books and should be careful to give proper weight to content as well as to appearance. They should develop a checklist of features to be checked. On the list should appear such factors as appearance, accuracy, completeness, organization, content, neatness, and quality of drawings and sketches. The teacher should not only grade the books but also enter comments which will help the student improve his future efforts.

Sometimes individual counseling on note-taking is necessary. The teacher should indicate all errors in grammar and spelling. Although the primary task may not be the teaching of English, it is a responsibility to point out students' deficiencies. It is especially important in the light of today's industrial needs when report writing and working from instruction sheets is becoming more important. It is well to remember that notes are as good as they are given, as good as they are used, and as weak as they are recorded. Teachers should refrain from giving too many notes. In every case the material should be sufficiently valuable to merit recording. The time consumed should be justified in terms of the usefulness of the material as well as the fact that it is not available in printed form.

Summary

"Teaching is not only a job but an opportunity for service."

There is a need for both individual teaching and group teaching. Although individual teaching might appear to be the better of the two, group teaching is used and offers certain advantages over individual teaching. We speak of teaching the group and instructing the individual because the teacher usually supplements his group lesson with further instruction to individual students. The skillful teacher makes wise use of group participation and interplay.

He makes provision for individual differences as well as for the fast and slow learner. He must provide instructional material to appeal to these two groups, although the bulk of his teaching is directed to the majority.

The notebook is an important teaching help, as well as an effective student aid. Why and how to keep a notebook and what material to include in it must be taught. The teacher must make judicious use of notebooks and neither neglect nor exaggerate their use.

Questions and Projects

1. What is meant by the term "individual instruction"?
2. What are some of the factors that will determine whether to teach the class or a small group?
3. What are some values that arise from group teaching?
4. How can the teacher provide for individual differences in his teaching?
5. Why is questioning an important skill in group teaching?
6. Make a list of checkpoints for group teaching.
7. Give several examples of how a teacher can make good use of student talents in group teaching.
8. Prepare a report on one of your classes which will show the differences among your students.
9. Choose a demonstration topic, develop a clear aim, and then show how you might provide at least three different ways of applying the topic.
10. State some values that notebooks might have in your particular area.
11. Develop a sample page that students might follow in keeping a notebook.
12. Develop a checklist which you might use in evaluating notebooks.

Sample Lesson for Study and Critique

It has been stated that the lesson plan is a flexible instrument. It is a guide that the teacher develops in order to organize the presentation of an adequate and effective lesson. No one plan can be labeled as "best." The best plan and best presentation depend on many factors. The skill of the instructor and the thoroughness with which he or she teaches the subject will determine the best lesson that can be given at a particular time or to a specific class.

A SAMPLE LESSON

The purpose of this chapter is to discuss a lesson presentation in its entirety and to include suggestions for variety in its development. This lesson is not intended to be accepted as perfect. It is presented as a typical lesson, and the alert instructor should be able to recognize many familiar techniques and to perceive opportunities for using additional ones.

This lesson is presented in playlet form. And the reader occupies an imaginary place as an observer.

The passing bell has rung, and a group of about 23 students enters a radio shop in a vocational and technical high school. They are first-term students. The students take their seats amid the usual confusion of small talk, paper lending, and pencil swapping. As the last bell rings, Mr. Smith calls the class to order with a cheery "Good morning, boys" and then quickly takes the roll. He moves to a long table that stands before the chalkboard and begins to speak.

Mr. Smith: "As I have told you before, the radio repairman does not build sets as part of his work; he repairs them. Now, when would a serviceman be called to repair a set? . . . Jack?"
Jack: "When the set is broken, I guess."
Mr. Smith: "Yes. We might add to that and say any time that a set is not functioning properly. This means that you as a serviceman must be able to repair sets quickly and as inexpensively as possible. Who tells the serviceman what is wrong with the set? . . . Sam?"
Sam: "No one; he has to find out himself."
Mr. Smith: "We call that trouble-shooting. That means that the serviceman must be able to diagnose the trouble and make a quick repair." (He holds up a radio chassis, facing the open back of the set to the class, so they can see the many components crowded into the chassis.)
Mr. Smith: "How easily can you see all the parts in this radio? . . . Henry?"
Henry: "I can only see the parts on top. There are a lot of them underneath."
Mr. Smith: "You are correct. Notice the number of resistors used in this set. How can you identify each one for its resistance value? . . . Jim?"
Jim: "Take them out and test them."
Mr. Smith: "We could do that but it will take lots of time, and we might not replace the same resistor in the proper location." (He then shows the group a box which is half-filled with approximately 100 different-size resistors.)
Mr. Smith: "Let us suppose the serviceman did locate the bad resistor. He knows there are several good ones in this box, but how can he recognize, quickly and easily, the one he wants? . . . Harry?"
Harry: "It will be pretty hard unless he marks them when he puts them in the box."
Mr. Smith: "How could he mark them? . . . Fred?"
Fred: "By writing the value on the resistor."

Mr. Smith: "What are some disadvantages of doing that? . . . Sam?"
Sam: "One of the numbers might rub off."
Mr. Smith: "Take another look at the chassis. Note the many positions of each resistor."
Tommy: "The number can't be read if the resistor is turned around."
Mr. Smith: "We need some kind of a marking system which will permit us to easily and quickly identify each resistor at any position it may be in."
Joseph: "Is that why there are strips on the resistors?"
Mr. Smith: "Yes, they can be seen from any angle and if, by accident, some of the color rubs off, there will still be color left. Our problem is to learn what each color stripe tells us." (He goes to the chalkboard and prints across the top of the left-hand board, "How to Read the Resistor Color Code.")
Mr. Smith: (Reads aloud as he writes.) "How to Read the Resistor Color Code! We have learned why color bands are used; now we are going to learn the color code. The idea of using colors to represent numbers or to identify something is not new. This is just another way of applying a very clever idea." (At this point, he holds up a large model of a resistor. It is about 18 inches long and about 5 inches in diameter. The model was made from a cardboard roll used for shipping linoleum. The aid was constructed several weeks before by one of the brighter students.)
Mr. Smith: "This is a large-scale model of a typical nonmetallic type of resistor. Notice the wires that extend from each end for making connections. Notice also the bands of color." (He noticed that George was doodling on a piece of paper and was paying little attention to the lesson. He brought George back into the lesson in the following manner.) "How many bands are there, George?"
George: "Uh, what did you say?"
Mr. Smith: "Help George out, Harry."
Harry: "There are four bands."
Mr. Smith: "Where are the bands located on the resistor, George?"
George: (Now attentive.) "They seem to be located at one end of the resistor."
Mr. Smith: "Right. They are placed at one end because each band indicates something and we must read each band in order. We read from the end toward the center."
William: (Raises his hand and is recognized by the instructor.) "Is that the only kind of resistor used in radios?"
Mr. Smith: "No, William, but to make it easier to learn the color code we will use this type. Once we learn the code it will be much easier to discuss other types. The color code we are going to learn today is the RETMA color code." (He adds RETMA in parentheses next to the title he had already placed on the board. He then slips two loops of string around each of the end wires of the model and hangs the

model by two chart hooks, so that the model hangs below the lesson title.)

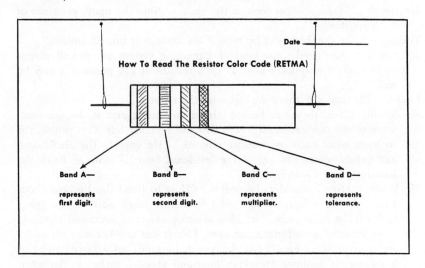

Mr. Smith: "Let us identify each band by labeling them A, B, C, and D." (He draws an arrow to each band and labels them A, B, C, D on the blackboard.)
"Band 'A' represents the first digit of the number. Band 'B' represents the second digit, Band 'C' represents the multiplier, and Band 'D' represents the tolerance of accuracy of the resistor."
"What *does* the word 'digit' mean? . . . Alex?"

Alex: "A digit is a number; I mean a single number like one, two, three, and so forth."

Mr. Smith: "Good, Alex. Now you should all remember our previous lesson when we stated that resistance in radio work can greatly increase. In fact it will often reach into the tens or even hundreds of thousands ohms. There would not be enough space for all digits in a number like 750,000; so we use a multiplier as the third band. The resistors with which we are concerned at this time are all rated in units of hundreds or thousands; so the multiplier method is quite acceptable. Let me give you an example. The first two digits might be 4 and 5. The multiplier is 1,000. What will the indicated value be? . . . Walter?"

Walter: "Four and five are multiplied by 1,000. The value is 45,000."

Mr. Smith: "Good. The fourth band gives us the tolerance of accuracy. Suppose the tolerance given is plus or minus 20%. What will the lowest possible value be? . . . Victor?"

Victor: "I don't know, Mr. Smith."

Mr. Smith: "Help us out, Tommy. What will the lowest possible value be?"

Tommy: "45,000 ohms minus 20% of 45,000 which is 9,000. 45 minus 9 is 36. The lowest possible value is 36,000 ohms."

Mr. Smith: "Good work, Tommy. What will the highest possible value be, Anthony?"
Anthony: "45,000 plus 9,000 or 54,000 ohms."
Mr. Smith: "Good thinking, fellows. You see the system works easily enough once you understand it. Of course you must be accurate in your calculations. That is why we stress mathematics so much. This is a good example of the practical use of math." (He then goes to the section of the chalkboard to the right of the first one used and enters the next heading.)
Mr. Smith: "We seem to understand the idea of the bands. Let us now learn the code." (He writes as he talks.) "Do not copy anything until

The RETMA Color Code Chart

Color	Value	Multiplier
Black	0	1
Brown	1	10
Red	2	100
Orange	3	1,000
Yellow	4	10,000
Green	5	100,000
Blue	6	1,000,000
Violet	7	10,000,000
Gray	8	100,000,000
White	9	1,000,000,000

you are told to.
"Notice that the color can indicate either a multiplier or a digit depending upon its position." There are two more colors that must be considered. They appear at the end of the resistor or on the fourth band. The two colors are gold and silver. These two colors or no color give us the tolerance code." (He adds the following information to the chart on the chalkboard.)

Tolerance Code

Gold +5%	No Color +20%	Silver +10%

Mr. Smith: "We now have all the information we need to learn the basic resistor color code. Let us try to change some colors into their correct digits. Give me the numbers of the following color bands. We will use only the first two bands."
Mr. Smith: "What is the number if Band 'A' is orange and Band 'B' is blue? ... Jack?"

TEACHING OCCUPATIONAL SKILLS

Jack: "Thirty-six."
Mr. Smith: "Good. Band 'A' is brown and Band 'B' is green.... Gregory?"
Gregory: "Fifteen."
Mr. Smith: "Fine. Let us try one more. Band 'A' is white and Band 'B' is black. What is the number?... Craig?"
Craig: "Is it 80?"
Mr. Smith: "Take a closer look at the chart, Craig, and be more careful when you read across."
Craig: "Oh, I see it. The number is 90."
Mr. Smith: Yes. Be careful that you go straight across when using the chart or you will make an error that could be serious. Of course, once you learn the chart you should not have to refer to it unless you are in doubt. Let us try some examples using the multiplier band. What will the number be if the first band is red, the second band is violet, and the third band is brown?... Larry?"
Larry: "Red is two, violet is seven, and brown means to multiply by ten. Twenty-seven times ten is 270."
Mr. Smith: "Good. Band 'A' is gray, Band 'B' is green, Band 'C' is orange. What is the number?... Gary?"
Gary: "Gray is eight, green is five, and orange is 1,000. That would be 85,000."
Mr. Smith: "Remember we are talking about resistance, therefore what units are we counting?... Walter?"
Walter: "Ohms."
Mr. Smith: "Here is a large chart with several problems on it for us to use in applying the color code." (He hangs the chart, which measures about 24" by 36", on a hook over the chalkboard next to the color chart he had already developed. There are five problems, presented by listing four colors to represent the four bands A, B, C, and D. The fifth and sixth columns are covered.)

Resistor Color Code Problem Chart

Band A	Band B	Band C	Band D	Tol.	
Brown	Green	Brown	None	150	±20%
Green	Black	Brown	Silver	500	±10%
Red	Green	Red	Gold	2,500	±5%
Green	Black	Orange	Gold	50,000	±5%
Violet	Green	Yellow	Silver	750,000	±10%

Mr. Smith: (Calls on various students for solutions and uncovers each answer as it is correctly given by the student.) "I have made up instruction sheets which I am going to give each one of you. Place your name and the date at the top of the sheet and enter it in your notebook. Complete the resistor color code on the sheet by copying the colors from the board into the left-hand column." (The class starts the work of completing the chart on the instruction sheet. While they work he removes the problem chart and quickly sketches five resistors on the chalkboard. He writes a number in each of the three bands and enters 5%, 10%, or 20% in the fourth band of each. He finishes the last resistor as the class finishes its work.)

CENTRAL HIGH SCHOOL

Radio Shop   **Mr. Smith, Instr.**

Name _____ **Group** _____ **Date** _____

Instruction Sheet No. _____   **Note No.** _____

Resistor Color Code Problem Sheet

You are to complete the Resistor Color Code Chart on this sheet, according to the Instructor's directions.

Resistor Color Code Chart

Color	Value	Multiplier
_____	0	1
_____	1	10
_____	2	100
_____	3	1,000
_____	4	10,000
_____	5	100,000
_____	6	1,000,000
_____	7	10,000,000
_____	8	100,000,000
_____	9	1,000,000,000

Tolerance Code

Gold +5%   Silver +10%

No Color, 20%

Mr. Smith: "You have probably noticed that there are two groups of problems on reading the values of resistors. The first group gives you the numbers, and you are asked to give the colors of the corresponding bands on the left-hand side of the page. The second group of problems gives you the colors, and you must find the number values and enter them in the right-hand columns. The problems I have placed on the board are the same as the first five problems in group one. I want all of you to work on the first problems of group one. Are there any questions on what we are going to do?"

Color Code Problems Group 1

Band 1	Band 2	Band 3	Band 4	Value of Resistor
3	4	5	5%	_____
2	4	8	10%	_____
7	3	1	None	_____
7	5	0	5%	_____
5	0	4	10%	_____
8	2	5	10%	_____
9	5	9	None	_____
6	0	6	10%	_____
3	5	7	5%	_____
2	6	9	None	_____

Color Code Problems Group 2

Band 1	Band 2	Band 3	Band 4	Value of Resistor
Orange	Orange	Red	Gold	_____
Green	Grey	Black	Gold	_____
Brown	White	Yellow	Silver	_____
Red	Orange	White	None	_____
Blue	Violet	Brown	Gold	_____
Violet	Brown	Black	Silver	_____
White	Blue	Red	Silver	_____
Green	Green	Brown	None	_____
Violet	Green	Blue	None	_____
Brown	Orange	Grey	Silver	_____

Peter: "Can we use the chart to do the problems, Mr. Smith?"

Mr. Smith: "Yes. I don't expect you to learn the chart without having the opportunity to use it and study it. I will expect you to learn it and remember it in the next day or two, however." (The boys start their work, and as they do he moves around the room checking the work of each boy. He makes comments and suggestions as he looks at each boy's work. Some are commendatory, some recommendatory. He gives extra help to those who need it and takes full advantage of the opportunity to check on his teaching and the students' progress.)

Mr. Smith: "I see that some of you have finished. Use the colored chalk to fill in the bands with the proper color of resistor one, Philip. You do the same for resistor two, John. Resistor three, Dan, resistor four, Robert, and resistor five, Conrad." (The boys go to the board and color the bands.)

Mr. Smith: "Let's all look up at the board now. Explain your solution, Philip."

Philip: "Well, I substituted the colors for the numbers which were 7%, 8%, 3%, and 5%. The colors are violet, gray, orange, and gold."

Mr. Smith: "Good work. Do we all agree? Next one, John."

John: "Well two is red, six is blue, six is blue again, but you didn't give another number, so I don't know what color to put in the last band."

Mr. Smith: "What does the absence of color in the last band mean, Tommy?"

Tommy: "It means that the tolerance is plus or minus 20%."

Mr. Smith: "See it indicated on the chart, John?"

John: "Oh yes, I forgot that."

Mr. Smith: "That is all right. We will work with the chart until we become familiar with all the information. Explain your answer, Dan." (Dan and then Conrad give their explanations of how they determined the correct color to use.)

Mr. Smith: (Notes the time and realizes there is only enough time for a summary of the lesson and assignment.) "Well, boys, I think you have enough information to start using the resistor color code. Let us check our work up to this point. Why must we have a resistor color code, Frank?"

Frank: "So we can identify resistors."

Mr. Smith: "Good. Why do we use the system of bands, Victor?"

Victor: "Because they are easy to read."

Mr. Smith: "True, but what other advantage is there in using bands, Walter?"

Walter: "Well, the bands go all around the resistor and we can see the colors no matter how the resistor is installed in a radio set."

Mr. Smith: "Yes. Remember we said that the value could be printed on the resistor, but when installing the resistor, the serviceman might turn it around so that the number would be on the underside and we would have a hard job reading the value, if we could read it at all. Each color has a specific meaning. What does the color of the first band give us, Craig?"

Craig: "The first digit."

Mr. Smith: "What does the color of the second band give us, Gary?"

Gary: "The second digit."

Mr. Smith: "What does the color of the third band give us, Anthony?"

Anthony: "The multiplier."

Mr. Smith: "What is the purpose of the multiplier, Jim?"

Jim: "We can read big numbers by multiplying the first two digits by 10, 100, 1,000, or 10,000, or whatever the multiplier is."

TEACHING OCCUPATIONAL SKILLS 116

Mr. Smith: "What does the color or absence of color indicate in the fourth band, Henry?"
Henry: "Well, if it is silver, it means plus or minus 10%; if it is gold, it means plus or minus 5%; and if there is no color, it means plus or minus 20%."
Mr. Smith: "What do we mean by plus or minus 5%, 10%, or 20%, Conrad?"
Conrad: "It means that the resistor reading is accurate to 5%, 10%, or 20% of the value of the resistor."
Mr. Smith: "Good work, class. As I told you the degree of accuracy necessary with this type of resistor is not extremely fine. Also, this is the basic color code; tomorrow I will show you more resistors. Our job now, however, is to learn the code. What is a good way to remember the code?" (The question is thrown open to the class. Several hands go up, and he calls on a student for his answer.)
Joseph: "We can practice by solving more problems."
Mr. Smith: "Yes. Suppose you complete the problems on the sheet I gave you. Use the chart if you must, but learn the code. Tomorrow we will check our answers and have a little quiz to put our memory to work. Later on we will pick resistors out of a box and check our readings with an Ohmmeter. Read the following pages in your text tonight: pages 124 through 127." (Bell rings and class is dismissed.)

CRITIQUE OF SAMPLE LESSON

The lesson presented above merits considerable study. It might be a good idea to study the lesson plan that Mr. Smith used in giving this lesson. His teaching performance did not just happen. It was the result of a carefully developed plan and included the construction of several visual aids. It also called for designing and duplicating the problem sheets that were distributed to the class. Furthermore, a lot of thought went into the manner of introducing the material. Mr. Smith also indicated a specific aim for the lesson and supplemented it by a simple plan which assured an effective lesson presentation. The plan developed for teaching this lesson is shown here in skeleton form:

Attention should be called to the fact that this lesson followed the plan fairly closely. Several characteristics of the plan will be explained for the purpose of emphasis. It is written in outline form with each step preceded by a number. The purpose of the number is to help the instructor find his place with a maximum of ease as he glances at the plan. It should be impressed upon the reader that this plan may be written in any one of several ways. A lesson plan should be the result of each teacher's own ingenuity and creativity. It may be well to discuss each part of the plan as the lesson progresses.

Instructor: _____ *Course:* _____ *Term:* ____ *No.* ____

Topic: Resistors in radio work.

   Aim: How to Read the Resistor Color Code (RETMA)

Preparation: Students   *Teacher*

1. Notebooks; previous reading and study of radio resistors.

1. Model of resistor
2. Resistor problem chart
3. Resistor problem sheets
4. Several radio chassis
5. Colored chalk

Motivation:
1. Develop need for repairing sets.
2. Point out need for troubleshooting.
3. Stress serviceman's responsibility to do a quick and effective job.
4. Display radio chassis and emphasize the need for an easy method of recognizing resistors.
5. Point out the quantity of resistors used.
6. Develop need for a simple, easy-to-read code.
7. Develop aim and place on board.

Presentation:
1. Show class model of resistor.
2. Point out bands. Why bands and not numbers?
3. Point out that bands are at one end, not center.
4. Why at one end?
5. Explain basic code; write RETMA on board.
6. Explain RETMA.
7. Hang model on board; draw lines to identify each band.
8. Explain each band; place on board.
9. What is a digit?
10. Explain multiplier.
11. Give example: 4000, 5000 and 1000.

Check and Test throughout:
12. Explain tolerance; give example.
13. What will +20% of 45,000 be?
14. Develop code chart on blackboard.
15. Have students solve several problems.

Band A	Band B	Band C
Orange	Blue	Brown
Brown	Green	Orange
White	Black	
Red	Violet	
Grey	Green	

16. Solve additional problems using problem chart.
17. Place five problems from problem sheet on board.
18. Call on students for answers to chart problems.

Application: 1. Distribute problem sheets. Give instructions for use.
2. Select five students to go to board to work on problems. Check work with class.

Summary: 1. Why have a resistor color code?
2. Why use system of bands?
3. What does each band represent?
4. Why a tolerance band?

Assignment: 1. Complete problem sheet at home.
2. Read and study text, pages 124 through 127.
R. C. A. Tube Manual
Slurzberg and Osterheld, *Essentials of Electricity for Radio and Television.*

The *aim* had been established. This was to acquaint students with resistors used in radio work. Other lessons might cover types of resistors, uses of resistors, and wiring in resistors.

Motivation. Here is an opportunity for each teacher to be as different as he wants to be. Mr. Smith used a developmental approach. He decided to create interest and introduce the aim by developing the need for a system of coding. In introducing the aim, which was to read the color code, he explained why the band system was a good one. There are undoubtedly many other ways to motivate the same lesson. He could have presented the class with a box filled with dozens of resistors or a board on which several dozen resistors were mounted. He could have related an experience that emphasized the need for knowing the color code, or he could have related the need to military requirements. The means of motivating a lesson are limited only by the resourcefulness of the teacher.

The aim was developed during the motivation, and Mr. Smith placed the aim on the chalkboard as soon as the class grasped the need for it. The title or aim on the chalkboard served to focus attention on the central idea or purpose of the lesson. It helped prevent digression or confusion because the students were reminded visually of the direction in which their thinking was to be directed.

Presentation. In this case, it might have been difficult to tell when the presentation began and when the motivation ceased as Mr. Smith proceeded. The transition from one part of a plan to another should be done so smoothly that only the teacher is aware of the change. The entire teaching performance should present a continuous, connected sequence of instruction. The professional instructor subdivides his plan in order to utilize the principles of teaching and the psychology of learning in the best possible manner. The lesson plan helps organize material for the best possible benefit to students.

The presentation phase of the plan included the essentials of information to be taught the learner. Mr. Smith included sample problems because he knew that it is difficult, under the stress of teaching a group, to make up simple problems as he proceeds. Noting specific problems in the plan aids considerably in keeping the pace from lagging. If necessary, the skilled instructor can change or add problems, but those he notes in the plan are definite and can be relied upon for demonstration purposes. Mr. Smith included key questions in his presentation because he knew that they would serve as springboards for other questions. The few he has noted are "starters," so to speak.

He also planned just when to utilize the appropriate aid. Introducing the aid at the wrong time may not be a cardinal sin, but an expert performance does not allow fumbling. The instructor who is sincerely interested in teaching knows that a well-taught lesson will pay handsome dividends in student interest and respect for him, as well as economy in his efforts in succeeding instruction.

Here again, as in motivation, there is a wide choice in the selection of method for presenting the lesson. The large resistor could have been drawn on the chalkboard instead of using a model. It could have been presented by means of a series of slides. The explanation of the bands could have been accomplished with the aid of a textbook or a radio handbook. The problem chart could have been constructed on a window shade and each succeeding problem made visible by pulling the shade a little lower. The color code chart could have been presented as a large poster rather than being developed on the chalkboard. It is most important to effective teaching that the teacher learn a variety of devices and skills from which he may make his selection.

It is very easy for the instructor to decide arbitrarily on a method of presentation, but he should take into consideration the ability level of the group, the needs of the group, and the aim of the lesson. It is quite possible that some instructors would criticize this lesson as being too complex or too simple. The determining factors are those just given. Actually the lesson can be tailored to fit the needs of several different groups by varying the degree of difficulty and changing the emphasis of the content. Good teaching techniques do not change, however, and should be utilized in all cases.

Application. Although it would seem that the application was introduced during the presentation of the lesson, it actually started with the distribution of the problem sheets. The solving of problems up to that point was included in the presentation to serve two purposes:

1. To test and check progress.
2. To assist in and reinforce learning.

Mr. Smith distributed prepared problem sheets because he felt that the aim of the lesson was to learn the code, not to copy problems. He also realized that motivating must be done in a subtle way. He motivated every time he complimented a student or the class on a correct answer. He knew from experience that copying from the chalkboard can be boring; therefore, to vary the procedure, conserve time, and assure uniformity and accuracy, he chose to use problem sheets.

Application of the material just learned is an important aspect of learning. Learning is strengthened by putting the knowledge to use immediately. The senses are stimulated, the mind is stimulated, and the power of memory is energized. Time is valuable in all educational activities. While the students work at solving problems, the instructor can walk among them and check for individual weaknesses that may appear. He can assist, offer comments, and generally maintain the close contact with his students which is desirable for good teacher-student rapport. He must carefully estimate the time, and thereby make allowances to complete the lesson within the prescribed period.

Summary. Mr. Smith used the last few minutes in the period to tie the ends together, so to speak. He brought out the highlights and main points of the lesson. He helped the class clarify its thinking by using a series of questions; other methods he might have used include writing the highlights on the chalkboard, having a student write them on the chalkboard, or promoting student discussion as a means of summing up the lesson.

Assignment. The assignment was simple, easy to understand, and meaningful. It gave the students something to do at home, or at least outside of the classroom. It called for initiative on the part of the students and helped them remember the code. Mr. Smith supplemented the assignment with reading and sought the suggestions of the students as to the best kind of assignment to give. The majority of students want to learn. They will volunteer, suggest, and participate in the lesson process when they are convinced of the need for the lesson, the sincerity of the teacher, and the ease with which material may be learned.

Learning, like good teaching, requires concentration. Teachers know that learning and teaching can be pleasant, rewarding, and highly effective if presented as a cooperative endeavor rather than as a conflict between teacher and student.

Reference. Mr. Smith noted references so that he could check his sources of authority and refer students to the sources for study on their own.

Instructional aids. Although instructional aids are discussed at length in Chapter 11, some comment at this point is appropriate. It is interesting to note that several aids were effectively used in this particular lesson. The use of such teaching aids stands foremost in the kind of teaching we are striving to promote.

The most effective aids are usually comparatively simple. The aids used in the lesson described were easy to construct, cost practically nothing, were made with school supplies, and, best of all, were made by the students themselves. In their long-range planning, teachers should include the construction of several teaching aids during the term. Students profit from the experience, future classes reap untold benefits, teaching becomes easier and better, and the entire direction is to upgrade instruction.

Summary

"Master teachers teach learners how to learn."

The purpose of this chapter has been to bring together the elements of teaching into a typical lesson unit presentation. Teachers should be able to recognize in this lesson many teaching techniques that are discussed in the text. It is recommended that this chapter be read more than once. The comments made in this chapter have been included as a method for provoking thought on the part of the reader.

Much has been said about creative and inspiring teaching in recent years. In fact so much has been said that many teachers might feel that creative and inspiring teaching is impossible for the average teacher. Nothing could be further from the truth. Occupational teaching is concerned with teaching accepted operations and information necessary to the application of the skills and knowledge. These operations and information taught belong to the realm of inspired and creative teaching.

A deliberate attempt has been made to include possible errors, as well as to include incidents which are typical. In either case, it is hoped that the reader will discover a great many points to think about, discuss, and improve. The important thing is to treat the material in the light of each reader's situation. He or she should ask: "How can I use these techniques in my occupational instruction, and how can I adapt them or improve upon them?"

Questions and Projects

1. What type of lesson was given?
2. What levels of education might the lesson suit?
3. How many questions were asked?
4. How many students were brought into the lesson in one way or another?
5. How did the presentation of the lesson differ from the lecture method?
6. State at least five advantages that might result from the use of the problem sheets.
7. List at least three other ways the teacher could have provided for application of the lesson.
8. Write a criticism of the lesson. Develop it for each phase of the lesson, such as motivation, presentation, etc.
9. Make a list of five places in the lesson in which, in your opinion, improvements can be made. Identify each part.
10. Design a problem sheet which can be used in the presentation of a lesson in your occupational area.
11. What further use can be made of the model of the resistor and the problem chart?
12. How would you handle each of the following situations if you were the instructor giving the lesson described in this chapter?
    a. One of the students offers a suggestion for memorizing the resistor color code by means of a simple memory device.
    b. A student asks a digressive question.
    c. A student suggests that it is unnecessary to remember the code because every handbook has the color code for easy reference.
    d. One of the students loses his problem sheet.
    e. One of the students has difficulty understanding the code.

Visual Aids

The dedicated teacher always has as his prime objective the efficient teaching of his students. He utilizes every device that will aid in achieving this goal. Teaching aids include, therefore, all devices ranging from the chalkboard to the filmstrip. The most common teaching aid, and one of the most effective when properly used, is the chalkboard. Although it is not a visual aid in itself, the chalkboard makes use of vision which, in conjunction with hearing, constitutes a powerful avenue of communication. Teachers in general, and teachers of technical and occupational skills in particular, can use the chalkboard in almost every lesson presentation. To neglect the proper use of this medium of instruction is to deprive the students of an excellent opportunity to learn. If a teacher feels deficient in his ability to draw, he should not delay in securing the proper training.

USING THE CHALKBOARD

The beginning teacher should start immediately to utilize the chalkboard properly. He should learn from the start certain correct techniques in its use; for example, he should work from left to right; observe proper margins and exercise neatness; provide himself with chalkboard tools such as a pointer, a straightedge, a triangle, and a compass. The chalkboard should be a motivating device as well as a learning aid. The teacher's work should be an example worthy of imitation by the students.

Some of the things which a teacher could place on the chalkboard at the appropriate times are:

1. Notes to be copied in student notebooks.
2. Lists of parts and their uses.
3. New terms and definitions.
4. Simple sketches of parts and devices.
5. Circuit diagrams.
6. Construction diagrams.
7. Graphs for different purposes.
8. Steps in performing an operation.
9. Maps, plans, and layouts.
10. Mathematical problems and solutions.
11. The day's date and class.
12. The day's attendance and percentage.
13. Reference numbers for notes, jobs, or information.
14. Lesson assignments.
15. Student application of a lesson or home assignment.
16. Simple quizzes and tests.
17. Safety slogans.
18. Cartoons that have learning value.

A simple drawing or sketch will provide the learner with the image needed for him to understand more easily the point being discussed. The chalkboard work will be limited in its effectiveness by the ability of the teacher using it. For example, a good lesson can be disrupted very easily by attempting to draw a complicated diagram during the class session. Such a drawing requires concentration and time, and the teacher who attempts to do it during the classroom session will soon lose control of his class. He will find that the time has elapsed without any appreciable teaching having been accomplished. When a complex drawing must be made, several procedures may be followed. One is to draw it on oak tag or suitable poster board. The alternative is to place the drawing on the board before meeting the class. The following list of chalkboard techniques will save time and help the teacher in making his chalkboard most effective.

Suggested Chalkboard Techniques

1. Keep the chalkboard in good working condition. Clean and wash it

regularly. Erase the board before washing it with water. Remove greasy stains with Fuller's earth. Assign a student to this task as a means of developing responsibility and earning credit.
2. Check lighting for good visibility from all sections of the area to make sure there are no dark spots or glare on the board.
3. Observe the work from the back of the room to be sure all your lettering and other work is legible and clear.
4. Develop drawings with appropriate notations as the lesson proceeds and thereby retain the attention of the students.
5. Stand to one side as the drawing is developed. It is highly incorrect to address remarks to the board.
6. Use explanations and questions as the sketch is developed.
7. Utilize a pointer to draw attention to special points.
8. Retain only relevant material on the board. All unnecessary material should be erased.
9. Highlight the work by underlining headings and by using color to accentuate parts and emphasize relationships. Shading often helps in delineating sections.
10. Arrange all chalkboard work in a neat, orderly, sequential fashion. It will help a student find his place should he be distracted momentarily.
11. Sharpen chalk to permit the drawing of fine lines as well as broad, heavy lines.
12. Construct plywood or masonite stencils for frequently used sketches, such as human heads, circles, ellipses, electrical symbols, engine parts, etc.
13. Mark off a small section at the left or right side of the board for notices, dates, attendance, and assignments.
14. Score or paint a section of the chalkboard in squares for developing graphs.
15. Observe the same requirements described for keeping good notebooks. Students trained in this way will learn neatness and order.
16. Maintain a good sense of balance and proportion when making drawings and sketches.
17. Place the aim of each lesson on the chalkboard.
18. Make pounce patterns of commonly used diagrams, graph squares, and other sketches that are involved and time-consuming to reproduce.
19. Use an oversized T square or right triangle to draw vertical or horizontal lines.
20. Construct an oversize yardstick with dimensions scaled to two or three times the normal size for easy transposition of dimensions and measured units on the board.
21. Train students in good chalkboard techniques to enable them to explain, illustrate, or solve problems when sent to the board.
22. Save time by taping prepared materials to the board instead of reproducing them. Develop your work around the material.
23. Use half-inch-wide colored tapes to mark off sections of the board.

24. Chalkboard work must be planned in advance as the board should never be left completely blank.

Although it is difficult to conceive of a modern classroom without a chalkboard, it is possible that circumstances might find a teacher without one. He should take all possible steps to provide at least a substitute writing surface until a chalkboard becomes available. One solution is to use large sheets of wrapping paper and heavy crayons; a twenty-four-inch, or even larger, scratch pad on an easel; or a masonite or transite board painted with three to four coats of dull black paint. These materials are inexpensive and quite suitable for temporary use.

CHARTS IN THE SHOP AND CLASSROOM

Charts are as necessary in a classroom or shop as a map is to a navigator. They aid the students to find their way and serve as another aid to teaching and learning. Charts represent in graphic form what otherwise would require reams of writing and hours of study. Statistics lend themselves particularly to charts. Bar graphs, line graphs, and figure graphs are usually very effective in demonstrating and making comparisons. Wall charts showing parts and functions can be developed by the teacher or secured from various manufacturers.

A teacher should make his own charts whenever possible because of the many advantages which result from doing so:

1. He can make the chart he needs for his class according to his own requirements.
2. He can make it as large or as small as necessary for his purposes.
3. He will develop skill in layout, printing, lettering, and drawing.
4. The skill developed in translating an abstract description into a visual image will help a teacher strengthen his ability to explain and simplify.
5. Students can learn, be motivated, and generally profit by assisting in the construction of charts.
6. Charts can be reproduced on a small scale by mimeographing or by other means for distribution to students.
7. Charts can be made for problem-solving by class participation. Several columns might contain the pertinent information and a blank column used for inserting the answers.
8. A chart might be made with the outline of the machine or piece of equipment lightly drawn and the main parts outlined in heavy color for emphasis.

> **ALWAYS BE CAREFUL!**
>
> Are you observing all safety rules?
>
> Let us all join in safe work habits.
>
> When a mechanic gets hurt, he loses income.
>
> A safe worker is usually a good worker.
>
> You suffer pain when you get hurt.
>
> Safety is everybody's business.
>
> Be alert to unsafe conditions.
>
> Every accident should be reported.
>
> Carelessness causes most accidents.
>
> An unsafe worker is also a hazard.
>
> Report unsafe equipment and conditions.
>
> Every oil spot should be wiped clean.
>
> Falls can be very serious.
>
> Untidy work stations invite accidents.
>
> Locate all fire extinguishers.

Some Other Types of Useful Charts

Charts that show:

1. Decimal equivalents.
2. Tap and drill sizes.
3. Wood screw sizes.
4. Wiring diagrams.
5. Construction details of houses.
6. Simple one-line drawings of scientific principles (schematic).
7. Steps in performing an operation.
8. Line diagram of a braking system, fuel system, or electrical system in an automobile.
9. Location of oil and grease cups on a machine.
10. Micrometer readings.
11. Sliderule readings.
12. Resistor color code problems.
13. Types of gears.
14. Styles of lettering.
15. Steps in tying knots.

16. Safety procedures and hazards.
17. Shop organization.
18. Shop rules.
19. Slogans and sayings.
20. Humor relative to the shop activities.
21. Materials, machines, and equipment not found in the shop.
22. Flow of material or parts.

A good chart deserves to be properly mounted on hard board or other good, sturdy backing material. Charts should also be properly stored when not in use. They should be labeled or indexed in such a way that they may be easily and quickly identified or located. The quality of a chart is as important as is the quality of any other visual aid. The new teacher will do well to choose his material wisely and have a few good charts, rather than many that are of questionable value. Charts, if worthwhile, should be used. The material they contain should be included in lessons introducing new material, during review lessons, or in tests.

POSTERS AND PICTURES

A poster is usually considered as an advertising medium. Much of this type of literature may be obtained from manufacturers. Charts are usually individualized, where as posters are often more general in nature. Both charts and posters serve a purpose, and the advertising which appears on many posters usually serves to introduce materials and names of companies providing certain services or products. It is advantageous for pupils to become acquainted with the manufacturers' products that they will use in the shop or occupation they have chosen. It is part of consumer education to learn of the products of many varied industries.

Pictures are, of course, ideal from the standpoint of accuracy and originality. When obtainable they are good; however, large pictures are expensive and the large-scale use of pictures is impossible. The use of slides in lieu of pictures is a most satisfactory educational technique.

WHAT MAKES A GOOD VISUAL AID?

All teaching aids should help the teacher to teach and the learner to learn. This may sound trite, but all too often visual aids, as well as other teacher aids, are showy, eye-catching, and attention-getting; and all too

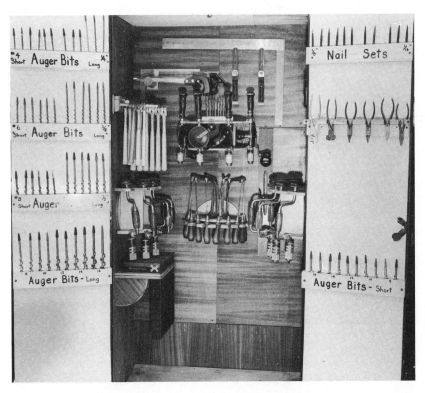

This orderly, well-identified tool storage area could also be used as a visual aid.

frequently they merely serve as window dressing rather than fulfilling their educational function. Visual aids should meet certain standards in order to realize their full potential as learning aids. The following should help the teacher evaluate his visual aids and prevent needless waste of time and effort in constructing new ones.

Characteristics of a Good Visual Aid

Although visual aids may differ in content, the characteristics of good aids should be common to all. A good visual aid should:

1. Clarify an abstract idea, show a sequence, explain a relationship, telescope a large part, or magnify a small part.
2. Depict hard-to-get parts, unusual parts, and things that are generally difficult to observe.
3. Be large and clear enough to be visible, without eyestrain, from any part of the room.
4. Be in color for contrast, to emphasize highlights, and to add interest.

TEACHING OCCUPATIONAL SKILLS 130

5. Include only necessary explanatory written material; avoid anything which will detract from the main purpose of the aid.
6. Be constructed of good material to withstand use and wear.
7. Be well-made and finished in a manner that will reflect good workmanship and skill. It should be attractive and professional in appearance.
8. Exemplify good design and proper proportion, and be built to scale. These relationships are important in achieving a desirable effect.
9. Show ingenuity: labels may be done in different colors; parts may be numbered and matched with the proper label at the bottom of the aid; ribbons or lines from the labels to the parts may be used in some aids where conventional labels cannot be used.
10. Be portable so that it may be easily transported to another location for use during a classroom presentation or an out-of-school talk.
11. Have surfaces protected with varnish, shellac, plastic spray, or plastic covers to permit easy cleaning.
12. Be properly stored when not in use. A tag or other means of quick identification should be devised.
13. Be properly and safely mounted. Wire is preferred to cord in suspending aids. If possible it might be well to bolt aids to walls. Aids should hang plumb and square.
14. Be titled for indexing and inclusion in lesson plans.

HOW TO USE VISUAL AIDS

Good visual aids become most effective when used properly. The following suggestions should be observed when using aids:

1. They should be displayed for easy reference and study by students.
2. Aids that are designed to meet a specific need should be displayed when appropriate to the topic. Displays that are inappropriate to the topic can be a distraction.
3. When using aids in a lesson presentation, keep the aid out of sight until ready to use it. The greatest interest will occur at first observation.
4. Use aids by referring to them. Do not merely show them.
5. Let the aid take the place of a chalkboard sketch, if possible. Aids provided with wire loops can be hung on chalkboard hooks over the place where the sketch would normally appear.
7. Develop paper instruction aids to correlate with the visual aid when possible.
8. Lesson assignments can be made which include study of the content of a visual aid.
9. Remove the aid when finished with it. Do not let the aid become a distraction during a lesson.

10. Encourage students to suggest and construct aids according to proper standards.
11. Good aids can sometimes be made better by including action. For example, gear trains that can be put into motion, simple radios that work, fluorescent circuits that can be livened, parts that can be hinged, and so on.
12. Especially good aids can be made by photographing the subject with a 35 mm. camera. The resulting transparency can be used as a slide for projection purposes.

Many teachers keep a supply of trade magazines and other literature in the shop for reference by the students. An important feature of a well-organized shop is a small reference library. It should consist of reference books, handbooks, and distributors' catalogs. The availability of such reading material under the supervision of the departmental instructor is a very valuable learning and teaching aid. As the supply of such material becomes more plentiful, or the literature no longer serves the original purpose, students are encouraged to remove appropriate pictures and mount them in their notebooks.

Summary

"A teacher's training is incomplete if he has not mastered chalkboard techniques."

The chalkboard is an essential aid to the teacher. New teachers should practice using the chalkboard in as many ways as possible. All the rules for neatness, sequence, visibility, and order should be applied. Students learn by example; therefore, the teacher's board work should be exemplary and his printing worthy of imitation.

Care of the chalkboard is important to secure maximum use. If a chalkboard is not available, teachers should find some substitute writing surface such as paper, large pads, or painted hard boards. The use of the board is invaluable in explaining principles and ideas. Writing notes, drawing diagrams, writing the lesson aim, labeling a sketch, or whatever other use a teacher makes of a chalkboard helps the learner focus his thinking as the presentation proceeds.

Charts, posters, and pictures are expanded applications of the chalkboard but are more permanent. When an often-used pictorial or visual representation is developed, it should be placed on a chart for repeated use rather than waste the time and effort of doing it over many times on the chalkboard. Some of the devices which the teacher uses with the chalkboard, such as the oversize right triangle, T square, and ruler, can also be used in constructing charts. Chart-making provides valuable experience in simplifying teaching material for easy understanding. Students are motivated and stimulated by good work as well as by taking part in the construction of teaching aids.

Questions and Projects

1. List ten ways in which you might use the chalkboard in teaching your subject.
2. A good lesson plan should contain not only key phrases and questions but also drawings that the teacher expects to use as part of his lesson. Indicate the chalkboard drawings you would propose for the teaching of a specific lesson.
3. Construct a chalkboard drawing aid, using heavy kraft paper or paperboard. Be prepared to demonstrate its use.
4. Construct charts for three of the following divisions of your teaching area:
    a. Showing a typical mathematical formula.
    b. Showing a tool with its parts properly labeled.
    c. Showing a cut-away view of the inside of a machine.
    d. Showing a typical electrical circuit.
    e. Showing the successive steps in performing a simple occupational operation.
    f. Showing the steps in performing a scientific experiment.
5. What factors should determine the type of lettering a teacher should use when writing on the chalkboard?
6. What can a teacher do to test the effectiveness of his chalkboard work?
7. What procedure can a teacher follow in storing charts, posters, and pictures?

Projections and Other Teaching Aids

The previous chapter dealt with the chalkboard, charts, posters, and pictures. They have one thing in common: They all serve as teaching aids. Each is different and perhaps unique, but all are pictorial. The advantages of using visual aids of that type extend to visual aids of almost any type.

All visual devices are vital aids to learning. They are not only attention-getters, but also interest-retainers. Visual aids present in concrete form what often is either difficult or almost impossible to describe adequately with words.

The image of visual exposure has a greater impact on the memory than words and is much easier to recall. The longer one teaches the more one will become aware of the difficulty in communicating with students. This concept of communication is a subtle one. Most new teachers will assume that correct English will guarantee mutual understanding. They fail to realize that meanings and shades of meaning in the spoken word contribute much to student comprehension. Visual aids carefully made and properly used assist in establishing the correct interpretation and relationships of the object or other material being taught. In short, words may confuse, but a good visual aid will clarify understanding.

USE OF MODELS IN TEACHING

The pictorial type of aids discussed in the previous chapter are limited when motion is necessary to develop thorough understanding. For example, the action of a piston rod on the crankshaft as it propels the piston up and down within an engine would require the use of several drawings illustrating the successive steps in the cycle. A simple, yet clear, written explanation would be necessary to properly describe each step of the cycle. This kind of chart or poster is good and can be used in many ways. It can be replaced, however, by building a simple model of the same thing. Carrying this one step further, the finest type of visual aid for demonstrating movement is the working model. The decision as to the kind of model to build depends on the subject, the aim of the course, and the need for the model. A model is superfluous when the real thing is available. Models are valuable when the real object or mechanism cannot be obtained; is not visible while in action; is too large to have in the shop; is too small to be easily seen; or is too expensive or fragile to permit handling.

Some objects need to be enlarged for group teaching. For example:

Slide rule	Water valve
Screwdriver	Tool bit
Micrometer	Printing type
Spark plug	Meter face
Resistor	Spark coil

Teachers of any occupational subject will experience situations that require enlarged models for complete understanding by the students. They will also find objects which are large and should be miniaturized or reduced for instructional purposess. For example:

Section of frame houses	Skylights
Engine parts	Machine parts
Safety scaffold	Extension ladders

Piping systems   Stairs and steps
Wiring systems   Aircraft ribs

Models can be made of wood, plastic, pressboard, metals, and other suitable materials sufficiently durable for the purpose. There is little excuse for not constructing models when the facilities of various school shops are available. The ambitious and interested teacher will develop many teaching aids that will reduce the usual wordy explanations and will definitely improve student understanding.

There are many commercial models available to teachers of science and biology which are examples of how different materials can be used to make the parts, and how color may be introduced to show the relationships more vividly. The teacher of occupational skills who has machinery and hand tools available to him can usually build excellent models that have the advantage of being suitable for his specific purpose and his students' particular needs.

Additional Types of Models

Models vary in kind to meet different needs. A teacher might build multiple models of an object showing the several stages of construction. When these are mounted on a display board, they produce a type of visual aid called a step-by-step display. This form of aid has many applications and will prove to be very helpful for student comprehension.

On the other hand, one might take a real automobile brake and cylinder assembly, mount it on a sturdy board, and have what is known as a working mock-up. This type of model is used extensively by industrial organizations when displaying their products in exhibits.

An effective aid may be developed by mounting on a display board the successive steps in such a thing as tying an Underwriter's Knot. Such demonstration boards lend themselves exceptionally well to the presentation of certain lessons. This kind of aid may be used by the student as a "do-it-yourself" in learning a particular skill. The number of teaching aids to be used is limited only by the resourcefulness of teachers.

With a variety of visual aids from which to choose, teachers should use the appropriate one to satisfy the need or, if necessary, develop supplementary aids. Various teaching aids create interest, stimulate more effective learning by the students, as well as heighten respect for the professional capabilities of the teacher. They are very valuable for stimulating student motivation. There are times when aids can be constructed by capable students as rewards and incentives. If a student

TEACHING OCCUPATIONAL SKILLS

participates in such a project, the teacher should be sure to give the student recognition for his ideas and assistance. When students suggest worthwhile aids, the teacher should not fail to accept such ideas. The cooperation of the teacher will encourage the student to develop a fine aid that will help him to learn more readily. Consequently, both student and teacher profit from the experience. The extra work will not interfere with, but will expedite, the student's progress in learning the essentials of his course. Visual aids developed by students are given renewed importance and status when the teacher uses or refers to them in lesson presentations.

FILMS AS AIDS

Films are another type of pictorial aid. They go further, however, in adding motion, color, and sound. When sound is added, the actual sound of a machine or process creates additional student interest. The introduction of a new voice is also an additional interest factor. Although referred to as films, they are just another type of projection aid.

The 16 mm projector adds variety to teaching and expands the range of knowledge occupational teachers can bring to their students. Courtesy of Bell and Howell, Chicago, Illinois.

By using this term we can properly include moving pictures, filmstrips, slides, and opaque projections. When projected on a screen, they are all valuable, yet each possesses a quality of its own. Unless motion is necessary to complete understanding, the slide film is satisfactory for the majority of teaching situations. Numerous fine training films in the various occupational areas can be obtained from the branches of the Armed Forces. Other interesting and instructive films are available through commercial sources. Many information films produced by industry are very good, but differ from the so-called training films referred to previously. Silent motion films are almost useless and, if used, should be used with great care to avoid misconceived ideas. All films will lose their value if improperly used, and the time devoted to them becomes time wasted in the absence of good methodology.

All films should be selected with care, and in all cases, teachers should preview them. Innumerable films are available on every conceivable subject for almost every occasion. They range in quality from excellent to mediocre. The teacher should exercise a high degree of selectivity when choosing films for instructional purposes; otherwise he will waste students' time with inferior instruction.

Previewing Films

It is very important that all films be previewed by the instructor before a showing. Failure to go through this process may result in embarrassment, ineffective use of film, or waste of time. Familiarity with the film content and the running time are factors on which the successful use of film depends. In some cases, training guides which accompany the film materially assist the teacher in the presentation.

The preview should assist in answering these questions:

1. Is the film pertinent to the lesson to be taught?
2. Is the sequence of presentation correct?
3. Does it show any incorrect ways of doing things or unsafe practices?
4. Is it too long for one showing?
5. Does it cover too much subject matter?
6. Is it too technical for student understanding?
7. Should it be shown more than once to convey its meaning?
8. What is the best procedure of presentation: teacher or student reading the captions?
9. What is the best time for the showing—before or after a presentation?
10. How may the film be connected with the course subject matter and with the student's previous experience?
11. What kinds of questions should be asked or assignments made following the showing?

TEACHING OCCUPATIONAL SKILLS

Suggestions for Better Use of Films

A list of worthwhile suggestions for using films:

1. Select an appropriate film.
2. Choose one that is apropos to the lesson.
3. Preview the film.
4. Choose a film which does not run too long.
5. Establish clearly in your own mind the purpose of showing the film.
6. Note the highlights of the film in your personal preview.
7. Prepare the class for the film; point out the highlights.
8. Check all equipment for smooth operation in order to permit good presentation.
9. Follow up with such things as questions, a quiz, a discussion, or a written report.
10. Note the characteristics of the film on a card file record.

Purposes of Films

The teacher should have a specific purpose in using every film, such as:

1. Motivate the class for course content.
2. Stimulate the class for lesson presentation.
3. Depict an industrial process.
4. Show an occupational skill.
5. Provide information about materials, processes, fabrication, construction, and manufacturing.
6. Explain scientific principles.
7. Portray the history of a principle, part, tool, machine, or process.
8. Introduce variety in teaching and relieve the class from usual routine.
9. Implement occupational guidance.
10. Substitute for field trips when they are not possible.
11. Bring into the classroom experiences that otherwise might have to be omitted.
12. Supplement safety instruction.

SLIDES

Slides are the projected version of pictures and charts. They have several advantages over charts because they are smaller and more easily stored. The modern, easy-to-use 35-mm. cameras have made slide-making so easy that teachers can produce their own color slides. They can bring into the classroom pictures of things and activities found in the various occupational areas.

The potential for this type of projection aid is seldom exploited sufficiently by teachers. Slides offer the advantage of comparatively simple projection equipment that is lightweight, portable, and easily and quickly set up. They can be used at any point in a lesson and can also be used for individual study by students. Slides require good photography and a planned sequence that includes essential points, just as in a good explanation or demonstration. The use of color in making slides will increase their effectiveness when color is important for realism.

Slides should be identified for proper sequence and presentation. They should be stored properly to prevent the possibility of loss. Since slide projections can be kept on the screen for as long as necessary and can be used as a basis for a class discussion, they may have a distinct advantage over motion pictures. In addition, teachers should use slides instead of continually using complicated drawings that are often time-consuming and boring to look at.

THE OPAQUE PROJECTOR

The opaque projector, larger and heavier than the ordinary slide projector, has several unique features that can be of great help to every teacher. Teachers very often find illustrations, pictures, or drawings which should be shown to their class group. This is easily done by placing the item on the opaque projector, which in turn will throw the image on a screen. The size of the image depends of course upon the distance between the screen and the projector.

A second important use of this projector is in the construction of charts. Material can be enlarged to chart size by throwing the image directly on a large sheet of drawing paper and tracing the object with a lead pencil. Color, shading, and other details can be added later. Small drawings can be quickly, easily, and accurately enlarged. These drawings may be used as visual aids, but teachers will also find this an easy method of making enlarged patterns for various projects where tracing and cutting are needed. The enthusiastic teacher will collect all kinds of worthwhile material and carefully mount it for use with an opaque projector, which is especially effective in projecting color.

THE OVERHEAD PROJECTOR

The overhead projector is unique among portable projectors in the manner in which it is used. It is the only machine that permits the

TEACHING OCCUPATIONAL SKILLS 140

operator to face the group while showing a slide. The body of the projector contains a light source that is directed upward. A heavy glass lies across the top of the machine, and the light passes through the glass to a reflecting mirror set at a 45-degree angle. The image is reflected from the mirror to the screen. The machine can be set for different size pictures by varying the distance of the projector from the screen. The lens can be easily adjusted for sharpness and clarity.

Black-and-white or color transparencies and teacher-made materials may be shown on the overhead projector. Courtesy of the Charles Beseler Company, East Orange, New Jersey.

Prepared slides can be used on this machine, or the teacher can write or draw on a transparent sheet of material that is provided by the manufacturer. Notes or drawings can be prepared before class or developed during the lesson. This arrangement makes it possible for the instructor to face the class while explaining the picture or while developing notes, working problems, sketching parts, making diagrams, labeling sections, or doing any of the things he would normally do at the chalkboard. An added advantage is that his work can be used over again at some future time rather than be erased, as it might be on a chalkboard.

Slides can be indexed and filed for repeated use, thereby saving valuable time. The one machine can be used for writing notes and projecting slides instead of using both the chalkboard and a projection machine. A common off-white window shade or a white wall will show a good picture; however, a screen is recommended for best results.

FILMSTRIPS

The filmstrip projector is the most versatile and most adaptable of the film type or projection type of aids. Most filmstrip projectors have the additional feature of being constructed to accommodate slides (2″ x 2″). This projector is light, portable, simple to use, and easy to repair. It can be set up in a minimum of time and with a minimum of effort. There is no disturbing machine hum, and the strip can be stopped at any point for discussion, question, or study. The film can be reversed to throw back to a previously shown frame for reference, or several frames can be passed over to give the teacher what he wants for the lesson at hand. There are many types; some are fan

The filmstrip projector is easy to set up, easy to use, and easy to store. It may be used either by the teacher in the classroom or by the student for self-instruction. Courtesy of Viewlex, Inc., Holbrook, New York.

cooled, and some can be operated by remote control. Regardless of type, all teachers should learn to use them and take steps to make a filmstrip projector available to their students.

Students should be trained in the use of the machine. They can set up the equipment for the busy teacher, store it after it has been used, and maintain it with a minimum of direction or instruction by the teacher. Many interesting things can be done with filmstrip projectors.

A regular film screen is preferred, but the picture may be projected on any glare-free surface if the surface is light and out of the direct sunlight. Some teachers have experimented with filmstrips by allowing absent students to study the films by themselves to make up for missed work. The same could be done easily with students who are ready to move ahead of the class or who wish to spend more time studying a particular film.

Suggestions for Using Filmstrips

1. Preview filmstrips the same as other films.
2. Develop a file of appropriate filmstrips.
3. Obtain through school supplies a selection of strips which can be woven into the presentation of the course.
4. Plan for the use of a filmstrip as carefully as you would any other lesson. If the filmstrip is to be part of a lesson, make the appropriate notes on the lesson plan.
5. Filmstrips are far more valuable when used as part of a lesson. Their use should be restricted to perhaps ten to fifteen minutes.
6. Make the filmstrip valuable; do not merely show it, but use it.
7. Prepare key questions about the film.
8. Prepare comments and explanations, applications, and relationships which should be pointed out as the film progresses.
9. Make notes on the lesson plan which will help improve the use of the filmstrip in future showings.
10. Point out the title and aim of the film.
11. Instruct the class on the proper viewing of filmstrips. They should study the picture while the teacher reads the captions.
12. Do not permit long periods of silence while showing a film. You will lose your audience.
13. Read captions in a clear voice at a moderate rate of speed. Be sure all can see as well as hear.
14. Do not allow note-taking while a film is being shown. Occasionally a special drawing or sketch might be copied by the class. Usually it is better to get on with the film and place the material on the chalkboard later.
15. Students sometimes should be called upon to explain some of the frames.

16. Filmstrips can be used for motivation, presentation, or review.
17. Develop quizzes based on films.
18. Remember, filmstrips are an aid, not a substitute for the teacher.
19. Use films for their educational value, not for entertainment.
20. Filmstrips should be integrated into the course of study to coincide with the needs of the majority of the students.

Some filmstrips are accompanied by records, which have a signal that coordinates the picture with the sound. These are valuable, and the suggestions above also apply to them. Go through the film once or twice to become accustomed to the signal, and thereby more easily and accurately synchronize the film and sound as you manually operate the machine. Filmstrips can be used the same way opaque projectors are used to make chalkboard drawings or charts from a film. The frame that you wish to reproduce can be flashed on poster paper and traced.

Film Record File

A simple card file of films should be organized by the teacher as part of his complete record. Each teacher can develop a card file to suit his particular needs. Every teacher should have a file of film sources cataloged by company and by film title. In order to do this, it will be necessary to send for catalogs listing the films available. A valuable reference text for sources is *Educational Film Guide*, published by H. W. Wilson Company. The guide lists films, sources, terms of loan, and brief descriptions about the offerings.

MAKING BEST USE OF TEACHING AIDS

Aids should not be used indiscriminately. Each aid offers a particular advantage. Teaching aids in all cases should be well constructed and finished in attractive colors. Despite the availability of many aids from commercial sources, teachers should learn to make their own (except films). The most effective teaching aid is the one for which the teacher has felt a need in order to clarify teaching points that have been difficult for students to grasp.

Suggested Aids for Specific Purposes

1. Chalkboard. To record sketches, outlines, technical words, and assignments.

TEACHING OCCUPATIONAL SKILLS

2. Books. To be used for assignments, reference, and background information.
3. Charts and graphs. To make comparisons or to show relationships.
4. Cartoons. To stimulate interest and develop proper attitudes, as well as to emphasize safety precautions.
5. Cutaways. To show interior structure and relationships of parts.
6. Exhibits. To display commercial products, examples of good workmanship, and sequence of operations.
7. Filmstrips. To show the sequence of operations, historical development, and desirable work habits and attitudes.
8. Illustrations. To show, by use of picture or poster or cartoons, objects which are not available for display.
9. Instruction sheets. To supplement the demonstrations and explanations of the teacher.
10. Mock-ups. To take the place of the real thing when economy of space is necessary.
11. Models. To take the place of the real object which is too small for instructional purposes or too large to bring to the instruction center.
12. Motion pictures. To be used when motion is necessary to the understanding of the specific operations involved.
13. Opaque projector. To be used when large charts or illustrations are not available or when enlarged sketches or drawings are necessary for class observation.
14. Pounce pattern. Should be used as a time-saver in placing complicated and desirable drawings on the chalkboard at frequent intervals.
15. Work manuals. To be used for specific jobs on standardized products such as automobiles, oil burners, and other commercially produced equipment and appliances.

Advantages of Visual Aids

In all cases a visual aid has one or more of the following advantages:
1. It may be used where the real object cannot be shown.
2. It may show objects stripped of their accessories, and thereby simplified.
3. It may be handled and examined for clearer understanding.
4. It may show parts that are ordinarily concealed.
5. It may be transported to a desirable location for instructional purposes.
6. It may show successive steps in a process, or the evolution of a machine or product.
7. It enables the students to learn by studying the visual aid without the teacher's presence.
8. It is an efficient supplement to a demonstration or other form of presentation.

Field Trip—A Form of Visual Aid

One of the most effective teaching aids, from the standpoint of learning and personal growth, is the field trip. It unfolds a panorama of visual experiences for the student which cannot be duplicated in any other way. The values derived from a well-organized field trip are so broad in scope that a discussion of them could be included in any one of several chapters. The field trip is being treated as a visual aid because it is primarily a medium of visual learning.

All visual aids are valuable because of the impact they have on the learner's power of imagery. Field trips offer the added advantages of realism and the opportunity for students to observe the integration of the multitude of operational skills and application of occupational information learned in school. Field trips satisfy two main concepts of educational theory: the motivation of the desire to learn and the actual learning.

Motivation. Field trips stimulate interest in and arouse curiosity about the occupation or subject as no other medium can do. Students are able to observe the actual duties, skills, and requirements of the occupation at first hand. They can develop an insight into the need for learning the information related to the job. By recognizing many of the tools, machines, materials, and processes of the occupation, students will develop a better understanding and appreciation of the school shop training they receive.

Learning the occupation. Students have the unusual opportunity to learn by observation. They also can watch the actual performance of the skills of the occupation. Industrial processes, relationships of operations to each other, and expert use of the equipment all tend to stimulate occupational interest. The on-the-job atmosphere is bound to affect the senses of the learner. Learning is strengthened by recall of facts learned and reasoning is induced by the observation of the actual situation.

A Field Trip Project

There are three phases to a field trip, all of which demand careful planning by the instructor.

Preparation. Instructors must make adequate preparations in order to insure the success of the excursion. The place to be visited should be related to the students' occupations and offer sufficient value to warrant the time and energy spent in organizing the visit. The timing of the trip is important and should take place at the point during the

Suggested Check List for Field Trip Planning

Check each item as it is completed.

1. Discuss the possibility of making the field trip with members of the class. Include cost, time, permission. _____
2. Make all necessary administrative arrangements and obtain permission from school authorities. _____
3. Make all necessary arrangments with responsible personnel at plant or institution to be visited. _____
4. Confirm and set all dates and time schedule. _____
5. Make arrangements for transportation. Public carriers should know about large groups so as not to interfere with regular commuters and other travelers. _____
6. Prepare record sheet for collection of money; give receipts. _____
7. Prepare written sheets for instructions for students. _____
8. Make arrangements for sufficient number of escorts. Ask teacher or/and parents. _____
9. Prepare students for trip:
    a. Discuss purpose of trip. _____
    b. Point out highlights to be observed. _____
    c. Discuss conduct during tour and in transit. _____
    d. Discuss possible hazards. _____
    e. Relate trip to course, processes, work, job opportunity. _____
10. Form class into group or groups at arrival. Check attendance. _____
11. Meet host and introduce group. Explain purpose of the visit. _____
12. Listen to instructions given by company guides. _____
13. Encourage students to take notes, make sketches and note questions to be asked. _____
14. Re-group at end of tour; check attendance; express thanks. _____
15. Report to school authorities on return to school. Make note of any important observations made which will help in future. _____
16. Follow-up the visit with a class discussion. _____
17. Prepare key questions to encourage student participation and explanation of highlights of trip. _____
18. Write an evaluation of the trip as to worth, information gained, student reaction, public relations. _____

course when the group has progressed far enough to appreciate and understand the many things they will see and hear.

The field trip starts with the instructor's correspondence with the business or industry to determine the time, day, and point of entrance to the place to be visited. An explanation of this type of teacher activity is discussed more fully in Chapter 15. It should be noted at this point, however, that teachers should acquaint themselves with the school administration's policy on these matters. They should learn the procedures concerning parent consent forms, handling of transportation, the costs involved, and other administrative details.

Students should be prepared for the trip. They should thoroughly understand the purpose of the visit and have some prior description of what they will see. Field trips are comparable to some films; they present so much that the instructor must prepare his group for the highlights. Of course the usual standards of good conduct and proper dress should be required. Instructors must be aware of the need for maintaining good public relations during the visit. It must be remembered that such groups are representatives of the school and consequently should be on their best behavior.

Participation. Taking the field trip should be a refreshing and exciting experience. Although trips are often tiring in the physical sense, the class should be mentally stimulated as a result of the experience. Most business or industrial organizations that provide student tours of their facilities have itineraries planned for visitors. They also have several of their personnel serve as guides for the group. Once the group arrives at the site of the visit, all directions and instructions given by the guides should be followed without digression. There is always the chance of accidents or injuries due to causes peculiar to the plant being visited. The students should be instructed to keep together and not stray from the group. As the tour progresses, the guides will usually present a running commentary on the things being observed. Students should be encouraged to make note of operations, equipment, or other points which strike their interest. Sometimes a question-and-answer period follows such a tour when the students can verify their reactions to things observed. Instructors, too, should take note of important things they observe as a basis for a follow-up session at the school. Since field trips are a valuable means of keeping up with technological changes, teachers should take full advantage of these trips.

Literature concerning the place visited or product produced is often distributed. Students should be asked to read, study, and report on such literature, as well as file it in their notebooks. Field trips give the instructor a vast amount of material for occupational guidance, and make the abstract description of working conditions and other occupational information more concrete and real to the students.

Follow-up. The impression and the depth of learning which affect a student depend on the immediacy with which he applies the new information and the kind of assignment he receives. The effectiveness of a field trip will depend on the follow-up. The key points of the trip should be emphasized through good questioning techniques to stimulate further thought about the highlights of the visit. It should become quite evident that the follow-up to a trip should take the form of a planned class session. It should be as carefully planned as any other lesson. The importance attached to a field trip by the students will be in direct ratio to the attention given to it by the teacher. Sometimes it is advisable to place a news item in the local newspaper concerning such a field trip to a local industrial organization. It is a gesture of good public relations.

Field trips are valuable learning media and should not be restricted to factories alone. Allied occupations as well as museum and public projects offer fine opportunities for learning. Trips and excursions present another means to diversify teaching. If a field trip is managed wisely from its inception through the follow-up session, it can serve to promote renewed interest in both the students and the teachers. When distributed carefully throughout the year, the trips break up the monotony of regular school work and provide an excellent learning situation.

Summary

"If a picture is worth a thousand words, use the right picture at the right time and save a thousand words."

The measure of a teacher's competence lies to some extent in the number of aids he has, the variety of aids he uses, and the way he uses them. Teaching aids, particularly visual aids, are a means of bringing variety into teaching. They are invaluable to learning and can help simplify a multitude of teaching situations, as well as help to solve problems. What one type of aid fails to do well, another can do successfully. Models are a good way of showing realistic samples of the real thing. Working models are often better than plain models. They can show the actual operation of a part, the relationships of parts, and can also be used in building a mock-up or developmental type of demonstration board. Models can be built not only by the teacher but also by students.

Films are another category of teaching aids which can be grouped together under the projection type. Each of the different types of films meets a different need, and each is valuable when properly used. Films should be previewed and special plans made for their use.

Aids are used as part of a lesson presentation. Some general suggestions for proper use of training aids are:

1. Select the proper and best type of aid for the lesson.
2. Prepare the class for the aid.
3. Plan for the use of the aid as carefully as you plan for any other aspect of teaching.
4. Use the aid to explain the lesson, and explain the aid as you present the lesson.
5. Follow all the rules for teaching a group, such as good visibility, hearing, and so forth when using aids.
6. Use aids confidently and smoothly.
7. Face the class, not the aid.
8. Index aids and store them, when not displayed, in a safe and easy-to-get-at place.
9. Continue to be interested in the improvement of all aids.
10. Always seek new and better ways of using teaching aids.

Field trips and excursions offer extraordinary opportunities to motivate a group as well as to teach many things about an occupation. Teachers are encouraged to plan field trips to industrial establishments related to their particular work, but trips do not have to be limited to industrial establishments only. Any visit that will be valuable in terms of occupational interest should be considered.

Questions and Projects

1. Carefully review the subject you teach and then decide on five models that will facilitate your teaching.
2. Construct at least two of the models listed in your answer to question 1.
3. Write two lesson plans, one information and one operation type, and include the use of a model in the plan.
4. Develop a list of several uses you can make of a specific working model you would like to have in your shop.
5. Develop a combined record card for (a) films (motion) and (b) filmstrips.
6. Develop an assignment sheet based on a film you might use.

7. Construct a chart from a textbook using the opaque projector, or from a filmstrip frame using a filmstrip and projector.
8. Add to the list of suggested techniques for using the visual aids discussed in this chapter.
9. Develop detailed directions to be distributed to students covering a field trip to a place of occupational interest.
10. Select at least 10 films that might be used in your specific instruction.
11. Examine catalogs of manufacturers of projection equipment and list the best projectors for your specific purpose.
12. Compile and maintain a list of film sources.

Testing as a Means of Evaluation

If a game of word association were to be played by the average person and he or she were given the word *school,* chances are that the words *test* or *examination* would inevitably occur as a response. It is said that those things which have the greatest impact upon our senses tend to remain with us the longest. Certainly that part of school life which involved the taking of tests remains with many of us. The announcement of a test always produced a certain flurry of excitement and as the day for a big test approached, nerves grew taut and students became anxious as they wondered what the teacher would ask.

Afterwards, the test was discussed and described as "fair," "good," "unfair," "it had everything we studied," or "nothing that we studied." Although there were many different ideas about the test and opinions as to the teacher's motives, most students were aware of the fact that the test was given to find out what they knew. The students' problem was to put on paper what they knew so the teacher could evaluate them. The teacher, too, had a problem. He was looking for a valid, fair, and equitable means of determining the students' progress by means of a test.

In brief, a test to most people is a device for finding out what students know. The teacher as a professional person must be aware of more than just that simple explanation. He must do more than find out what students know; he must use tests and quizzes to evaluate and measure student progress, as well as his own teaching success. In order to do this he must overcome two major obstacles:

First, he must devise tests that are clear enough to the student to elicit the answers required and that are within the framework of what has been taught.

Second, he must free his students from the usual mental stress of test-taking so that they can devote their entire energies to the test.

A test should measure or evaluate what a student knows and really understands. A test that relies on the recollection of facts alone should be treated as just a written recitation of facts. The teacher who ascribes to such a test enough weight on which to issue a grade—one that will pass or fail a student—will be seriously in error. Teachers must understand the limitations and implications of each kind of test and then use it with discretion.

In the area of occupational training it is imperative to give due value to the importance of knowing how to do things. The best paper test is but a poor substitute for a performance test. Teachers in industrial arts, vocational education, or technical education at any level are in the unique position of being able to test more accurately than teachers of almost any other subject area. It is important to recognize this fact in order to arrive at a fair and equitable final grade for each individual student.

Measurement of students' progress throughout a given course is the responsibility of the instructor. Such measurement must be objective and based on factual evaluation rather than on personal impression or generalities. True measurement must be based on many things not the least of which is understanding. Tests should serve the following main purposes:

1. Reveal to the teacher what the students have learned.
2. Help students learn.
3. Reveal to the student his weaknesses and his strengths.
4. Provide an incentive for improvement.

5. Become a basis for grades.
  6. Help the teacher evaluate his teaching and serve as a basis for improvement.
  7. Serve as a means of evaluation for guidance and special help.

There are other values and uses for tests in the area of administration. Test results should be carefully recorded for use during parental interviews or for use by the supervisor or principal. Such records are objective and are valuable in presenting a clear and fair picture of student progress.

TYPES OF TESTS

If the functions and purposes which have been ascribed to tests are to be realized, then the teacher must become familiar with the variety of tests which can be given, skilled in the art of constructing the tests, and experienced in the uses and application of each of the types of tests that are available. In general there are three common ways of testing:

  1. Practical or performance tests.
  2. Oral or verbal tests.
  3. Written tests.

Performance Test

The practical or performance test is a good means of testing in any occupational area. It calls for a display of both understanding of the skills of the occupation and the performance of the actual operational skills of the work or job. A job within the occupational area is first selected which includes many of the skills that have been taught. The student is then given the time to make up such things as materials lists, drawings and sketches of the finished product or job, and a list of tools and equipment. Next, the student proceeds to do the job within a reasonable time limit set by the instructor. This kind of practical testing places the premium on such factors as:

  1. Approach to the job.
  2. Selection of correct tools and equipment.
  3. Planning for the job or project.
  4. Application of safe practices.
  5. Sequence of steps in achieving success.
  6. Quality of workmanship.
  7. Accuracy of work.

8. Pace of working.
9. Skill in problem-solving.
10. Neatness and housekeeping.
11. Use of proper tools.

Each teacher can develop a checklist for his own field to include any of the points above and, in addition, those points that are peculiar to his occupational area of instruction. It can be readily seen that practical testing is time-consuming, somewhat costly, and requires close supervision and the development of a variety of jobs, each of which must include as broad an application of the occupational skills as possible. Performance testing is more practical with small groups. The large-size classes, which are often encountered, tend to make performance testing too difficult to use successfully. The importance of this type of testing cannot be overlooked, however, and teachers of occupational skills should realize that one of the end results of their instruction lies in the student's ability to perform. The next best thing therefore is to develop a system of evaluating and grading each job or project, which in itself is a test of the skills and information learned in order to do the job. This viewpoint is important and will be discussed more fully in the section on grading.

Oral Tests

Oral tests are somewhat limited in use because of their nature. Oral testing can be done with a group as part of the application of a lesson when checking for understanding, or it may serve as a form of review and recall of facts. Because each student is asked a different question, there is no basis for any fair comparison and the teacher has no means of determining how each student would answer all the questions. There is, however, an important use of oral testing which teachers should realize. Every teacher will have students who have reading difficulty. Very often such students are able to do good shop work and understand principles. However, their poor reading ability becomes a stumbling block, and they fail to perform well in the usual forms of testing. It would be unfair and unprofessional to allow these youngsters to fail because of a reading block. These students can be tested orally in private by the teacher. Safety tests, review quizzes, and other tests can be administered in this fashion.

Written Tests

The third type of test is the most commonly used and also the most commonly misused type of test. Planning is at the very core of good teaching, and planning a test is no exception. It is imperative that teachers understand each type of written test, of which there are two main types: the essay and the objective.

Let us first discuss the objective test. Objective types of questions and tests have become more popular and are more widely used than any other kind because of their particular adaptability to the testing of occupational skills and knowledge. They are free from the subjectivity of the traditional essay type of question, are easier to answer and to score, and do not require a high degree of literary skill in written expression. Because of the latter reason, they are quite popular with students. It is evident on further examination that the objective tests offer an ideal solution to the testing problem of teachers of occupational skills. They are most valuable, but should not be used to the exclusion of good, properly designed essay types of questions. A good program of testing must be based on variety, balance, and planning.

Some of the more common types of objective questions are:

True-false	Completion
Multiple choice	Matching
Short-answer	Recognition

All these forms call for a minimum of writing and require less thinking and organizing on the part of the student than the essay type of question. They usually ask for facts and the recall of specific information. They require usually one short answer. To some extent they can be answered by guessing. Very often they can be scored by using a scoring key or stencil. They also permit a more extensive sampling of the work without incurring the hardship of analyzing each answer for actual meaning. They do not penalize the test-taker for poor writing, spelling, or composition. They can be given and scored within a very limited period of time. They are more palatable to take and as a consequence encourage more frequent testing, which can be advantageous to both student and teacher.

The warning has already been given to balance the types of questions used. It is important that teachers be aware of the limitations of objective types of questions. They do require more time and care to prepare. More of them are required. They ask for recognition and recall and can be answered by circling a number, or writing a letter, or writing a word or phrase in a designated place. They deprive the student of the opportunity for organizing thoughts, expressing ideas, solving problems, or using reasoning in developing an answer. The premium is sometimes on memory rather than on understanding. It is up to each teacher to recognize these points and to use all questions wisely.

THE TRUE-FALSE QUESTION

The true-false question is the simplest of the objective types of questions. Because it is so familiar, many new teachers place too much emphasis on it. The element of guessing is greatest in the true-false type and must be evaluated with that thought in mind. It is a very good device for creating interest, introducing a new unit of instruction, and reviewing for a larger, more comprehensive test.

At least 50 to 100 items are necessary to achieve a valid result. The rate of answering is approximately five to seven items per minute. The following format is typical of this form of test.

Example of True-False Test

School Name_____   Department_____
Woodworking_____   Instructor_____
Name_____Date_____Mark_____

Review Quiz

Instructions: Read each of the following statements carefully. Some are true and some are false. Indicate your selection by placing a circle around the T or F in the right-hand column.

Example: Wood should be sanded with the grain.   (T)   F

1. Pine is a softer wood than mahogany.	T	F
2. A ripsaw is used to cut wood with the grain.	T	F
3. Soft woods are used for furniture.	T	F
4. Most mahogany comes from the south.	T	F
5. A hacksaw is used to cut out scrolls.	T	F

Suggestions for Construction of True-False Tests

1. Let the sequence of true and false items be irregular and follow no pattern.
2. Include only one point in each statement.
3. Construct simple, plain statements.
4. Statements should be factual, not ambiguous.

5. Division of true and false items should be about equal.
6. Do not let one statement give the answer to another.
7. Give instructions on answering the statement.
8. Place answer columns to right side for easy marking.
9. Give an example of how to answer the statement.
10. Do not use double negatives in constructing statements.
11. Do not use statements that are partly true.
12. Do not use absolute language, such as never, always, all, etc.
13. Use correct English in constructing items.
14. Do not include items that are not relevant to the intent of the test or are not within the range of the instruction given.
15. Construct an answer key for easy scoring of each test.
16. Discard and replace items which prove to be unsatisfactory.
17. Try to place the main thought at the end of the statement.

THE MULTIPLE CHOICE QUESTION

The multiple choice question can be used to enable students to use judgment and knowledge in selecting the correct answer. It can be used to cover a broader scope of the work and calls for recognition rather than simple recall of facts. It gives a greater opportunity to apply reasoning and makes pure guessing more difficult and less effective. Items consist of statements or questions which pose a problem, followed by a choice of solutions or answers.

Multiple choice types of questions are more valid than true-false. Approximately 50 or more items are considered necessary for obtaining reliable results. The rate of answering is approximately four to five a minute, depending on the complexity of the items. The following example is typical of this type of test.

Here are some suggestions for constructing multiple choice questions:

1. Three choices are too few, and five choices are too difficult to devise.
2. Choices should be plausible, not completely irrelevant.
3. Do not permit any pattern of correct choices to develop.
4. Do not use words in the original statement which will give a clue to the correct choice.
5. When using an incomplete statement, let the blank which the correct choice will fill be at the end.
6. If a word is common to all choices, place the word in the statement.
7. Have the student place the number or letter of the correct response in the right-hand column for easy scoring.

TEACHING OCCUPATIONAL SKILLS

Example of Multiple Choice Test

School Name_____

Department_____

Electrical Wiring_____ Section_____

Name_____ Date_____ Mark_____

Marking Period Examination—Armored Cable

Directions: Each of the following statements or questions is followed by four possible answers. Read the statement and answer each carefully. Place the letter of the answer you select in the right hand column.

Example: The number of bends permitted in one run of armored cable is,

    a. Four bends   c. Six bends
    b. Unlimited   d. Eight bends   __b__

1. Armored cable should be strapped every,
    a. Five feet   c. Four and one-half feet
    b. Two feet   d. Six and one-half feet 1._____

2. Armored cable is supplied in rolls of,
    a. 500 feet   c. 250 feet
    b. 100 feet   d. 200 feet   2._____

3. The white conductor of a two-wire cable may be, live when used as,
    a. Feeder   c. Identified wire
    b. Branch wire   d. Switch leg   3._____

---

    8. Avoid the use of underlining or circling answers. If overlapping takes place, it will be difficult to mark the answer intended.

    9. Do not use long, involved statements or questions.

    10. Do not make a multiple choice question out of an item that limits choices.

THE SHORT-ANSWER TYPE OF QUESTION

The short-answer type of question satisfies to some degree both the requirement of objectivity and the clear, concise essay type of question. Guessing is almost eliminated, and the student can be given the opportunity to express himself, solve a problem, reason, and think. This type of test is not too difficult or time-consuming to prepare and

Example of Short-Answer Test

School Name_____ Department_____

Occupational Area_____ Term_____

Title of Test_____ Index No._____

Name_____Date_____Mark_____

Instructions: Read each statement or question with care. Write the appropriate answer in the space provided. Be brief but be understandable.

Example: State three measuring devices used by the machinist.
    a. Micrometer   b. Scale   c. Calipers

1. The machinist makes considerable use of decimal equivalents. What is the decimal equivalent of (a) ⅛, (b) ⅝, (c) 7/16?

    a. _____
    b. _____
    c. _____

2. A ¾" hole must be laid out in the center of a steel block which is 8" square. List four hand tools needed to do this.

    a. _____
    b. _____
    c. _____
    d. _____

---

can be easily scored. It permits the inclusion of a broad range and diversity of test items. Many students in shop and laboratory type of subjects prefer this type of test.

The rate of answering short-answer questions depends on the subject material and the complexity of the test items. Remember that the student must write the answer, and there will be differences in the speed with which they write and the ease with which they find the proper words to express their thoughts. Fifteen or more items should be included.

Here are some suggestions for constructing short-answer questions:

1. Construct clear, simple sentences.
2. Construct sentences that give specific instructions.
3. Keep all spaces the same length.
4. Adapt the short answer to include a variety of areas, such as:
    a. Simple explanations.
    b. List of steps.
    c. Names of parts.
    d. Solutions to problems.
    e. Labels for drawings.
    f. Names of symbols.

SOME VARIATIONS OF SHORT-ANSWER-TYPE QUESTIONS

1. Complete the following chart by filling in the characteristics and uses of each type of pipe used in pipe-fitting and plumbing.

Type of Pipe	Characteristics	Uses
Black Iron		
Galvanized		
Brass		
Lead		
Copper		

2. State a specific safety rule which applies to the use of each of the following items:
   a. Step ladders _____
   b. Straight ladders _____
   c. Floor vise _____
   d. Soldering iron _____
   e. Knife _____
   f. Hammer _____

3. Write in the spaces the names of the parts of the fluorescent tube corresponding in letter to the part.

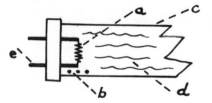

a. _____

b. _____

c. _____

d. _____

e. _____

g. Advantages of certain processes, parts, or uses.
   h. Lists of materials.
   i. Functions of parts.
   j. Reasons, principles, safety.
5. Weigh the answer to each part of the question and ascribe a value to each part so that the total will be a round number.
6. Use the right-hand answering column whenever possible for quick and easy scoring.
7. Be prepared with an answer key.
8. Include sketches, diagrams, illustrations, and other drawings when possible to add interest, clarity, and value to the test.

THE COMPLETION TYPE OF QUESTION

The completion type of question is closely related to the short-answer type in that it requires only a word or very short phrase to give an answer. However, the difference between them is that the completion type of question will complete a sentence, whereas the short answer is independent of the original sentence. Completion types of questions require accurate information and usually a recall of facts. It can be used to obtain a broad sampling of subject matter. The word which correctly completes the sentence should be placed in the right-hand column for easy marking. All spaces should be of equal length so that the line or space will not be a clue to the missing word. The test is of the objective type, but teachers should be careful not to write sentences that call for opinion instead of fact. Opinion types of questions become subjective and often lead to disagreement over the answer.

The missing word should be the key word, the name of a tool, a principle, unit of measurement, part of a machine, function of a part, name of a process, trade term, etc. Try as much as possible to place the key word near the end of the sentence, and always construct sentences which are grammatically correct. The rate of answering depends on the material, complexity, and other facts that always arise when students are asked to frame an answer and then to write it. Use 15 or more items for dependability.

Here are some suggestions for constructing completion types of questions:

1. Construction of completion types of items is similar to true-false items except that completion items are always correct.
2. Use correct sentence structure.
3. Do not omit more than three words in a sentence, and less if gram-

TEACHING OCCUPATIONAL SKILLS

Example of Completion Test

School Name_____

Department_____   Occupational Area_____

Name_____Date_____Mark_____

Review Quiz in Radio Theory

Directions: Read each sentence carefully. When you have decided on the answer which will complete the sentence completely, place the answer in the right hand column.

Example: The prefix meaning thousand is _____.   Kilo

1. The unit of electrical pressure is_____.   1. _____

2. The silver tip on a resistor indicates a tolerance of _____.   2. _____

3. The mathematical relationship between electrical pressure, current and resistance is called _____.   3. _____

4. Sound is magnified in the radio receiver in the _____ circuit.   4. _____

5. Vacuum tubes are rapidly being replaced by _____.   5. _____

4. Place blanks beyond the second half of the sentence for easier reading.
5. Make all blanks the same length.
6. Provide for easy and quick scoring by placing answer blanks in right-hand column.
7. Construct sentences in your own language; do not use texts or other books for obtaining sentences.
8. Try to use items that call for only one correct answer.
9. Be prepared to accept alternate answers if correct.
10. Let the answer include only material relevant to the topic, not extraneous terms.
11. Provide answer blanks in the right-hand column which are long enough to accommodate the answers.
12. Prepare a scoring key.
13. Be prepared to change sentences that students find vague or otherwise confusing.
14. Avoid "give away" words before the key word to be inserted.
15. Be careful not to use words in sentences which are answers to other questions.

THE MATCHING TYPE OF QUESTION

The matching type of test can be used when the teacher wishes to test students' ability to identify terms, parts, definitions, etc., and to properly associate them with their companion terms. The premium is on recall and recognition and, consequently, the use of matching types of questions can be of value in learning associations. The familiar form is to construct two columns, one of terms, the other of definitions or dates and events, or inventors and inventions, parts and functions, tools and uses, materials and characteristics. It is a good idea to construct one column with two or three items more than the other to discourage guessing or answering by elimination.

The maximum number of items should not exceed 10 to 15 because time is needed to scan the lists, make comparisons, and choose the correct answer. The rate of answering is hard to determine, therefore each teacher should check his class, subject, and material in order to estimate the time to be allowed.

Example of Matching Test

The left-hand column lists the names of famous inventors; the right-hand column lists a series of inventions. Study both lists and match the inventor with the invention by writing the letter corresponding to the inventor next to the number of his invention. You should have ten pairs when finished.

A. Boyle	1. _____ The electric light
B. Edison	2. _____ Wireless telegraphy
C. Bell	3. _____ The air brake
D. Zworykin	4. _____ Law of gas volumes
E. Steinmetz	5. _____ Telegraph
F. De Forest	6. _____ Electrical and mathematical genius
G. Faraday	7. _____ Father of television
H. Westinghouse	8. _____ The electric generator
I. Marconi	9. _____ The vacuum tube
J. Morse	10. _____ The transformer
	11. _____ The self-starter
	12. _____ The telephone

Here are some suggestions for constructing matching types of questions:

1. Keep items homogeneous rather than cover many diverse areas.
2. Construct neat, orderly columns.
3. Do not include as extra items material which is completely irrelevant.
4. Do not permit matching by underscoring because such answers are too confusing to score.
5. Do not construct a matching type of question with less than five items.
6. Arrange the question so that all of it will appear on the same page.
7. Give specific and clear directions for answering the question.
8. Construct or prepare an answer key as has been recommended for all objective types of questions.

THE ESSAY TYPE OF QUESTION

Essay types of questions are often referred to as power questions; and when carefully and properly constructed, they should test for real knowledge and understanding. Essay questions, when loosely worded and poorly prepared, can become quite subjective and confusing to the test-taker. When they are constructed to request specific information, however, they offer a means of evaluation which cannot be achieved with objective types of questions.

It might be well to define the words *objective* and *subjective* at this point. According to a dictionary, one of the meanings of the word objective is "directing the mind or activity toward external things without reference to personal sensation; grasping and representing facts as they are; unbiased by prejudice or temperament." Subjective means "the illusory quality imparted by the individual mind; an impression."

A good test, in order to be valid and reliable, should be one which can be evaluated without prejudice, bias, or otherwise influenced by personal impression. It is very easy to become impressed with the quantity of writing in answering a question, the style rather than the content, or the fact that the student is such a "good" boy, rather than with his capability as a student. Another criticism of the traditional essay type of question or test lies in the difficulty on the part of the test-taker to clearly comprehend the intent and meaning of the question. Such questions as the following do not clearly indicate the response expected by the teacher:

1. "Tell what you know about the transformer."
2. "Describe plexiglass."

3. "How do you cut a taper?"
4. "Tell what happens when high-test gasoline is used in a car."
5. "What is a Pittsburgh joint?"

Yet, the questions listed above contain material for good, thought-provoking, and challenging problems to be solved. The thing for the teacher to do in each instance is to ask himself what has been taught, what should have been learned, and what should be asked in specific areas of the topic in question. For example, each of the questions above might be rewritten in several different ways, such as:

1. "Explain the principle of operation of the simple transformer."
2. "State the four main characteristics of plexiglass as applied to its use in industry."
3. "Give a step-by-step procedure in making a simple taper, including the necessary formulas."
4. "Give the advantages of high-test gasoline in engine performance."
5. "Make a series of simple sketches with labels to illustrate the method of making a Pittsburgh joint."

In each of these questions an attempt has been made to limit the scope of the answer to definite parts of the main topic. The student is relieved of the tension and waste of time which usually accompany guessing what the teacher wants. It is often said that essay types of questions are easy to construct and difficult to score. This is true of the traditional form, but should not be true of a well-stated, essay question. No question or test is "easy" to construct. It should not be a cumbersome task or take many hours of work to construct, but neither should a test or question be devised on the spur of the moment or between classes. Inspirations can come to a person any time, but to implement them takes time.

Example of Essay Test

1. Most car owners know that a thin oil should be used in cold weather and a heavy oil should be used in hot weather.
   a. List four different factors that a trained automotive mechanic should consider in selecting the proper engine oil for a vehicle. (4 points)
   b. Explain the importance of each of the four factors you listed in part a. (16 points)

ESSAY TYPES OF QUESTIONS

Should	Should Not
1. Call for knowledge.	1. Be vague.
2. Require thought and reflect understanding in the answers.	2. Be too broad.
3. Be clear and easy to comprehend.	3. Permit answers open to argument.
4. Call for problem-solving.	4. Ask for opinion instead of fact.
5. Be constructed so that all the answers can be graded on the same basis.	5. Be difficult to mark.
6. Be varied and call for sketches, steps, illustrations, explanations, etc.	6. Be a test of literary skill instead of subject-matter understanding.
7. Be specific.	

PREPARATION OF TESTS

The following tests are fine examples of what an enthusiastic and devoted teacher can do. In lieu of using some of the more common types of tests, he displayed ingenuity and capacity for work by devising these original forms applied to his particular subject. They particularly appeal to students because of their structure and their pictorial feature. The same ideas can be applied to practically every area of vocational education. Such forms can be used repeatedly; therefore, the professional teacher can quickly recognize their value and justify the time it takes for their construction.

The teacher should determine whether the test is a quiz, review, unit test, weekly test, final examination, or pretest. The pretest, which has not been discussed up to this point, is usually an objective type of test utilizing true-false or multiple choice items which cover in a broad way many simple fundamentals, mathematics, principles, tools, machines, materials, equipment, etc. of a given occupational area or related field. The test is not meant to examine, but to sample students' previous knowledge of the topic so that the teacher can organize his teaching in accordance with the needs of his class.

The most valuable source of test material is the lesson plan. Lesson plans represent the refinement of all the teachable content of the course. Work sheets, assignment sheets, project sheets, job sheets, and other instructional material have their origin in the teacher's lesson plans. It is logical, therefore, that the same sources should be the reference for tests and test questions. Tests may include things learned

Recognition Type Questions

1. Recall of auger bit sizes by number.

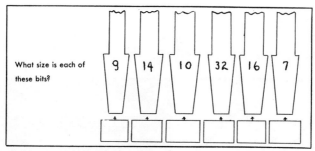

2. Recall of names of geometric figures for area and volume problems as applied to various occupations.

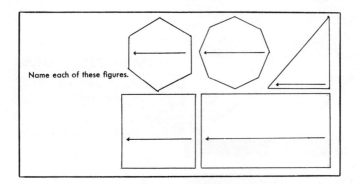

3. Recall of proper names of operations of an occupation.

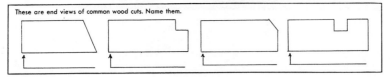

through assignments, practical application, research, homework, projects, and other learning experiences. However, all of them should have been included somewhere in the teacher's lesson plans. The lesson plan can serve not only as the basis for instructional material, but also as the basis for various tests.

Quizzes lend themselves well to motivating instruction and can be part of a lesson. Objective tests that require approximately ten minutes to complete are especially appropriate for the purpose. A teacher might plan to use a true-false, multiple choice, short-answer, or completion

TEACHING OCCUPATIONAL SKILLS 168

Recognition-Type Test

Machine Shop   Common Hand Tools

Name_____ Class_____ Date_____ Grade_____

Instructions: Write the correct name of each tool in the space next to the corresponding number at the bottom of this page. Check your work.

1_____ 2_____ 3_____ 4_____
5_____ 6_____ 7_____ 8_____
9_____ 10_____ 11_____ 12_____
13_____ 14_____ 15_____ 16_____
                17_____ 18_____

type of quiz as the application of a lesson. These types of tests can be easily and quickly administered. They permit the interchange of students' papers, and thereby can be marked in class. Grades may or may not be recorded, depending on the decision of the individual teacher. When tests are to be used in this manner, it should be noted on the teacher's lesson plan under "Teacher Preparation." When a

Recognition-Type Test

Test on Hand Tools   The Plane

Name_____Date_____Class_____Mark_____

Instructions: The instructor will assign a plane to you. Write down the name and the size of the plane in the top circle. Study the plane and examine it carefully. As you recognize and recall each part, write its name in the circle whose arrow points to the part.

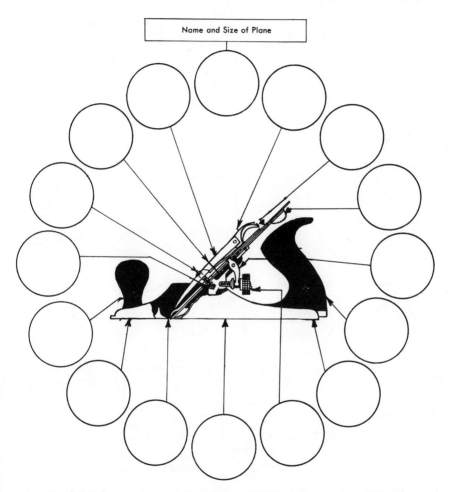

test is to be given at the end of the week or month or at the end of the unit of instruction, it should be noted in the teacher's weekly plan.

If a quiz is to be developed, perhaps 50 true-false statements or 25 to 50 multiple choice statements will serve the purpose. If, on the

Recognition-Type Test

Woodworking Test   Common Mouldings

Name_____ _____Date_____Class_____Score_____

Instructions: The sketches below are of commonly used wood mouldings. Each has a number. Study the mouldings and the list of names at the bottom of this sheet. Write the correct number of the moulding next to the name of that moulding.

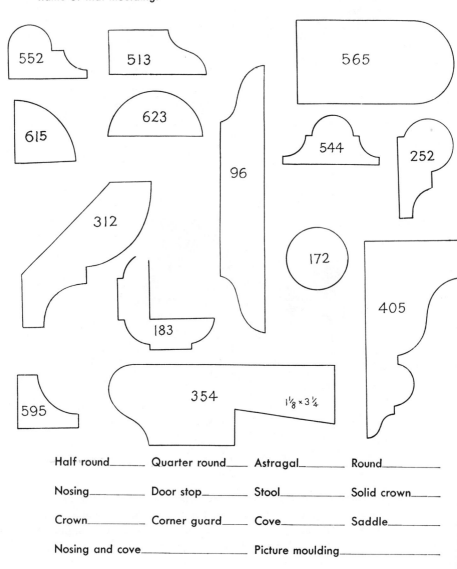

Half round_____ Quarter round_____ Astragal_____ Round_____

Nosing_____ Door stop_____ Stool_____ Solid crown_____

Crown_____ Corner guard_____ Cove_____ Saddle_____

Nosing and cove_____ Picture moulding_____

Multiple Choice Tests

Creative teachers can find means of varying standard formats, yet accomplish their objectives in testing. Shown below is an unusual application of multiple choice questions which has appeal and learning value because it is different. The test is marked by means of an overlay type of scoring key.

Each of the following sentences has three answers, but only one is correct. Write the correct answer in the circle alongside the question.

Saws are sharpened with an oilstone, file or rasp. ○	A plane, a knife or a chisel is best for making a chamfer. ○
A drill, a brace or a bit actually makes the hole in wood. ○	Glue, nails or screws are used most for fastening. ○
Which do you make first: a working edge, face or end? ○	White pine, oak or poplar is a hard wood. ○
A marking gauge, a rule or a try square is used for scribing lines. ○	Which is best for marking: a pencil, a rule or a knife? ○
A back-saw, a rip-saw or a crosscut saw cuts with the grain. ○	Lumber is sold by the inch, foot or yard. ○

other hand, an examination is to be developed, then a variety of types of questions should be included. An examination should include such elements as:

1. Safety questions.
2. Problem-solving.
3. Use of related mathematics and science.

TEACHING OCCUPATIONAL SKILLS

Multiple Choice Type Tests

Shown below is an overlay type of scoring key for the multiple choice type test illustrated on page 171. Overlay keys are easily made from heavy paper or oak tag. They can be made for many other types of tests, depending on the ingenuity of the teacher.

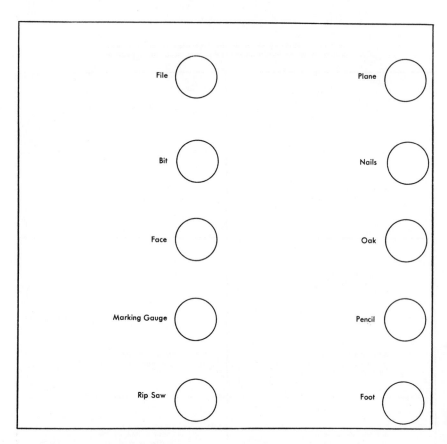

4. Knowledge of parts, functions, and uses.
5. Tools, materials, equipment, and machinery.
6. Drawings and diagrams.

Testing for proficiency in any of these areas can be done by including a combination of essay, multiple choice, matching, or any of the variations of the short-answer types of questions. Another examination might utilize the essay, completion, and matching types of questions. A balance can be achieved by using an essay question and a combination of objective types of questions. The use of variety in planning tests adds interest, gives students of various levels of ability and capacity the satisfaction of having achieved at least partial success, and gives the teacher a broad sampling of results for intelligent analysis and diagnosis.

Develop first the general framework of the test by constructing an outline, then determine what will be included, and finally decide which types of questions will best suit the material. Take into account the time available or time required for the test. When students become familiar with a standard form, they will be able to proceed with the test and not waste time becoming acquainted with new and different arrangements of material. It is important to remember that the examination is meant to test for subject content, not cleverness in outwitting the instructor or ability in wading through extraneous material.

It is advisable to have all test scores total 100 points. Each part should be weighted according to the importance of the question, the complexity of the answer required, and the length of the question. Each weight, however, should be a round number and each part should be assigned a whole number. Assigning weights and values of ¼ and 3½ and other such mixed numbers makes scoring most difficult and adds nothing to the test. A choice of questions is desirable, and partial credit for correct steps and procedures add to the value of the test. If, in the instructor's opinion, a question or several questions deal with vital and important material, then those questions should be made mandatory and the remaining ones provide a choice.

Many teachers use a code number for each examination so they can compare class progress each succeeding term. Examinations may be used more than once when used at different times, and far enough apart so that students do not recognize them. Always include instructions for taking a test and clearly indicate the numerical value of each question. Teachers sometimes have students place the answers on a separate sheet. It is more desirable to have the work done on the test paper so that both question and answer are together. This procedure will make study and review more meaningful and valuable. Routine tests should be considered an integral part of every course, and they belong in the students' notebooks as a record of the work done and as a source of study material.

Administration of Tests

Avoid the error of assuming that students know how to take a test; that they will conduct themselves properly during a test; or that they will carefully read all the instructions and understand them. Teachers should not assume that all they need do is distribute the tests and students will know just how to proceed. Each test is different, each has a different purpose, and each should be explained

In supervising a test, a teacher should stand behind or to one side of the class.

and instructions given. For this reason, it is better to give each student a copy of a test than to write the questions on the board or read them aloud to be copied by students. Remember that everything a teacher does to improve his teaching skill will make teaching more rewarding to the teacher and more effective for the students. Also remember that as teaching skill improves, classroom problems decline.

Hints on Improving Tests

1. Plan every test carefully. Determine clearly:
    a. The purpose of the test.
    b. The material to be covered.
    c. The time available.
    d. The place in the class period when it should be used.
    e. The type of test to use.

2. Choose a means of duplicating which will produce a clean, legible copy. Provide space for answers when laying out the test.
3. Decide on a uniform heading for all tests with a code number or other means of classifying and indexing the tests. Include instructions and examples.
4. Run off more than enough copies for immediate use to provide copies for future use.
5. Give students prior notice so they can study and prepare for the test, especially if the test result is to be recorded and used as a basis for a grade.
6. Test on what has been covered or assigned, *not* unknown or unfamiliar material. Do not go in for "tricks." Tests can become learning and measuring devices only when teachers develop confidence and trust on the part of the students.
7. Ask students to remove all books, notes, and other material from desks and tables. Remind them to sharpen pencils, check pens for ink, and secure rulers and other materials needed for the test.
8. Announce the time allotted for the test. If the test is expected to take 45 to 60 minutes, announce when five minutes remain.
9. Distribute papers face down. Have students simultaneously turn papers over and instruct them to fill in the heading completely.
10. Read the instructions to the class; explain them if necessary, and check to be sure everyone understands. Advise the class to answer first those questions which they are most sure of, then to proceed to the more difficult ones, and in that way avoid wasting time.
11. Start the test and time it from the starting signal.
12. Supervise the test. Do not leave the room, read a book, or otherwise leave the class to its own devices. Have an extra supply of paper if needed.
13. When the allotted time has elapsed, collect the papers while students are still seated.
14. Depending on the nature of the test, students may exchange papers, mark, and return them to the owners, or collect them for further check by the teacher.
15. Mark and return test papers promptly. When test papers are not returned for three or four days or even a week, interest is lost, continuity is broken, and much of the educational benefit is wasted.
16. Review tests with the class. Point out errors and weaknesses, as well as accomplishments. Plan to retest if a serious weakness becomes apparent.
17. Ask for comments and suggestions about the test. Take steps to correct shortcomings in test construction. Try to improve the items, the form, and general construction for future use.
18. Do not use the test as a weapon or form of punishment. Many students become apprehensive simply because it is a test. Teachers

should do what they can to ease students' minds so they can concentrate on the test.
19. Take some of your own tests a term later. See how plain and understandable they are. Many glaring faults may be evident.
20. Accept advice—in fact, ask the older, more experienced teachers for it.

These hints are meant to be general in nature. Not every test or quiz needs to be so formal. However, the procedure of preparation, construction, duplication, and administration remains the same. There is no simple formula for testing in all areas or under all circumstances. Each teacher must know his students, analyze his objectives, and implement a testing program which will be consistent with the needs of both. The best way to become skilled in testing is to construct tests of all types. Learning by doing applies to all, students and teachers alike. The skilled person becomes so only through repeated efforts.

Summary

"Tests are the proving grounds of learning."

All teachers should determine how much and how well their students are really learning. They must test their methods so that they will be valid and reliable. They must measure students' performance and knowledge. They must evaluate understanding as differentiated from recall of facts. A method of evaluation and measurement must be as objective as possible and must not be influenced by impressions or personal likes and dislikes.

Tests should serve a number of functions, such as:

1. Reveal weaknesses to students.
2. Indicate deficiencies to the teacher.
3. Stimulate a desire for learning.
4. Help to determine grades.
5. Serve as a basis for guidance.
6. Measure progress in the course.
7. Assist teachers to analyze difficulties.
8. Be of sufficient variety to appeal to the range of individual differences found in the average class composition.

The methods of testing include oral quizzing, written tests, and practical tests. Oral quizzing has limited value as a basis for evaluation other than in a lesson or as a means of checking. It can be used with students with reading difficulties. The practical or performance test, although probably the best of the lot, is sometimes too involved. It requires extensive preparation and a selection of test jobs or projects plus the tools and sufficient material to administer it. When performance tests are used, teachers should develop special check sheets including all the factors on which the job is to be evaluated. In lieu of performance tests, teachers should keep careful records of jobs, projects, and other practical applications of student performance in the occupational area. All jobs done in a shop are tests in themselves because they show the degree of skill possessed. These factors are all important in the final evaluation and grading.

The types of paper tests are divided into two main areas: the essay type and the objective type. The essay type is the traditional form of written test which calls for detailed explanations and the ability to express oneself well in written form. Unless care is taken, essay type of questions can easily become subjective. Essay questions can be made objective by limiting and defining the responses required. Skill in constructing essay questions should be cultivated because they require thought, problem solving, judgment, and reasoning. Real understanding and knowledge may be reflected in the answers. This form of question provides both a learning experience for the student and a valuable measuring instrument for the teacher.

The objective types of tests usually call for recall of facts, short answers, and often promote guessing. The main types are:

1. True-False
2. Multiple Choice
3. Completion
4. Matching
5. Recognition

Construction of objective types of questions usually requires more planning and time. Sometimes they are more difficult than essay questions. Most students at all levels of occupational instruction prefer them. They are economical in time for both student and teacher. A wide range of information can be covered, facts can be emphasized, students cannot bluff, and answers are not open to disagreement.

Quizzes can be constructed using any one of the types of questions described. On the other hand, examinations should use several different types in order to inject enough variety and selection to appeal to all students. Teachers should develop answer keys for each test for easy and quick scoring. When tests are several pages long, they may be marked by scoring all similar pages at once. This method will simplify marking and economize the teacher's time, because each page becomes familiar and the scoring becomes more objective. Although tests should total 100 points, the number of questions need not determine the weight of each question. Weights should depend on the importance as well as the amount of work done in answering them. Assign weights in whole numbers because odd numbers or fractions will not only be more difficult to tally but will also increase the chance of error.

Administration of tests is important and should not be either haphazard or neglected. Instructions and explanations should be given. The use and purpose of the test should be clear to the students. Students should be put at ease, they should be instructed in how to take the test, and room conditions should be checked. Test papers should be returned promptly and reviewed to correct errors and to help students find their weaknesses.

Teachers should work at test construction. They should use a standard heading or other device as adopted by the school or department. If there is none, the teacher should develop one of his own which will best suit the situation.

Questions and Projects

1. What are five values derived from taking a test?
2. What are five values derived from giving a test?
3. List five disadvantages of the traditional essay type of question, and develop five techniques to overcome the disadvantages.
4. Construct five essay questions that can be used in your teaching.
5. What are the characteristics of objective types of tests?
6. Construct:
    a. 25 true-false statements.
    b. 10 multiple choice questions.
    c. 10 short-answer questions.
    d. 10 completion types of questions.
    e. 10 matching types of items.
    f. 10 recognition types of items.
7. Develop a uniform heading for your tests.
8. Construct a quiz that can be used as part of a lesson.
9. Construct a short-answer quiz using diagrams as the basis for the answers.
10. Draw up a list of requirements by which a good test may be judged.
11. Make up a true-false test of 50 items to be used as a pretest.
12. Why should test results be recorded whether or not they are to be used for grading?
13. What might either of the two following test results indicate?
    a. 30 students—20 above 90, 10 above 80.
    b. 30 students—20 below 70, 10 below 50.
14. Make a list of techniques in administering tests.

Instruction Sheets as Aids to Learning

If we could observe a typical school group engaged in some type of shop activity, we might hear the students asking questions such as these: "I have finished, Mr. Rogers. What do I do next?"; "I was in the other school one month before I transferred here."; "My project is all finished. May I start the next one now?"; I have time left over, so may I do another job like the last one?"; "Where can I find the information about this material?"; "I was absent for two days and I want to catch up."

We might read the teacher's mind and find that he is thinking: "I wish they would give me just a few minutes to check the supplies. Tom is going to be finished long before the rest of the class. What can I give him to do that will be worthwhile? Jimmy is so slow he will be left behind if I don't find some way for him to follow the instructions after I have given them to the group. Harry needs to improve his reading skill. How can I give him material to read that is appropriate and related to the occupation for which he is preparing? I wish I had some kind of form that the boys could use to estimate their job costs and material needs. Bill is a good boy with a natural curiosity to find out things for himself; if I had some experiments for him to perform, he might become at least temporarily interested and satisfied. I think I will develop some test report forms similar to those in industry." We could go on and on listing questions teachers ask themselves. Similar questions arise in the many instructional areas as teachers try to discover ways to solve the problems that they encounter when attempting to teach occupational skills and information to groups.

INSTRUCTION SHEETS

Much has been said and much has been written about instruction sheets. Many comments have been favorable, while many others have been unfavorable. Instruction sheets, when well-constructed and properly used, can fulfill many functions. They can:

1. Serve to clarify instruction.
2. Give specific instructions.
3. Supplement verbal instructions.
4. Supply additional information about the skills being taught.
5. Permit students to progress at their own rate.
6. Encourage initiative and train students to follow written instructions.
7. Reinforce the slow student's previous learning.
8. Enable the new or late student to pick up the work already taught.
9. Permit the student, without very much assistance, to do additional jobs of the same difficulty in order to improve his skills.
10. Help the student to help himself.

In general, anything that helps the teacher to help the student learn might be called a teaching aid. Instruction sheets are a printed type of teaching aid; in the same sense, a book is a teaching or instructional aid. It is almost impossible, however, to obtain books that fulfill the needs of any one teacher. Teachers of occupational skills soon find that such instruction is almost individualized in terms of their area, class, facilities, student needs, and their own occupational experience. If instruction sheets can be developed which will meet the requirements of the learner as described above, then they can be valuable and should be used.

The criteria by which instruction sheets may be judged should be based on the quality of the sheets and the manner in which they are used. *No instruction sheet can replace the teacher, even the best sheet can only supplement the teacher.* Well-developed material of this kind should stimulate student thought, as well as show how to approach the work to be done. The successful worker and the successful student need facts and information, as well as manual skills. They must be able to combine these intelligently so that they can keep abreast of technical changes and solve trade problems intelligently. Instruction sheets should give specific instructions with step-by-step procedures on how to do a job or operation. In addition, they should include information necessary for the successful completion of the task at hand.

Instruction sheets probably require more careful preparation than any other type of teaching material. They must be clearly written in language that is direct *in meaning* and easily understood. Any student should be able to read and interpret the instructions with a minimum of difficulty. Instruction sheets place a premium upon the instructor's ability to express himself in written form. He can and should use the outline form, give step-by-step instructions, and supplement them with diagrams and illustrations wherever they will be of value. It is important to note at this point that the development of lesson plans is a valuable experience in writing instruction sheets. The skill involved in developing the presentation or procedure part of a plan can often be used as the basis for an instruction sheet.

Some of the more common types of instruction sheets are:

1. Job Sheet. This form of instruction sheet gives directions for doing a series of operations involved in a complete job. It may include considerable detail or it may consist of a working drawing or a blueprint.
2. Operation Sheet. This type of instructional material is limited to the teaching of a single basic operation of an occupation. As a rule, it is used in the preliminary phase of a training course when the learning must progress one step at a time. Its main objective is to establish a uniform method of performance and encourage the correct habits in the performance of the particular skills.
3. Information Sheet. This type of sheet contains factual information essential to the intelligent completion of an operation or job. It is either a review of the teacher's instruction or a supplement to what the teacher has presented. In some cases it becomes the property of the individual student.
4. Assignment Sheet. This teaching tool is used as a follow-up to the teacher's instruction. It may consist of a number of problems to be

solved, a series of questions to be answered, references to be consulted, observations to be made, or directions for an assigned job to be performed.
5. Project Sheet. This is a sheet that contains all the elements for doing a job or constructing a finished product. It lends itself particularly to the industrial arts areas and exploratory type of classes in junior and senior high schools.
6. Experiment Sheets. This type of instruction sheet is especially valuable in the laboratory where students can perform a series of tests or trial problems in order to demonstrate and prove scientific principles, facts, or formulas. Although especially valuable in the laboratory, any teacher can utilize the same techniques to help his students learn certain principles or prove certain theories.
7. Work Sheets. This term is being used in this text to designate the miscellaneous sheets that can be developed to meet unique needs. Examples of this type are sheets on which students make up a bill of material for large job costs. Sheets of this kind, with a variety of problems, can be used for extra tasks, for home assignments, or for use during the application of a lesson.

Although each sheet may vary in its detailed content, all the sheets should possess certain common characteristics:

1. A statement of the purpose of the sheet.
2. A uniform heading with a title, index number, and area classification.
3. A list of tools, materials, and equipment required.
4. A step-by-step procedure to be followed.
5. Necessary safety precautions to be observed.
6. Some thought-provoking questions.
7. Simple illustrations and diagrams when possible.
8. Reference books and other texts for further study and check.
9. Attractive layout and organization.
10. Faultless reproduction on a good grade of paper.

Value of Instruction Sheets

Instruction sheets should assist in the three important phases of teaching vocational subjects by:

1. Explaining how to do the work.
2. Giving information essential to the successful completion of the work.
3. Questioning to stimulate student thinking about the work performed.

Despite the obvious advantages of instruction sheets, certain disadvantages have been registered against them because:

1. In some cases they enumerate the steps in doing a job, but they do not explain how to perform these steps.

2. They are not clearly written; therefore, they are difficult for students to understand.
3. It is difficult for some people to interpret printed instructions.
4. Students will seek the needed information from co-workers rather than read the instructions themselves.
5. Teachers find it difficult to motivate students to use instruction sheets.
6. The sheets are so complete that the students need exercise no initiative in doing the work and need give little thought to the doing if the directions are followed.
7. Students fail to give their undivided attention to the teacher's demonstration or explanation because they know that an instruction sheet will be distributed following the teacher's presentation.
8. The reading ability of many students is unfortunately limited; consequently, mistakes in doing the work are inevitable.

Although teachers consider that the above statements represent faults of instruction sheets, a careful analysis will show that these so-called faults are really due to poor teaching and inadequate instruction of students at some point in their previous training.

There has been some criticism of job sheets because of a misconception of their construction and use. A job sheet used in industry by the skilled worker would be highly inadequate in a school that proposes to train intelligent learners. The industrial job sheet consists of a list of the required operations arranged in the sequence considered best for mass production. It is generally used by the job setter and not by the individual skilled worker or machine operator. In this case the worker is supposed to follow standard procedure and, therefore, needs to do little thinking about the job. This is not the type of job sheet which should be used in a school where intelligent mechanics are to be trained.

Shortsightedness is often responsible for the nonuse of instruction sheets. Too many teachers are indifferent to the development of instructional material because of the time required in addition to their regular school hours. Although the development of instruction sheets is not an easy job, it is one that pays high dividends in terms of efficient teaching and effective learning, with economy of time to both teacher and student. Instruction sheets do not miraculously eliminate all difficulties or relieve the teacher of his responsibilities, but they do help to lighten his burden. At first the inexperienced teacher will probably find it difficult to write definite instructions on how to perform the operations involved in their occupation in simple, clear, unequivocal English. However, with considerable persistence plus a model sheet as a pattern, it is possible to become quite adept at writing instructional material.

Many projects in technical education are written up on instruction sheets.

There has been considerable emphasis placed on the fact that students will not read instruction sheets. Consequently, many teachers make too little use of written material in their classes. The failure of students to read those sheets is an excuse rather than a reason for the nonuse of this type of teaching aid. Since boys literally wear out such magazines as *Popular Mechanics* and *The Craftsman,* there is little justification for saying that students will not read well-presented material. If instruction sheets are simply and attractively presented, the average student will be eager to read them and to follow them. Another important consideration is the value the teacher places on instructional sheets as demonstrated by the way he uses them.

It is a well-known fact that every class has students who rebel against reading directions. The manual activities of the shop are more agreeable to many learners than the mental effort required to comprehend the printed page. Since there are numerous reasons why students refuse to read or are unable to comprehend instruction sheets, teachers, once again, must rely upon the psychology of individual differences to cope with the situation.

Students may have been allowed to develop careless reading habits in the elementary school. The ability to comprehend printed matter may never have been fostered within many students in their formative years. Moreover, these pupils will likely never learn to read if it is not required of them. Many, if not all, occupations require some reading ability and good instruction sheets can promote reading skill and at the same time familiarize the student with occupational terms. Perhaps the teacher himself may be guilty of not giving the necessary background information or of giving vague and inaccurate directions in his instruction sheets. A teacher must always be alert to these and other situations which cause this valuable teaching aid to become ineffective. Patience, thoughtfulness, and persistence must be employed if the use of instruction sheets is to be profitable.

Advantages of Instruction Sheets

A list of the advantages of instruction sheets is a persuasive argument in favor of their use. They serve to:

1. Economize the teacher's time and eliminate unnecessary oral explanations and repetition of instructions.
2. Illustrate careful preparation on the part of the teacher.
3. Enable a teacher to effectively instruct a group of learners who are working on different assignments.
4. Allow a teacher to simultaneously instruct students on diffent trade levels.
5. Motivate the learning through an appeal to the sense of sight, since drawings and illustrations are usually included.
6. Enable a student to progress as rapidly as his individual ability will enable him. The faster students are not retarded by the slower ones.
7. Permit a student to continue his work when the teacher is absent or when the teacher is preoccupied with other members of the class.
8. Eliminate the possibility of misunderstanding which always exists when instructions are given orally.
9. Remove the excuse of "fooling around" by students.
10. Develop uniform habits of workmanship.
11. Encourage self-reliance on the part of the student.
12. Prepare the student for industrial emplyoment, where written instructions are very common.
13. Provide a permanent work record for a student's notebook.
14. Serve as a reference for review of the work.
15. Are convenient to use and easily stored.

Developing Instruction Sheets

Now that the advantages and disadvantages of instruction sheets have been listed, the precautions that should be observed in developing this type of material will be discussed. Each type of sheet will be discussed individually. While there are factors common to all the instruction sheets, there are certain points that should be noted specifically in connection with each one.

The suggestions listed below are valuable in developing the various kinds of instruction sheets.

1. Use language that is simple and easily understood by an adolescent student. Do not use words or phrases that are unusual or ambiguous. Some people recommend a conversational style with frequent use of the second person because this practice is more appealing.
2. Supplement the words with sketches and illustrations for greater clarity. The illustrations may save many words.
3. Avoid crowding the sheet.
4. Give specific directions that are clear and concise. However, do not sacrifice clarity for conciseness.
5. Limit each instruction sheet to one piece of paper, if possible.
6. Avoid the inclusion of irrelevant material. Include only necessary information for the intelligent completion of the work.
7. Be consistent in the use of the word *teacher* or *instructor*, and also *student* or *pupil*. Preferably, use *teacher* and *student* throughout.
8. Separate points, items, or paragraphs by numbers or letters.
9. Formulate questions that challenge the thinking of the student. A school's chief function is to make students think and to stimulate initiative.
10. Space the various divisions of the sheet, such as the title, purpose, sketches, and text in order to produce a well-balanced and attractive aid.
11. Vary the typing between lower case and upper case letters and use underlining to emphasize or to distinguish between headings, subheadings, and content.
12. Exercise discrimination in the choice of material to be included in an instruction sheet. There is a probability of "loading" the sheet with a considerable amount of irrelevant information. The chief purpose of instruction sheets is to aid the student in doing the work and to increase his knowledge and ability to exercise judgment.

DEVELOPING JOB SHEETS

Directions for doing production jobs in industry consist of drawings and specifications which include such data as the name, code number and the use of the job, material to be used, finish required, and possible delivery date. Rarely does the job ticket or drawing give the procedure for doing the job because the skilled worker who receives the order knows the steps to be taken. In the school the situation is different. The novice learner does not know how to plan his work. A plan must be given to him, especially in the early part of his training course. He must be told the specific things he has to learn and the standards by which his progress will be evaluated.

The job sheet is not intended, in itself, to teach the trainee how to perform the required operations. It is assumed that the student will receive adequate instruction from the teacher's demonstration, and the instruction sheet will serve as a reminder. As the trainee advances to more difficult jobs, he should be required to write out his procedure or to state it verbally to the teacher. In all cases he should secure the teacher's approval before he starts the job.

Steps in Writing Job Sheets

1. State the aim as a specific thing to be done.
2. Supplement the aim by a brief statement covering the purpose of the job and an explanation of its nature.
3. List the tools, materials, and equipment needed to complete the job.
4. List in their correct sequence the steps involved in doing the job.
5. Include all necessary illustrations to aid in doing the job and to clarify any anticipated difficulties.
6. Indicate precautions to be observed and directions by which to check the accuracy of the job.
7. Suggest references that may prove profitable for a better understanding of the work.
8. Pose only such questions as are considered necessary for checking the completed job and the students' understanding.

The amount of detail placed on a job sheet may be gradually reduced as the student progresses in his course. Ultimately the job sheet may appear only as a drawing or blueprint that approximates the form in which jobs are assigned in industry.

The following list is composed of typical trade jobs for which job sheets could be written:

Machine Shop	Cutting a spur gear
	Making a slip bushing
Printing	Printing a letterhead
	Printing an admission ticket
Auto Mechanics	Relining brakes
	Repairing a blowout

Plumbing	Installing a sink
	Replacing a vent pipe
Shoe Repair	Replacing worn heels
	Replacing a shoe tongue
Dressmaking	Making a blouse
	Making an apron
Millinery	Making a beret
	Making a felt hat
Beauty Culture	Giving a manicure
	Giving a permanent wave

A series of *instruction sheet* layouts is presented here for examination. They vary somewhat in design; however, they all achieve the same result. The elements of good form exemplified in these samples apply to all instruction sheets. The individual instructor must select the form that best suits his purpose for the content involved.

WRITING OPERATION SHEETS

The operation sheet is confined to one operation or one step of a job. It explains the "how-to-do." *Making a bushing* would be a job, while *straight-turning the outside diameter* would be an operation. The operation sheet is usually distributed to the student when he is individually ready for it, and always after a complete demonstration by the teacher. The following suggestions will prove valuable when writing operation sheets for training purposes:

1. List in the proper order the steps involved in performing the operation indicated in the title of the sheet.
2. Use the correct occupational and technical terminology.
3. State the instructions in clear, concise English.
4. Indicate the safety precautions to be observed.
5. Depict the different steps by good illustrations.
6. Pose several specific questions that will challenge the student's thinking concerning the completed operation and its application to other phases of the work.

The instructions on this kind of sheet should be so clear that even the slower students will be able to go ahead with the process in a workmanlike manner and with a minimum of help after the teacher's initial demonstration.

Almost every household gadget or piece of mechanical equipment purchased today is accompanied by a leaflet of instructions which is comparable to the operation sheet. Usually the directions are written

Job Sheet — Job No. ____ Sheet No. ____

MACHINE SHOP

Name of Job _____
Aim _____

Tools | Materials

Drawing

Steps in Procedure
1.
2.
3.
4.
5.
6.

Questions
1.
2.
3.
4.
5.

School Name _____ Location _____

Assignment Sheet — Unit No. ____ Sheet No. ____

RELATED MATHEMATICS

Topic _____
Objective _____

Problems
1.
2.
3.

References _____

Calculations _____

School Name _____ Location _____
Student Name _____ Section _____

Operation Sheet — Unit No. ____ Sheet No. ____

SHEET METAL SHOP

Operation _____
Aim _____

Order of Performance

Sketch or Photograph — 1.

Sketch or Photograph — 2.

Sketch or Photograph — 3.

Questions _____

School Name _____ Location _____

Assignment Sheet — Unit No. ____ Sheet No. ____

RELATED SUBJECTS

Topic _____
Objective _____

Procedure _____

Recordings

Conclusions _____

School Name _____ Location _____
Student Name _____ Section _____

clearly enough to enable the purchaser to assemble or operate the device without a demonstration. The success of correspondence instruction during the last half-century is further evidence of the popularity of self-teaching instruction sheets. It would be profitable for beginning teachers to consult such types of material for helpful suggestions in writing their own instruction sheets. The following operations in various occupations are typical of those for which operation sheets may be developed.

Sheet Metal	Soldering a seam
	Mitering a corner
Machine Shop	Knurling a set screw head
	Facing stock in a lathe
Carpentry	Planing across grain
	Nailing flooring
Dressmaking	Overcasting a seam
	Making a hand-rolled edge
Plumbing	Wiping a joint
	Installing a trap
Printing	Adjusting guide pins
	Justifying a line
Cabinetmaking	Setting saws
	Turning a chair leg

WRITING INFORMATION SHEETS

Information sheets, as the name implies, are sources of information about the jobs being done and the materials being used. They are used to explain the *why, where,* and *when* rather than the *how* of jobs, materials, and equipment. They should supplement the teacher's instruction but should not replace the teacher. The sheets should explain necessary factual information in an interesting way that will encourage students to read them. The following list indicates topics that could be covered by information sheets.

Plumbing	The various kinds of solder
	The causes of water hammer
Dressmaking	The different types of silk fabrics
	Bias binding and its uses
Beauty Culture	The advantages of shampoo over soap
	The types of bristle in brushes
Machine Shop	Kinds of tool steel
	Kinds of abrasives
Woodworking	Kinds of wood and their uses
	Grading of sandpaper

Electrical	Capacity of electrical wire
Installation	AC versus DC current

In all cases the information sheet should give essential facts, show differences, explain principles, or otherwise provide information that will be helpful to the intelligent completion of an assignment.

The following hints will be helpful when writing this type of instruction material:

1. Treat a single topic only and state specifically what it is.
2. Relate and integrate the information with the student's knowledge and experience.
3. Use as many illustrations as are necessary to clarify the facts presented.
4. Aim to make the layout attractive. Do not crowd it. If necessary, use more than one sheet.
5. Remember, these sheets will form a reference handbook for the learner.
6. Specify desirable references by chapter and page number.

Teachers should not fail to develop sheets of this kind. Such valuable information will increase student understanding and competency. These sheets are necessary to supplement the teacher's efforts whenever there is a need for specialized occupational or technical information. There are two reasons why it is psychologically sound to present this kind of information in limited quantities at one time. First, if the amount of information distributed at one time is restricted to a single topic, confusion is avoided and the student is aided in his concentration. Second, if the material presented at one time is not voluminous, the student does not feel overwhelmed by it and consequently will not be discouraged from reading it.

WRITING ASSIGNMENT SHEETS

This type of instruction sheet gives the student specific assignments as a follow-up to the teacher's demonstrations or other instructional efforts. It consists of organized directions for performing certain skills, completing specific jobs, reading pertinent references, making intelligent observations, performing experiments, or carrying out special investigations.

The assignment, regardless of its type, should be given immediately after the instructor's presentation. It is at this point when interest is greatest and the need for follow-up most apparent. Recalling the student's memory span and the laws of learning, the importance of this suggestion will be realized. In a great many situations the assignment is in the nature of acquiring related industrial or technical information. Such information is essential to the retention and thorough comprehension of the skills and processes involved in shop instruction. This point might be exemplified by instruction on the use of a slide rule. Immediately after the teacher's presentation, the students should be assigned a series of problems to solve which will provide an opportunity to exercise their recently acquired knowledge. When developing this kind of instructional material certain ideas should be common denominators:

1. State specifically the task to be performed.
2. Prefix the assignment with an introductory statement of the purpose, as well as the need for the knowledge or skill to be acquired.
3. Include one or more completed examples of the type of problem to be solved.
4. Give the exact name of the book or magazine which is to be used for reference, the name of the author, the chapter, and the page numbers.
5. Indicate the form in which the data are to be recorded. In many cases provision should be made on the assignment sheet for the entry of the data.
6. Include illustrations that will clarify doubtful points when necessary.
7. Prepare the student for the assignment by using oral discussion to create interest or otherwise motivate the student's efforts.

Typical topics for assignments in the various trades are the following:

Upholstering	Secure samples of synthetic textiles suitable for use in reconditioning lounge furniture for a club.
Dressmaking	Observe the style trends in ladies' suits shown in the local stores.
Sheet Metal Work	Investigate the chemical reaction that takes place when sheet iron and sheet copper are adjacent to each other.
Plumbing	List the necessary pipe fittings and other needed parts for a particular installation.
Electricity	Record the readings of a voltmeter when different kinds of materials are used for resistances.
Carpentry	Estimate from a blueprint the quantity and sizes of the lumber needed for a specific job.
Machine Shop	Figure the necessary offset required for turning a given taper.

The purpose of the assignment is to tell the learner what he is to do and how he is to do it. Any or all of the following instructions might appear under the caption *Assignment:*

1. Answer a list of questions already prepared by using a text, handbook, manual, or specially prepared instruction sheet.

2. Make a sketch, drawing, or diagram.
3. Complete a sketch, drawing, or diagram.
4. Label or color a sketch, drawing, or diagram.
5. Do a job for which instructions are provided.
6. Do an experiment according to instructions.
7. Study an assignment in a text, handbook, periodical, manual, trade literature, or notebook.
8. Go to the library to do reference or research work on a tool, machine, process, inventor, or history of the occupation.
9. Prepare a graph from data compiled.
10. Study a filmstrip or view a movie, then report on it.
11. Visit a supply house to get prices of materials.
12. Inspect a sample of material, a display, a model, a mock-up, a cutaway, a photograph, a completed part, or an entire machine.

When assignments include the use of specific texts or other books, the assignment should follow the same procedure used in listing references. For example:

Durbhan, W. E. *Fundamentals of Carpentry*, Vol. 11. Pages 133-146.

Assignment sheets may vary widely in form and content depending on the ingenuity of the person who writes them. In the last analysis, their chief purpose is to stimulate the student's thinking about the practical application of his knowledge and skill. The progressive teacher will spend time and effort in the development of assignment sheets because they are a valuable medium of instruction. In all cases they should be clear, specific, realistic, and relate to the work of the course.

The instruction sheets presented on the following pages are typical examples of the various types of paper teacher-learner aids that can be developed by teachers of occupational subjects.

PHYSICAL MAKE-UP OF INSTRUCTION SHEETS

Although the content of instruction sheets is of vital concern, the physical make-up is a very important factor in creating interest in them and increasing their use. Unfortunately, too many instruction sheets currently in use are not a credit to the schools or the instructors. They are illegible because of inferior duplicating procedures; they have poor layout; and frequently, they are inadequately illustrated. Much of the difficulty may be attributed to a lack of knowledge of the factors involved in planning and layout.

OPERATION SHEET **Unit 1**
Sheet No. 4

Operation: Splicing

Aim: How to Splice a 16mm. Film

Most "splicers" enable you to perform the basic steps necessary to make a permanent splice. In some cases the splice is made diagonally across the film. In others, it is at right angles to the film.

In all instances it is necessary to (1) trim the irregular broken edges, (2) remove the emulsion from one end, (3) cement ends together and (4) clamp momentarily. The following procedure describes these basic processes as they are performed on the Craig splicer.

Procedures

1. *Insert Film*

Insert and clamp both ends of film in clamps "A" and "B". Care should be taken to have film lined up on sprocket hole pins with the dull or emulsion side up.

Clamp "B" slides on a bar and for this operation, should be in the extreme right-hand position.

The cutting blade "C" is swung forward out of the way while inserting film. See Figure 1.

2. *Trim Film*

Swing cutter blade "C" forward and down, trimming both ends of the film square and parallel. See Figure 2.

3. *Scrape Off Emulsion*

Return cutter blade to original position and remove emulsion by several quick strokes of the scraper "D". See Figure 3.

4. *Cement & Clamp Splice*

Apply cement to cleaned portion of film, shift film in clamp "B" to left-hand position placing film end on the cement. Snap clamp "B" over latch "E" applying pressure for a minute or two. See Figure 4. Unclamp film by releasing latches on "A" & "B" and lifting upper plates.

Illustrations

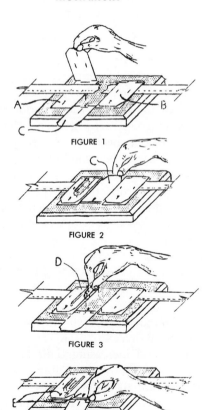

FIGURE 1

FIGURE 2

FIGURE 3

FIGURE 4

Central High School

Industrial Arts Department

ELECTRICAL SHOP

Signal Wiring   **Part 1, Bell Wiring**

Information Sheet No. BW 1.0

    All mechanical fields whether trade or technical make use of drawings and diagrams to represent objects and devices used in doing a job. Extensive use of symbols is utilized because symbols tell in picture form what might take many words to describe. Mechanics and engineers need only glance at a symbol to immediately understand the written message it conveys.

    The purpose of this information sheet is to introduce you to some of the symbols of the commonly used devices in bell wiring. You must learn them in order to be able to follow your job sheets.

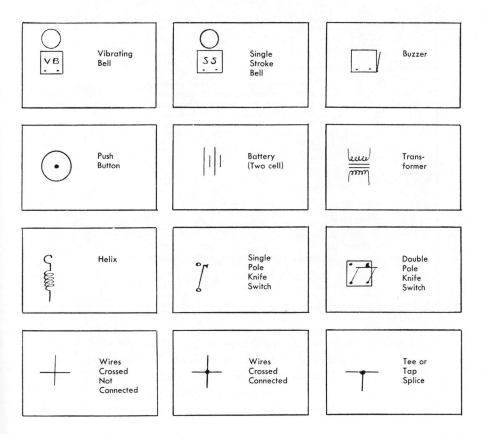

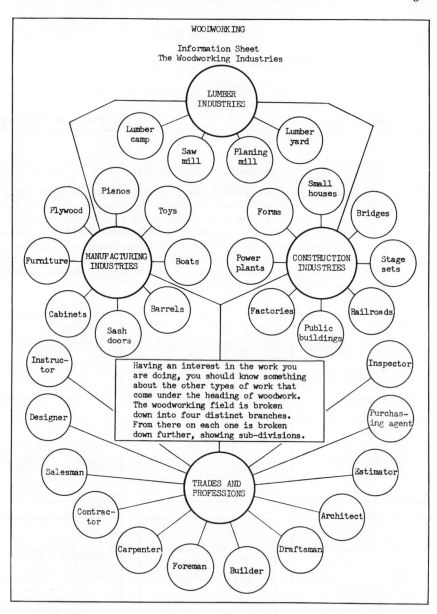

There seems to be no justification for a lack of knowledge and skill in the reproduction of instructional material by the various duplicating processes. Manufacturers of duplicating machines provide instructional service in the operation of their equipment. This service is available without charge, and there is no excuse for not taking

Instruction Sheets as Aids to Learning

UNIVERSITY OF THE STATE OF NEW YORK
STATE EDUCATION DEPARTMENT

Division of Vocational Education   Bureau of Industrial and Technical Education

Sheet Metal Work   UNIT 1SM-T9   Beginner's Course
Trade Theory Series   MACHINE PROCESS   Sheet No. 1 of 2

DESCRIPTION OF BURRING MACHINES

OBJECTIVES OF UNIT

1. To compare turned and burred edges.
2. To describe burring machines.
3. To describe the adjustments of burring machines.

INTRODUCTORY INFORMATION

The burring machine is a rotary machine used to form narrow edges on discs, covers, cylinders, and irregular pieces. (Fig. 1). These edges are called burred edges and the process of making such an edge is called burring. Burred edges may be used for double seams, set-in bottoms, etc. The burring machine is often called the "thin edge" machine in the Sheet Metal Trade.

FIG. 1 BURRED EDGE

COMPARISON OF TURNED EDGES AND BURRED EDGES

A turning machine makes a somewhat rounded edge while the burring machine produces an edge with a sharp radius. Since the burred edge has a sharp radius, it must be made narrower than a turned edge on the same size disc to avoid becoming wavy. In a similar manner, burred edges must be narrower on small diameter discs than on large diameter discs. On small light work, burred edges should not be over 1/8" wide. While a wider edge can be burred on a cylinder than on a disc, burred edges should be made narrower when used for double seaming.

A good burred edge is made by turning the operating handle rapidly after the first revolution of the job, holding the work steady, and not raising the job too fast.

DESCRIPTION OF BURRING MACHINES

The burring machine consists of a frame and two rolls connected by gears and turned by an operating handle. (Fig. 2). This frame is attached to a standard which can be clamped to a bench.

The rolls are made of heat-treated steel and screwed on the threaded ends of the shafts. The upper roll is disc-shaped while the lower roll is cylinder shaped with a recess near the outer end. (Fig. 3). The upper roll is moved by a crankscrew to clamp the metal while the edge is being burred. The alignment of the rolls is adjusted by means of a knurled screw at the end of the shaft.

advantage of it. In addition to the knowledge and skill necessary to operate the machines, it is essential that the recommended stencils, ink, and other accessories be used in lieu of cheaper substitutes. If

| Sheet Metal Work | UNIT 1SM-T9 | Beginner's Course |
| Trade Theory Series | MACHINE PROCESS | Sheet No. 2 of 2 |

DESCRIPTION OF BURRING MACHINES

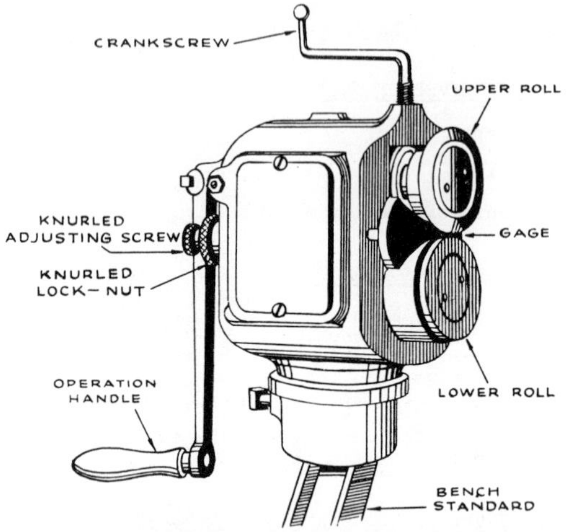

FIG. 2 BURRING MACHINE

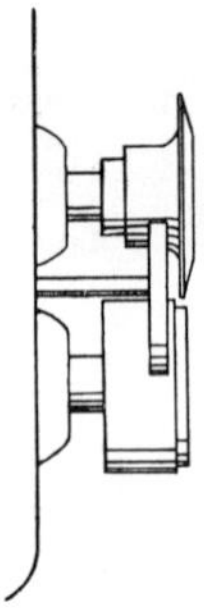

FIG. 3 ROLLS

The machine shown in Fig. 2 has a capacity of 22 gage and lighter mild steel. Machines of this capacity are available with rolls 1½" in diameter which will burr an edge 3/16" or less, or with rolls 2-1/8" in diameter which will burr an edge ¼" or less. Larger hand and power-driven machines, are available to burr heavy gage metal.

Universal rotary machines with a throat similar to a beading machine are available which have interchangeable rolls for burring, beading, crimping, turning, and wiring. This machine is desirable in shops where the different types of rolls are not often needed.

DESCRIPTION OF THE GAGE ADJUSTMENT

The width of the burr is determined by the distance from the face of the gage to the inner edge of the upper roll. (Fig. 4). The gage is moved by a knurled screw and is held in place with a knurled lock-nut.

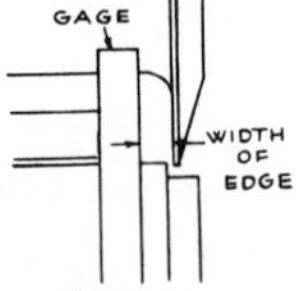

FIG. 4 GAGE SETTING

SELECTED REFERENCE

Selvidge & Christy-------Instruction Manual For Sheet-Metal Workers

teachers hope to train students in good work habits and have an appreciation for standards of achievement, they can ill afford to place before them examples of poorly planned and slovenly produced instruction sheets.

199 Instruction Sheets as Aids to Learning

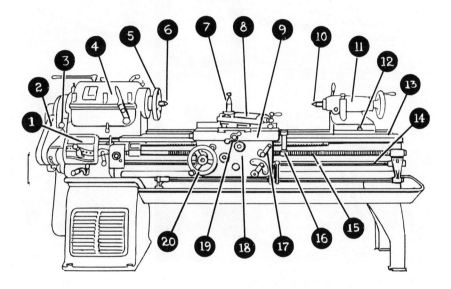

UNIVERSITY OF THE STATE OF NEW YORK
STATE EDUCATION DEPARTMENT

Division of Vocational Education | Light Machine Operation | Bureau of Industrial and Technical Education

TEST 29   LATHE PARTS IDENTIFICATION

INSTRUCTIONS: Write the number of each lathe part opposite its proper name listed below:

( ) Tailstock   ( ) Spindle sleeve
( ) Gear guards   ( ) Gear box
( ) Headstock   ( ) Apron
( ) Driver plate   ( ) Hand wheel
( ) Tool post   ( ) Bed
( ) Back gears   ( ) Carriage
( ) Compound rest   ( ) Set over screws
( ) Live center   ( ) Half nut lever
( ) Dead center   ( ) Cross feed handle
( ) Reverse lever   ( ) Thread dial indicator
( ) Lead screw   ( ) Feed rod

The overall impression that these sheets create depends upon a neat and attractive layout. Such an effect may be secured by the proper arrangement of the component parts. Careful thought must be given to each sheet if satisfactory results are to be obtained.

TEACHING OCCUPATIONAL SKILLS 200

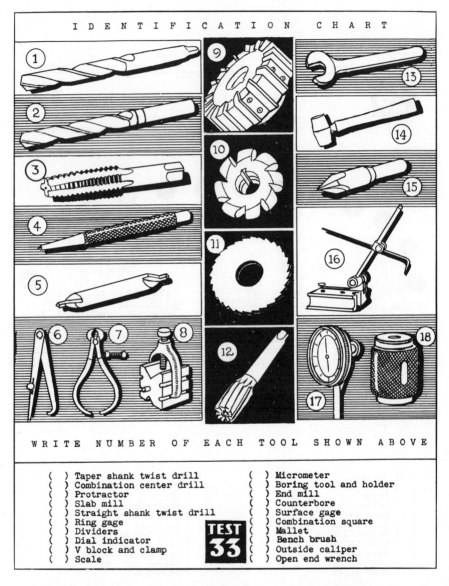

Crowding, the outstanding fault, may be avoided by thinking through the entire layout at the time the material is written. Although it is desirable to use one sheet for one unit of instruction, it may be necessary to use two sheets to avoid a crammed appearance.

The skeleton illustrations of instruction sheet layout given previously are more effective than word descriptions. Several arrangements of the text and illustrations are depicted; these are only suggestions

Central Junior High School

Industrial Arts Department   Area: Wood

Project No. 4   Man's Bureau Caddy

This little caddy will be an attractive addition to your bureau top. It will be handy for keeping cuff links, tie clasps, rings and other personal articles in one location. The finished caddy can be painted, stained or varnished to suit your needs. Check with your instructor on how to finish the job.

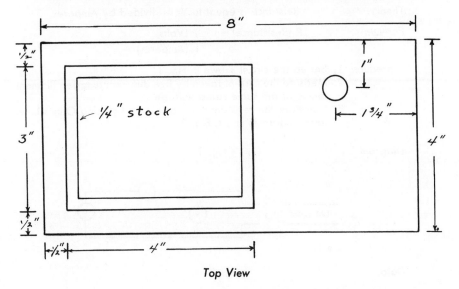

Top View

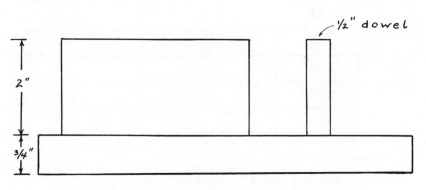

Side View

Plan Your Work. Decide on the finish you want, then select the lumber for this job. Decide which tools will do the best work.

Central Technical High School — Physical Measurements
Technical Electricity — Experiment Sheet

MEASUREMENT OF RESISTANCE

Aim of Experiment: To determine the Resistance of an incandescent lamp by the volt-ammeter method.

Theory: Resistance is equal to Volts divided by Amperes.

Formula: $R \text{ (Resistance)} = \dfrac{E \text{ (Volts)}}{I \text{ (Amperes)}}$

Procedure:
1. Set up the circuit shown in Fig. 1.
2. Measure the current taken by five different tungsten filament lamps at the same rated voltage.
3. Calculate the resistance of each lamp by using Ohm's Law. Record data in chart, Fig. 2.

Diagram: Fig. 1.

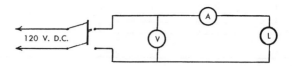

Data: Fig. 2.

Lamp Watts	Volts	Amperes	Ohms
25			
40			
60			
100			
200			

Check Your Math.!

Summary:
1. Draw a graph of Resistance vs. Watts.
2. Which has more resistance: a 25 W. or a 60 W. lamp?
3. Refer to your graph and determine the R. of a 150 W. lamp.
4. Which would have less resistance: a 500 W. or a 1,000 W. heater?

Central Vocational and Technical High School

Building Trades Department

ELECTRICAL INSTALLATION

Third Term Wiring, Signal Work   Part 1, Bell Wiring

Job No. BW 5.0

When a means of signaling must be provided at two different entrances in a dwelling, different sounding signals must be used. The most common combination used is a bell for the front door and a buzzer for the back door. This job is a good example of a typical installation of the type described.

Specifications: Install and connect a bell and buzzer in a one family house. The bell is to be controlled by a P.B. at the front door, the buzzer by a P.B. at the back door. (This is an example of two parallel circuits.)

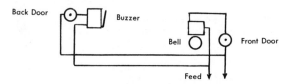

Assignment No. BW 5.0

1. Copy this job into your notebook as in previous jobs. Do the job.
2. Copy the following questions and answer them in your notebook.
   a. What could be used in place of the bell?
   b. What signal device do you have in your home?
   c. What is the basic difference between a bell and a buzzer?
   d. Where should the bell and buzzer be located in the house?
   e. How can the sound intensity of a buzzer be changed?

because no hard and fast rules may be given. The sections of the sheet as well as the illustrations should be separated by properly spaced margins if the material is to have eye appeal. The instructor must use imagination and resourcefulness when planning instructional material of this kind if he wishes it to receive favorable student reaction.

INSTRUCTION SHEETS AS VISUAL AIDS

There is an ever-increasing tendency to use visual aids for all kinds of instruction. The fact is universally accepted that a "picture is

Example of Instruction Sheet for use in Industrial Arts Shop

Area: Electrical   Instruction Sheet No. El.

HOW TO TIE AN UNDERWRITER'S KNOT

Step 1: Separate wires for a distance of about 3 to 4 inches.

Step 2: Loop one of the wires around the other one, working to the left.

Step 3: Loop straight wire around end of first loop.

Step 4: Bring wire of step 3 into first loop.

Step 5: Pull both wires tight. Knot can easily be moved up or down.

Name of School

Refrigeration Shop

Domestic Units   Work Sheet

The refrigerator service man must become familiar with every type of domestic unit made. This includes the controls and characteristics as well. Troubleshooting these units will become much easier when the service man learns the data about each unit.

INSTRUCTIONS: Copy the following form in your notebook and use it as a guide to obtain the data on one of the units assigned you by the instructor. Show your completed work to the instructor for checking.

REFRIGERATION MOTOR DATA SHEET

Name of Unit_____ Serial Number_____

Motor: H.P._____ Volts_____ Amperes_____ Frame_____

　　　　Type_____ R.P.M._____ Locked Rotor Rating_____

Starter: Manufacturer_____ Type_____

　　　　Size_____ Rating of Thermal Units_____

Switch: Size_____ H.P._____ Type_____ Amperes_____

　　　　Size of fuses_____ Size of wire used_____ Type wire____

Other Controls: Type_____ Purpose_____

Comments:_____

Voltage at Switch_____ Voltage at Motor_____

Amperage: At Start_____ On Running_____

Megger Reading for Insulation Test_____

Other Information:_____

Note Condition of: Belts_____ Pulleys_____ Couplings_____

　　　　　　　　　　Mounting_____ Cleanliness_____ Lube_____

Name of Service Man_____ Date_____

　　Make a neat wiring diagram of the unit, and include it in your notes. Identify the unit. Have your work checked by the instructor.

worth a thousand words." Therefore, well-developed instruction sheets should include illustrations to help in the interpretation of the text. A majority of people assume the "show me" attitude, which in turn makes illustrations necessary whenever it is possible to include them. It is often difficult and time-consuming to explain mechanical devices and occupational information verbally. However, a sketch, a drawing, or a photograph will tell its own story. Illustrations will transpose irksome learning into a pleasant experience. Evidence of the validity of the above statements may be found in the wide circulation of picture magazines, tabloid newspapers, and comic books.

There is a wide variety of illustrative material available to the ambitious teacher in addition to his own handmade sketches or drawings. Industry, business, and publishers recognize the value of eye appeal; consequently, all mechanical textbooks, scientific books and trade catalogs, trade periodicals, and instruction manuals are liberally illustrated. All of these publications are source material for teachers. It is highly probable that if a teacher is persistent enough, he will always be able to find an illustration of the exact treatment of a subject he desires, such as a cross-sectional, schematic, halftone, phantom, or exploded pictorial reproduction. As a rule it is better to use the commercially published illustrations because of their excellent quality, provided they may be adapted to the teacher's needs. Such material is usually prepared by professional photographers and draftsmen, and thus is properly shaded and "touched up" for satisfactory reproduction.

Permission to use such material may be secured from the publisher merely by asking for the privilege. Seldom will such a courtesy be withheld by a manufacturer or publisher. Although it is not necessary to state copyright acknowledgment on instruction sheets, it is sometimes advisable. If the sheets are prepared for sale, the copyright acknowledgment must be included. The commercial copyright rules are usually suspended when the material is used for educational purposes.

A good illustration is one that best conveys the ideas of the writer. In some cases it may be a line drawing, while in other situations a photograph is necessary. Often a well-executed line drawing is to be preferred to any other type of picture. The resulting contrast of black and white is very effective, particularly if shading and different weights of lines are used. This fact is true whether the reproduction is done by one of the common types of office duplicating machines or by the photo-offset process. The latter process permits the duplication of halftones without difficulty. There are times when only the photo-offset process can be used because of intricate things to be portrayed. In all cases, the illustrations should increase understanding and not serve as mere decoration.

METHODS OF PRODUCING INSTRUCTIONAL MATERIAL

There are numerous ways of duplicating instructional material. These methods include the use of the letter press, the multigraph, the mimeograph, the photo-offset or lithograph machine, and the blueprint or one of the liquid reproducing processes. Although all these methods of reproduction have their value and place from the standpoint of cost, it is necessary to choose the processes that are best suited for school use. Consequently, the following methods are selected for further description: blueprinting, mimeographing, and photo-offset. Information on the other duplicating techniques may be secured from the manufacturers of the necessary equipment.

Blueprint. This method of duplicating is very desirable and easily accomplished. The preparation of the original drawings takes time, but not out of proportion to the time necessary for the other processes. A simple printing frame of the proper size may be used, with natural sunlight, if a blueprinting machine is not available. But this disadvantage is offset by two advantages: (a) the durability and physical appearance of the blueprint for shop use, (b) the fact that blueprints are used in industry. Schools will find it advantageous to approximate the conditions in the business world whenever possible.

Mimeographing. This process is very common because mimeograph machines are available in most schools. This method of reproducing is most economical from the standpoint of time and materials. Its use is confined to text material and line drawings. The distributors of mimeograph machines have a comprehensive treatise on the process, and in addition will give individual instruction on the use of their equipment. Teachers should avail themselves of this service and learn to make and use their own stencils.

Sometimes it is desirable to use intricate drawings on instruction sheets. Even the expert will find it most difficult to make the drawings. In such cases the photo-chemical process, developed by the A. B. Dick Mimeograph Company, may be used. A sensitized stencil has been developed that acts as a photographic plate. After it is exposed to the original drawing and properly developed, it can be placed on the mimeograph machine and copies produced in the same way as an ordinary typed stencil. The necessary equipment for this process is not too expensive considering its utility. If a school has a limited number of such jobs, it is possible to have the stencils produced by the equipment manufacturer at a reasonable cost.

Offset process. This is a very effective method of producing instruction material, and it is relatively inexpensive. As a rule, schools do not have the facilities for doing this work; however, some of the larger institutions have found it economical to purchase the necessary machines for this purpose.

The one outstanding advantage of the offset process is the variety of material which may be prepared through its use. It is possible to cut drawings and halftones from printed sources and paste them on the original dummy sheet. It is also possible to add or delete identifications. In the former case the additions may be placed on white paper and pasted in the appropriate position, while in the latter situation a piece of white paper may be pasted on the parts or printing to be eliminated. These changes do not show on the final offset copy.

Color on instruction sheets. There are times when color will enhance the use or appearance of instructional material. It may be desirable to identify certain sections of a drawing by using different colors to distinguish parts, lines, and dimensions. The color combination may be secured by the use of the mimeograph or liquid type of duplicating machine. This effect is very easy to accomplish at practically no additional cost over the plain black-and-white combination. These processes are carefully explained in the literature of the machine manufacturers, and they are highly recommended if they are used with discretion.

USE OF INSTRUCTION SHEETS

Duplicating processes have been made so simple that teachers may learn how to produce them skillfully within a short time. Furthermore, the cost of the duplicating equipment has been lowered to a point where individual teachers or groups of teachers can purchase the necessary facilities if the school will not do so. Consequently, there appears to be no excuse for teachers not providing their students with well-designed, neat, and carefully processed instruction sheets.

There are several ways to use instruction sheets. First, sheets should be filed and indexed in a manner that will make for easy inventory and distribution. A numbering system should be adopted similar to the one suggested for lesson plans (2.00, 2.01, 2.02, 2.03,

3.00, 4.00, etc.) in which additional sheets may be added without losing the numerical continuity. Although some teachers give the students a copy of the sheet to keep in their notebooks, most teachers use the sheets on a loan basis. Copies of instruction sheets which are in current use should be protected by placing them in plastic envelopes. A check system should be developed for easy counting at the end of each shop session. Careful use and storage of such material should be encouraged. As part of shop organization, the teacher should determine the extent of the work to be done and make available only a sufficient number of sheets for immediate needs. There is no point in distributing large numbers of this material when they are not needed. Careless use of material will promote careless habits and damage to the sheets. The teacher who develops good shop organization will find that his instructional material will last for a long time if properly handled. Students will have as much regard for the sheets as the teacher shows that he has.

Teachers should not make the error of passing out sheets and then expecting the student to do the rest. He must follow up with individual instruction. It must be remembered that these sheets supplement the instructor's efforts. Material that appears on them should be taught, referred to, and included in quizzes and tests. Assignments should be specific, clear, and easy to follow. Teachers should check carefully to see that they are carried out completely and correctly. Students should be instructed in the proper use of the sheets, and from time to time selected copies may be given to them to keep and enter in their notebooks.

Summary

"Good instruction sheets serve the student in the same way maps guide the traveler."

Instruction sheets are a definite aid in learning as well as in teaching. They should not be used indiscriminately nor drawn up without planning. They serve many purposes when wisely used and are especially valuable in teaching occupational skills to groups of students with varied interests, backgrounds, and abilities. They supplement the instructor's efforts and provide a means of individual written instruction. They permit students to progress at their own rates of speed and complete extra jobs and projects, save the instructor unnecessary and repeated instructions, and help put students on their own. There are many types that can serve different purposes. It is up to the individual instructor to develop the sheets he needs for his class in terms of the occupational area and level he teaches as dictated by the students' needs.

Form and content are both important, as well as how the teacher uses the instruction sheets. He should carefully plan a sequence and variety of jobs and projects, including sheets that provide the required and pertinent information and operations necessary for doing the job or project. Other sheets should be developed for assignments, experiments, testing, and collecting data as the specific occupational needs dictate.

The shop program should be organized to include a good, sound, simple system of storage and distribution of instruction sheets. They should be well-duplicated, indexed, filed, and protected in transparent envelopes. The teacher must stress the importance of these sheets, and by so doing impress their worth and value upon his class. He must not rely exclusively upon them as the sole source of teaching, but must keep in mind that instruction sheets serve to supplement his teaching. The teacher does not supplement the instructional material.

Questions and Projects

1. Make a list of written instructional aids you can use in your shop.
2. Develop a job sheet or project sheet which you could use with beginning students in your area of instruction.
3. Develop a standard format for instruction sheets in your teaching situation.
4. Write a list of experiments which your students could perform in order to help them learn the theory or the principles of your occupational area.
5. Develop two experiment type of instruction sheets based on the answer to Question 4.
6. Develop two sheets of each of the following types:
    a. Operation.
    b. Assignment.
    c. Information.
7. Develop an instruction sheet that will show the students in your subject how to evaluate a completed job.
8. Develop a parallel list of at least ten advantages and ten disadvantages in using instruction sheets.
9. Develop a list of ten or more techniques on the best use of instruction sheets.

10. Three simple principles of teaching are:
    a. Present material one step at a time.
    b. Present material from the simple to the complex.
    c. Present material in a good learning sequence.
11. List the titles of ten instruction sheets, and explain how you would provide for the principles listed above in each title.

13

Rating Student Performance and Progress

There has been considerable controversy in recent years concerning the rating of students and the granting of grades to indicate progress. Some educators discredit grades because they claim education should not be a matter of grades, marks, promotion, and diplomas. They feel that the education a person can obtain is the thing to be valued, not the prize in the form of a grade. It is true that at times too much emphasis may be placed on grades; nevertheless, there is considerable justification for granting grades. The millenium has not yet been reached when grades and marks can be dispensed with entirely as some educators would prefer. People are ranked, graded, judged, rated, and classified in all walks of life, and part of the school's function is to prepare young people for life ahead. It would seem reasonable, therefore, to expose youngsters to this sort of process while in school.

WHY RATE STUDENTS?

Ratings or grades result in pupils being promoted or held back, praised or censored, granted honors or penalized, as well as guided toward and recommended for jobs. Therefore, ratings play an important role in the everyday school life of the student, and subsequently in his adult life when he is employed. Grades and ratings are granted for a number of reasons, such as:

1. To comply with administrative demands. The granting of grades is a general school requirement and serves as an administrative tool.
2. To provide a running record of each student's progress. A conscientious and capable teacher should know at all times the relative standing of each of his students. This information is made available through granting grades on the work students accomplish.
3. To inform the students how well or how poorly they are progressing in their work. Students should be continually advised of their achievement. Notice of failure should not come as a surprise at the end of the term.
4. To advise parents concerning the success or failure of their children. Frequent and close contact with the parents is desirable, particularly when the children are not showing satisfactory effort and progress.
5. To indicate to the teacher his relative success in teaching the information and skills of his subject. The ratings are not only the measure of the student's achievement in tests and work assignments, but also an index to the teacher's skill in teaching.

TYPES OF RATINGS

There are varied forms of rating plans, many of which may be adopted with slight modifications. In all cases the rating plan should be devised to evaluate specific things, whether these be the quality and quantity of achievement or the personal characteristics and attitudes of the individual student. Regardless of the rating system that is used, grades depend to a large degree on the judgment of the person doing the rating. It is natural that some guesswork is involved, as well as the personal feelings of the teacher.

This weakness of the rating procedure is highly criticized by some professional educators, but they have been unable to devise a simple and satisfactory substitute system devoid of the objections they register. The faults in the existing rating schemes are not as serious as they would have us believe. The element of injustice implied is largely eliminated and the teacher's evaluation is made satisfactorily reliable if the single grade given is supported by a detailed analysis of the factors involved. A highly complicated rating plan is unnecessary for practical purposes. Furthermore, a system that is too complicated falls into disuse within a relatively short time.

Many times a teacher makes the mistake of granting to a student a single or blanket grade that usually includes the quantity and quality of work done, plus the teacher's reaction to the student's personality characteristics. Usually the grades are expressed in such generalities as *satisfactory, unsatisfactory, excellent, good, fair, poor, failure,* or A-B-C-D-E. Such grade symbols are vague or indefinite and do not give a very clear picture of the individual's ability and character. These composite grades are difficult to defend if they are challenged by the student, by the school administrator, or by the parents. This fact is particularly true if the student is capable and intelligent but somewhat troublesome because of peculiar or antagonistic attitudes.

It is easy to conceive of a boy who does "A" work but who has negative personal characteristics that antagonize the teacher. In this case a composite grade of "C" given by his teacher may classify him as a less-than-average student. In fact he is a capable student whose deportment is unsatisfactory or whose attitudes are undesirable, and the teacher has reflected his personal reactions to the student by giving a blanket grade of "C". The reverse of this situation is possible, in which case the student rates very high from the standpoint of behavior although his achievement is low. Teachers are influenced many times by the student's good behavior and, consequently, grant a higher rating than the pupil's work merits. In this case the boy may do "C" work, but he may have fine personal qualities and, again, the teacher is influenced and grants the boy a reasonably high grade of "B" or "A".

In both cases the rating is not a valid estimate of the individual's achievement and personal characteristics. This situation, therefore, demands that teachers rate the quantity and quality of work done by the student separately from the personal characteristics and attitudes of the student.

This dual rating plan is not only fair to the student but also enables the teacher to point out in detail the student's strong and weak points, whether they be in the work done, in his work habits, or in his social attitudes.

Rating Student Work

If the rating of a student's work is separated from the rating of his personal characteristics, it is necessary to consider different factors for each type of rating. When appraising the work done, certain qualities of the work must be judged. This fact is particularly true in the field of vocational and practical education in which jobs, projects, and exercises are produced. In all cases it is advisable to rate the work immediately following its completion and to record the grade granted on each assignment.

The factors to be used as the basis of judgment are numerous and depend upon the occupation or type of work being done. Mechanical drawings should be rated for neatness, layout, dimensions, lettering, arrowheads, and weight of lines; a printing job for selection of type face, line justification, layout, and the number of proofreader's corrections necessary; a dressmaking job for fit, style, finish, matching of stripes or design of material; modeling of clothing for confidence, aptitude, style sense, showmanship, and grooming. Each trade, occupation, or subject taught will require rating factors applicable to that specific kind of work. An adequate rating plan includes as many evaluations as there are separate factors to evaluate. The instructor must decide arbitrarily how much weight to give each factor in his rating scheme. For the sake of convenience, the sum of the maximum weights should equal 100 points.

Rating Student Characteristics

When rating vocational school work, particularly in the early stages of the training course, the student should not be expected to duplicate the workmanship of a skilled craftsman. The work should be graded in relation to the work to be expected from students of that age, experience, and grade level. Toward the end of the training course, however, the vocational student should approximate the journeyman's quality of workmanship, if not the quantity.

Usually unfavorable student reaction to grades may be reduced or eliminated by a personal conference. It is the teacher's responsibility to explain thoroughly the rating plan in use, and thereby gain the cooperation of the students and remove the idea that education and going to school is a matter of just getting grades.

On the other hand, when rating individual student characteristics, it

TEACHING OCCUPATIONAL SKILLS

is necessary to establish rating factors such as cooperation, appearance, aptitude, promptness, and ability to get along with people. It is evident that a careful and valid evaluation of the student's characteristics and work necessitates a breakdown of the factors involved. Specific rather than general criticisms of the student's work and attitudes should be made. Such criticism should help to remove the difficulties and improve the quality and quantity of the work, as well as improve the individual's work attitudes. It is not sufficient to rate a student A, B, C, D, or E in any one characteristic without an explanation. Adverse student reaction to grades may be reduced or eliminated if students understand the meaning of the factors on which they are rated. Furthermore, an arbitrary rating, without comment, may be destructive to the student's self-respect and self-confidence. The symbols used should designate a specific gradation of the characteristic or attitude on which the rating is based. This point is exemplified in the following table.

SYMBOLS AND GRADATIONS

	90-100 A	80-90 B	70-80 C	60-70 D	Below 60 E
Aptitude	Very industrious	Good worker	Usually busy	Idle at times	Lazy
Reliability	Trustworthy	Reliable	Satisfactory	Irregular	Unreliable
Application	Very quick	Apt	Average	Slow	Very slow

The rating factors or characteristics to be selected depend on the type of work, the subject, and the point of view of the teacher. Some teachers may choose to divide the factors into work traits and character traits as a matter of convenience. In this case a random classification may be as follows:

Work Traits

1. Accuracy.
2. Speed.
3. Safety.
4. Care of tools and equipment.
5. Neatness.
6. Workmanship.
7. Dexterity.

Character Traits

1. Aptitude.
2. Industriousness.
3. Reliability.
4. Resourcefulness.
5. Cooperation.
6. Interest.
7. Conduct.

Although it may be desirable to use most of the traits listed above, it is not advisable. If too many factors are used, the system becomes cumbersome, and consequently a burden to the teacher. Therefore, an individual teacher or a particular school or a department within the school should select the factors on which the students are to be rated. After the factors or characteristics to be used are selected, the various gradations of the characteristics or factors should be decided. This step is necessary in order to establish a rating scale.

It was indicated above that a grade of A, B, C, or D, or 90, 83, 72, or 60 means little in itself. If a descriptive word can be used to represent each of these letters or numerical values, then the grade is more meaningful to students and parents. Usually a five-point scale is sufficient for all practical purposes. Listed below are a number of rating factors or characteristics with corresponding gradations. Sometimes it may be difficult to select suitable words that give the desired shade of meaning and that avoid an overlapping of terminology. However, after considerable thought a satisfactory scale may be evolved. The following suggestions may be helpful:

Aptitude: very slow to learn—learns with effort—learns readily—unusually bright.
Quality of work: poor—fair—good—above average—superior.
Knowledge of work: lacking—meager—moderate—well-informed—complete.
Industry: lazy—needs urging—fairly steady—plodder—hard worker.
Confidence: timid—overconfident—confident—self-reliant—excellent.
Interest: not interested—mildly interested—quite interested—enthusiastic.
Reliability: unreliable—irregular—satisfactory—dependable—trustworthy.
Cooperation: rebellious—antagonistic—self-centered—tolerant—very cooperative.
Manner: unpleasant—indifferent—agreeable—gracious—winning.
Judgment: bad—lacking—reasonable—sound—unusual.

The succeeding step is the assignment of values to each of the factors according to one's judgment. Assume a situation in which it is decided to use the following factors with maximum point values assigned to each as indicated:

Accuracy	30 points
Speed	20 points
Neatness and order	15 points
Care of tools	15 points
Attitude	10 points
Aptitude	10 points
	100 points

If a five-point rating scale is to be established, it is necessary to assign point values for each division of the scale. In this case the five divisions might be as follows:

Below 60	60-69	70-79	80-89	90-100
E	D	C	B	A

This rating scale will enable the teacher to assign grades according to letters A, B, C, D, E, or in numerical values within each point on the scale, for example, 65, 76, 85, 92, 96, etc. When the meaning of the grades is understood it makes little difference whether they are expressed in the form of letters or numbers. In most cases, numbers are more convenient because of the ease with which individual differences may be indicated. It is then necessary to assign a given number of points to each factor in the division it falls under on the scale. These will be arbitrary figures scaled down from the maximum point values listed above. The result of this operation will produce a rating scale that will appear as follows:

NUMERICAL EQUIVALENTS	Below 60	60-70	70-80	80-90	90-100
RATING FACTORS	E	D	C	B	A
Speed	very slow 10	slow 14	good 16	rapid 18	very rapid 20
Accuracy	inaccurate 15	careless 24	average 26	accurate 28	very accurate 30
Neatness and order	slovenly 8	unsatisfactory 9	satisfactory 11	very neat 13	extra neat 15
Care of tools	wasteful 7	negligent 9	average 11	good 13	excellent 15
Attitude	indifferent 5	passive 7	interested 8	eager 9	enthusiastic 10
Aptitude	unfit 5	slow 7	fair 8	capable 9	adept 10
TOTALS	50	70	80	90	100

In the table above there is a greater point spread between the D and E column of the factors *speed* and *accuracy* than between the other columns. This provision was made because the least capable students in manual activities invariably are inaccurate and are particularly deficient in the amount of work accomplished.

If a greater number of rating factors are used than are indicated in the table above, then a different distribution of point values must be made. A satisfactory way of testing such a rating scale is to rate two students in the old-fashioned way by saying one is an "B" student and the other a "C" student. Then carefully check these students on each of the factors on the rating scale.

The *first* student is given the following ratings:		The *second* student is given the following ratings:
20	Speed	10
26	Accuracy	30
10	Neatness and order	11
12	Care of tools	13
10	Attitudes	7
9	Aptitudes	7
Total 87		Total 78
Grade "B" as per scale		Grade "C" as per scale

Invariably the total number of points will indicate that the student ranks about the position in which you originally placed him by subjective rating. The advantage, however, of this detailed rating scale is the teacher's opportunity to show the rating to the student or parent and to indicate definitely where improvement should be made.

The first student is evidently a rapid worker, but in his haste he sacrifices accuracy, neatness, and care of tools, as shown by the objective rating.

The second student is very slow but apparently meticulous in his work, although slow to learn and somewhat neutral in his attitude to his work. This plan also enables the teacher to take care of the shades of difference in the ability of students. Two students may be comparable in certain respects, but one is slightly better than the other. This difference may be indicated by varying the number of points granted for each of the factors involved.

Another form of rating plan (illustrated on page 220) includes more factors but involves less work for the teacher. In this case the card is designed to accommodate four ratings. In shop subjects three or four ratings per year are adequate. There is not a sufficient change in a student's skills and attitudes to warrant a greater number of grades for administrative record purposes.

In this case the student may be advised of his deficiencies, as

Name: George Casey Subject: Woodworking III Department: Ind. Arts
Year: 19 Instructor: C.E.A. 1st period B 2nd period ___ 3rd period ___ 4th period ___

Degree of Attainment

Characteristics	90 to 100 A	80 to 90 B	70 to 80 C	60 to 70 D	Below 60 E
Accuracy	Very Accurate ①2 3 4	Accurate 1 2 3 4	Fairly Accurate 1 2 3 4	Inaccurate 1 2 3 4	Careless 1 2 3 4
Speed	Very Rapid 1 2 3 4	Rapid 1 2 3 4	Good ①2 3 4	Slow 1 2 3 4	Very slow 1 2 3 4
Application	Very Industrious ①2 3 4	Good Worker 1 2 3 4	Fair Worker 1 2 3 4	Poor Worker 1 2 3 4	Very poor Worker 1 2 3 4
Initiative	Very Progressive 1 2 3 4	Progressive ①2 3 4	Passive 1 2 3 4	No Evidence 1 2 3 4	In- different 1 2 3 4
Knowledge of Work	Excellent 1 2 3 4	Very good ①2 3 4	Good 1 2 3 4	Fair 1 2 3 4	Poor 1 2 3 4
Neatness	Very neat 1 2 3 4	Neat 1 2 3 4	Fairly Neat ①2 3 4	Untidy 1 2 3 4	Solvenly 1 2 3 4
Reliability	Trustworthy 1 2 3 4	Reliable ①2 3 4	Satis- factory 1 2 3 4	Irregular 1 2 3 4	Un- reliable 1 2 3 4
Aptitude	Adept 1 2 3 4	Capable ①2 3 4	Fair 1 2 3 4	Slow 1 2 3 4	Stupid 1 2 3 4
Confidence	Excellent ①2 3 4	Self- Reliant 1 2 3 4	Confident 1 2 3 4	Lacks Confidence 1 2 3 4	Timid 1 2 3 4
Cooperation	Very Cooperative 1 2 3 4	Tolerant ①2 3 4	Self- Centered 1 2 3 4	Antago- nistic 1 2 3 4	Rebel- lious 1 2 3 4
Conduct	Exceptional ①2 3 4	Very Gentlemanly 1 2 3 4	Well Behaved 1 2 3 4	Trouble- some 1 2 3 4	Unsatis- factory 1 2 3 4

NOTE: Place a circle around 1, 2, 3, or 4 according to rating period. Indicate at the top of card composite rating for each period and final grade in spaces provided.

Remarks _____

well as his satisfactory characteristics. Although references are made to these types of ratings as being subjective and not scientific, they do lend themselves to satisfactory interpretation. The student can understand why he received a certain grade and even the least educated parents can comprehend the situation without difficulty. This is a far more effective rating system than one expressed in percentile rank, deviations, and other educational terminology with which neither the students nor the parents are acquainted. It is not proposed that the rating card illustrated here be used as a report to the parents, although an abridged form of the card would be very satisfactory.

This type of rating scale has several advantages:

1. It is objective rather than subjective.
2. It permits the granting of a grade that can be supported by detailed analysis.
3. It removes the possibility of the teachers being accused of giving a low grade to pupils he does not like.
4. The terminology is simple and understandable.
5. It enables the teacher to indicate the weakness in a student's performance or attitudes, and to suggest remedial techniques that the student and parent comprehend.
6. It separates the rating of work performed from the work attitudes of the student.
7. It is sufficiently inclusive but not involved.

It is possible to achieve the objectives of rating as stated in the first part of this chapter, if the ideas presented are modified to meet the existing conditions in a school or subject.

OTHER AREAS OF EVALUATION

The evaluation of any student based on accurate, objective methods is important regardless of the grade level or the objective of the course. One of the prime meanings of grades to parents is the indication they give for success in the work they represent. The mark or grade which appears on the report card will be a composite of achievements. Up to now we have discussed grades based on the performance of occupational skills. Other factors entering the picture are notebooks, tests, quizzes, and possibly class marks based on participation during class or shop activities.

If a teaching device is to become important, it must be given value. If a notebook is to be kept by students, for example, the teacher should give it value by inspecting it periodically and grading it. The rating should enter into the student's final grade or evaluation. Quizzes and tests should also have a bearing on the final grade.

Neither one test nor one evaluating process should be the criterion for passing or failing a student. A final grade should be a combination of several things. Of course, as has been stated, the teacher should explain his method of assigning grades so that students clearly understand what is expected of them and can easily explain the bases for grading to their parents. Once this is done, teachers can rest easier, knowing that their students will understand that grades are earned, not given by an instructor.

The problem is to weigh the factors fairly. Many instructors of occupational skills believe that the mark based on shop skill and competency should weigh two or three times the quiz averages or test marks or notebook marks. The theory is that the major part of the student's time is spent learning skills, and that although the notebook may be neat and handsome, it does not compare with skill performance in future value and use. Another argument is that tests and quizzes are usually paper devices, and as such are liable to all the weaknesses of any paper tests, such as reading difficulties on the part of the test-taker or poor questioning techniques on the part of the teacher. It has been noted time and again by teachers of vocational subjects that those students who are not proficient in test-taking may be highly skilled in performing the skills of the occupation. To weigh all aspects of the training course equally would be unrealistic. A typical attempt to assign a final grade might take the following pattern:

Final test	83
Quiz average	78
Notebook mark	85
Shop mark	86
(Three times value	86
of quiz marks)	86
Class mark	75
Final grade	83

Compare the same grade with one obtained by weighing each part equally.

Final test	83
Quiz average	78
Notebook mark	85
Shop mark	86

Class mark	75
Final grade	81

It would seem that two points are not very important; however, there are examples when the difference will be more than two points and can easily make the difference between passing and failing or attaining honor roll standing or not. In schools where honor rolls and other such systems are used, students learning occupational skills should be given the opportunity to achieve high standing.

Each teacher must study the needs of his group to determine the best method of marking and grading students. It is quite possible that the system one teacher uses will not apply in another situation. Teachers should strive for fairness, objectivity, and simplicity whenever possible. Grades should be recorded and be open to inspection. When a teacher uses any kind of secret system, then he will be under suspicion, whereas a simple, open system will stimulate students, show them their shortcomings and weaknesses, and make grading easier and more palatable.

THE PROGRESS CHART

Student progress should not be a deep, dark secret. Although the instructor must assign grades and marks, he should be more interested in seeing his students improve than watching them experience failure. A visual means of noting student progress, which is available and easily understood by both students and teacher, is the progress chart. It is a most important element of good shop organization and management. There are many desirable results that should be obtained from its use.

Benefits Derived from the Use of Progress Charts

1. Increase understanding because they are visual.
2. Simplify comparison within the class.
3. Motivate students to keep up with at least the average progress.
4. Serve as another basis for evaluation by the teacher.
5. Give students a means of self-evaluation.
6. Provide reference facts during conferences with parent, student, or supervisor.
7. Show a group-by-group comparison of progress.
8. Enable a term-by-term comparison of classes.
9. Help the instructor in timing and projecting the term's work.
10. Permit a means of recording jobs or projects completed.

Each teacher will find it an advantage to develop a progress chart that fits the needs of his particular occupational area. There are some elements of construction which should be included in all progress charts:

1. Clear, simple identification.
2. Designation of the occupational group.
3. Periods the group is in the shop.
4. Teacher's name.
5. Term and year.
6. Simple explanation of chart.
7. Directions for use.
8. Column for students' names.
9. Extra space for new students.
10. Horizontal columns for entering marks or symbols to denote completion or partial completion of jobs or projects.
11. Means of noting prolonged absence or assignment to duties which account for seemingly poor progress.
12. Good form, neat layout, and dignified appearance.

How to Use the Chart

Among the many deails with which students can assist the teacher are the entries on the progress chart. Instructors can assign this duty to the shop foreman, class secretary, or some other member of the class. The instructor can keep a double check by approving each completed assignment before permitting the assigned student to make the entry on the progress chart. Adjustments in the design of the progress chart must be made according to the occupation under consideration. Many instructors have each student make his own entries on the chart. This method has merit in that the student must observe his progress in relation to the rest of the group every time he makes an entry. Instructors should consult the progress chart daily. Students lagging behind can be helped or advised, and students progressing rapidly can be challenged with extra work or can help the teacher in various ways.

The graphic presentation of student progress which shows the fast, the slow, or the average is sufficient for the purposes intended. The inclusion of final grades, test marks, and other notations that might tend to be a source of criticism or embarrassment should be omitted. The primary purpose of the progress chart is to motivate students and to help in self-evaluation. It should not be used to detract from those two worthwhile goals.

Summary

"There is no better incentive for learning than a fair and enthusiastic teacher."

Grades and marks are necessary in any teaching situation. Although teachers should stress the value of learning rather than emphasize grades, evaluation of one kind or another is essential. The problem is to develop a system for arriving at grades which will take into account the skills, attitudes, customs, and requirements of the occupational skill. Grading should also take into account the student's performance on tests and quizzes, as well as his notebook if one is used. The ability to read and write is important and necessary in varying amounts in the different levels of every occupational area. A student's performance in all areas, therefore, will help determine his future choice of job level, as well as point out areas of weakness and strength.

Teachers must study many systems and develop one that works best for them with accrued benefits to their students. They should develop checklists for noting each skill or trait which the occupation requires. They should explain the system to the class and keep all records accurately so that students can be properly guided and advised from time to time. The system may be modified by school policy: Grades may be numerical or alphabetical, or may be issued quarterly or every third period. Regardless of the individual school policy, however, each teacher can develop his own system for granting grades and still conform to the required procedures for the reporting and recording of grades.

Questions and Projects

1. State five reasons for giving grades.
2. Give several reasons for the elimination of grades.
3. Develop a list of factors you would use in evaluating occupational skills.
4. Develop a system of grading for the skills listed in the answer to question 3.
5. Develop a checklist for grading a job or project in your occupational area.
6. Develop a checklist of factors for arriving at a class mark.

7. Students in a shop situation usually share many duties, such as housekeeping, crib attendance, foreman, and so on. First note whether or not students should be graded in the performance of these duties; then substantiate your viewpoint.
8. Develop a record card that will help you record a student's progress during a six-week period so that you can arrive at a final grade.

14.

The Teacher's Role in Guidance

The words "guidance" and "counseling" are as well-known today as the word "teacher." There are a few people, however, who do not understand the need for offering guidance services in the school. The mobility of the American family, the great need for and the emphasis placed upon higher education, the complexity of the ever-changing world of work, and other social changes that are taking place—all add up to a frequently bewildering and frightening future for high school students. A guidance system attempts to help these students. A counselor is a person who devises a guidance system and who, using his specialized training and experience, carries out the function of helping students.

The counseling function is an outgrowth of a vocational guidance movement that started in the early 1900's when Frank Parsons wrote

Choosing a Vocation, in 1906. He maintained that the growth of an industrial society would develop more complex jobs that would require different kinds of preparation. He realized that persons seeking jobs had to know more about the requirements and characteristics of jobs and, in addition, had to know more about their own talents and abilities in order to get these jobs. Therefore, Parsons stated that it is the duty of the vocational counselor to bring the job and the job applicant together. It is important for teachers of occupational skills to understand the beginnings of vocational guidance. Professional vocational counselors must study the various occupational fields to learn about jobs and requirements. Since the vocational teacher knows the requirements of the job field for which he is training his students, he can become a valuable partner to the vocational guidance counselor.

Vocational guidance should not be oversimplified, however. The world of work in Parsons' time was vastly different from the world of work today. The number, types, and kinds of jobs, ranging from the unskilled and skilled to the technical and professional, have expanded to such a degree that the *Dictionary of Occupational Titles* was developed by the United States Department of Labor to catalog and classify what now approximates 40,000 different jobs.

The concept of a job has also changed. We now talk of training and retraining a person some four or five times in his lifetime of work. The implications are serious for vocational training if it is to meet the challenge of a changing world of work. The narrower the training, the narrower the opportunity for employment; the broader the training, the broader the opportunity for employment. The scope of vocational offerings must be expanded if occupations are going to change in skills and technical information during a worker's lifetime. Vocational training must change its methods and concepts to keep up with this occupational change.

THE NEED FOR GUIDANCE

There are many other influences that threaten the security and affect the thinking of young people: the threat of war and possible extinction, the possible demands of military service, the struggle for status and recognition, the powerful pressures to go to college. Another threat to their security is the effect automation may have on their career plans. About the only fact that emerges from the many investigations into the effects of automation is the uncertainty about the effects of automation. Some experts believe that an expansion of business will create jobs, while others believe that automation will eliminate not only jobs but whole classifications of jobs. It is important to note that the severest effects of automation have been felt in the unskilled job areas and that the most recent labor projections disclose a continuing need for skilled, technical, and professional types of labor.

Professional guidance becomes a necessity for all young people when they are burdened with such pressures and threats to their security. A well-trained and well-informed vocational teacher is even more valuable when he can offer them this professional guidance. Vocational teachers must keep abreast of job changes and refinements throughout their teaching careers. In addition, they should be able to interpret and communicate objective information concerning these changes to students and parents.

THE COUNSELING PROCESS

Basic to effective counseling is the rapport or relationship which exists between counselor and counselee. This is true of the trained counselor or of the informal counselor, such as the vocational teacher. Two essential principles are often given for successful counseling. First, each counselor must be sincerely interested in the counselee or client. Second, the client must have confidence in the counselor.

Counselor and counselee relationships must be warm and sincere; these personal qualities are usually found in the majority of vocational teachers. Furthermore, when we consider the environment of the shop or laboratory, which lends itself to a certain freedom and informality, it becomes more understandable why so many vocational and industrial arts teachers have succeeded with boys and girls when other teachers have failed.

Young people, like adults, relax when they are doing what they like to do and are successful at it. When students are confident, can relax, and know that their teacher is truly interested in them, the teacher has an exceptional opportunity for informal guidance.

Vocational teachers may counsel their students individually when the shop is in session or in groups during the presentation of a lesson. This counseling could include some of the following points of information:

1. Requirements for entrance into a vocation.
2. Wages and benefits in industry.

3. Union affiliations.
4. Apprenticeship programs and requirements.
5. Civil Service opportunities.
6. Opportunities for self-employment.
7. Opportunities for further education.
8. Career opportunities in supervision, middle management, and management.
9. Opportunities to become teachers, either in industrial arts or the vocational field.
10. Ancillary opportunities in related job fields.
11. Automation and the possible need for retraining.
12. Getting started on the job.

The counseling process for vocational teachers is primarily informational and often includes firsthand experiences and knowledge. The teacher's objective observation is important because an experienced craftsman can recognize dexterity, agility, and the "feel" for a job. By questioning and testing, he can gain valuable insights into a student's aptitudes and abilities for given job skills. This informal method of evaluating a student can be quite valuable when combined with formal testing by a trained counselor. Vocational teachers should learn, therefore, to be thorough and objective in all phases of student appraisal and evaluation. They should consult with school counselors on special or unusual problems. In fact, vocational teachers should consider counseling as a further career in education.

Many steps can be taken to keep students abreast of information, and to make them aware of the importance of their choice of vocation. Teachers can, at the same time, keep informed themselves. There are a number of organizations that are extremely valuable in providing information that will help vocational teachers and counselors to keep up with job and training trends. Some important sources of information are:

1. Ford Foundation Grants in Vocational Education.
2. American Council on Education.
3. National Committee on the Employment of Youth.
4. Bureau of Labor Statistics, U.S. Department of Labor.
5. Office of Education, Department of Health, Education, and Welfare.
6. National Education Association.
7. American Vocational Association.
8. U.S. Department of Labor.
9. Carnegie Corporation of New York.
10. State Departments of Labor.
11. U.S. Government Printing Office.

The addresses for each of these can be obtained from the school counselor or from the library. Some material can be posted on the shop bulletin board. Many organizations will send attractive posters, booklets, and flyers which can be used as teaching aids. Birth dates of inventors or other persons who have made important contributions to their fields should be noted in class, on the bulletin board, or in the school newspaper.

Vocational teachers can cooperate in assembly programs devoted to vocational guidance. Career guidance programs in which successful people are invited to speak to students about their fields are another important means of informing and motivating vocational students.

PERSONAL RELATIONSHIPS IN COUNSELING

There are several personal relationships in counseling which teachers must be aware of. The first, and most important, is with the student; another is with the professional counselor. There are others, such as relationships with the administration and the staff, with agencies, and of course, with parents. Generally teachers will come in contact with the student and counselor more frequently than with the others.

There is an essential rule in all relationships which every teacher should abide by: the respect for confidentialities. Personal information is privileged information and should be treated with the utmost discretion. Communication with professional counselors should be kept on a professional level; washrooms and lunchrooms are no place to discuss personal pupil problems. Casual conversation should not include information which, although seemingly valuable in understanding what motivates a student, is really only a contribution to the vicarious thrills of ordinary gossip. Students need a confidant, and teachers should not betray that trust.

Teachers should be discreet in their discussions with parents. Students frequently confide in their teachers because they feel that teachers are their friends. Often parents are intolerant toward adolescent problems and erroneously ridicule their children instead of listening to them understandingly. Information of a comparatively unimportant nature, sometimes passed on to other people by teachers in violation of a confidence, causes turmoil instead of helping to bring about a solution to a problem. There is no easy answer to the problem. Teachers must exercise judgment according to individual cases and, at the same time, must recognize and respect the responsibility and integrity of parents.

Teachers should not be absolute in counseling or guiding young people. They should explain facts and expose students to choices, but they should not become authoritarian and arbitrarily dictate actions for students to follow. Teachers may recommend actions and help to guide students, but in the final analysis students must learn to make correct decisions for themselves. Making decisions based on information and good judgment is essential to maturity, and teachers play an important part in developing young people when they help them broaden their horizons. The best counselor is frequently the best listener. Teachers can help students to detect flaws in their plans by showing them alternate choices and by giving them career information. When given a direction that they do not understand or see no reason for, students have been helped very little. On the other hand teachers can, by listening and questioning, help students develop insight and the ability to think and reason through to a solution.

Teachers should not hesitate to learn more about guidance from the guidance counselor. Counselors are trained and can help teachers understand many of the statistical entries on a student's cumulative record card. These entries, however, should be used with caution. Scores should be weighed against other factors.

For example, many teachers accept reading grades without finding out the grade in which the reading test was given. If John Doe has a reading grade of 7.7, his tenth-grade shop teacher might feel that he is behind in reading. A closer inspection of John's cumulative record would reveal that he took the test in September of the seventh grade. Therefore, he was actually above average in reading ability. If John were at or above grade level in reading ability up to the eighth or ninth grade, based on a series of reading tests spread over a four- or five-year period, his teacher might assume that he is a fairly good reader and at grade level in his tenth year.

There are similar examples of other test results. It is not the purpose in this chapter to delve deeply into the area of tests and measurements. It is important, however, that teachers be alert to consistent patterns of test results and, more important, consult with trained counselors before they attempt to interpret results.

In return, counselors are interested in vocational teachers' reports and evaluations, because of the time and environment factors inherent in shop teaching. In most cases vocational shops are four periods in length and, as has been pointed out, the more informal environment of the shop permits a more accurate observation of a student's skills and of his personal relationships with other students in the group. The freer relationships and atmosphere which prevail in shop often influence the attitude of the student toward a more positive approach to learning. Clues to the causes of poor attendance, poor achievement, or poor interest are often discovered by shop teachers. With proper help from the attendance coordinator, the counselor, or other guidance personnel, many students can be motivated to continue schooling and to renew their interest in school.

USE OF STUDENT RECORDS

Entering grades and comments on student records is one of the responsibilities of vocational teachers. Records are used for many years after a student leaves school; teachers should keep this fact in mind when entering comments and characterizations. Comments should be accurate and objective. Teachers must assess the validity, value, and implications of entries. Although they are usually cautioned against making exaggerated comments that are open to misunderstanding, teachers are not usually cautioned against overrating a student. This happens when a student's manners, pleasantness, and cooperation are rated to the exclusion of vocational course achievement. Another weakness of teachers is to be influenced by the marks of other teachers. Teachers often seek comfort in what has been called the "central tendency," in which all marks are neither high nor low, but are comfortably within the so-called average range. It is not easy to be objective, for we all react to others as they react toward us, but teachers must be able to separate personality traits from occupational competency in arriving at a true evaluation of a student.

Since the counseling aspect of vocational teaching is becoming increasingly important, a list of valuable reference texts and books is given at the end of this book. They should become part of a teacher's professional library and should be supplemented from time to time with new and current literature.

PERSONALITY TRAITS

Teachers of occupational skills must be concerned with the personal development of their students, as well as with their occupational development. Adolescents are sensitive and perceptive. Since students learn to socialize in school as well as outside of school, teachers must be understanding and mature in their relationships and must exemplify good personality traits themselves.

Some of the traits that a successful teacher might display are:

1. The ability to wield influence in a democratic way.
2. The ability to create and maintain interest in everything he teaches and does in the teaching situation.
3. The ability to be humorous and to accept humor. Although he should handle his work conscientiously, he must not take himself too seriously.
4. A pleasant and even temperament, coupled with the ability to see the bright side of things.
5. The ability to develop confidence in himself and his students.
6. An enthusiasm in his profession, his class, and his work, accompanied with patience.
7. Qualities of leadership. Adolescents look for direction, and the teacher should be an important guide.
8. Qualities of integrity and sincerity. A teacher should personify the ideals he teaches.
9. Personal habits of neatness, promptness, self-control. He should be able to do the things he asks of his students. He should practice the good habits he expects to inculcate in his students.
10. The ability to adapt himself to other personalities and other viewpoints. Tolerance and a broad viewpoint should be a part of his character traits.

In the list developed above there are many of the qualities and attributes which students will include in lists they make up when asked to describe qualities they admire in teachers. From time to time such lists are published in newspapers or professional publications. They are valuable in that they serve as guides for ascertaining what students are thinking. Teaching and learning are a concomitant endeavor, and what is good for one is usually good for the other.

The authors have often advised their teacher trainees to try to turn back the hands of time and recall the characteristics of their favorite teachers, as well as the teachers they did not particularly admire. Clues to successful teaching have often been discovered in this way. Many teachers find that it is beneficial to sit with the members of the group when several students are at the chalkboard. There are, after all, two sides to the room, and it might be a good idea to look at the room from the student's side.

Let us look at a typical list of teacher qualities that students admire. The list is a composite of various lists and does not purport to include every desirable quality.

Qualities Students Admire in Teachers

Sense of humor	Easy to understand
Patience	Capacity to organize
Fairness	Ability to explain
Firmness	Friendliness
Sincerity	Personal interest
Honesty	Tolerant
Integrity	Even-tempered
Knowledge of subject	Understanding
Neatness	Well-groomed
Courteousness	Respects other opinions
Good voice	Good speech
Energetic	Willingness to listen

In studying such a list one soon becomes aware of certain needs that are common to learners, particularly at the school level. There is a plea for understanding. There is a plea for guidance, and there is a desire for the teacher to be considerate and to display qualities that earn the respect of the learners. Teachers should realize that respect must be earned. Although the profession of teaching is one of the highest callings, each teacher must earn his own share of the respect which the profession generally receives.

HOW IMPORTANT ARE GOOD TEACHER QUALITIES?

One might question the importance of the qualities that have been listed above. One might argue that, after all, opportunities for learning the skills involved in the performance of the various occupations are provided in the curriculum. The course of study prescribes the work to be done, and the teacher sets the standards for the successful completion of the work. Although this is true, it is not the whole story. There are two other aspects of the teaching picture which must be explained. First, proper atmosphere for learning is essential in the consideration of the learning process. Students should be able to concentrate on the problem of learning without dealing with a teacher's idiosyncrasies. They should be free of as many distractions as possible.

The other aspect involves the problem of teaching attitudes and values. A lesson plan can be developed for almost every subject, topic, and aim, but how does one write a plan on integrity? When does one know when he is preaching and no longer teaching? One of the competitive forces with which teachers must contend is the popular notion that it is not what you know, but whom you know. Another shibboleth is the one about honest larceny, i.e., it is all right if you do not get caught. Teachers are seriously involved in the battle of character training and the instilling of moral values. How will the teacher accomplish his goal? Will a lecture on integrity get the desired result? After all, teachers are educated people, and as one neophyte teacher once remarked, "Surely, students will take my word for it." But is it enough to talk about such things as honesty, respect, cooperation, democracy, understanding, honor, trust, or should such values be inculcated by application and practice? Of course we must live by these values if we want them to apply. There is no double standard in teaching. The standard we want our students to observe must be the same standard that we, as teachers, observe. A teacher must exemplify the qualities he wishes to inculcate in his students. When he realizes and implements this ideal, then the words *sincerity, integrity,* and *cooperation* will begin to take on real meaning.

Getting along with students is often established by the students, reactions when a teacher meets his class for the first time. He should greet them cordially and sincerely. All too often teachers receive advance reports about the groups they are to teach and, as a result, they betray by voice or manner their fear of the group or their regard for the group. During the first session the purpose of the course, as well as the aims and objectives, should be explained. The standard of work should be described and also the sincere belief that all the students will be able to achieve and benefit from the work. Start developing the confidence of the students from the beginning. Be prepared and organized, have something for the students to do every session. Motivate by being enthusiastic and helpful. Be ready with suggestions to help each student progress at his rate and at his best level. Recognize and acknowledge individual differences.

Although the general conduct and standards of performance are essentially the same for all, allow for differences of ability and rate of speed. Do not neglect the shy student, nor leave the bright student completely on his own. Bring everyone into the "act" whenever possible. Ask questions of students, learn their likes and dislikes, their aptitudes and interests; learn their problems and their ambitions. Avoid embarrassing students before others. Use the private talk for discussing shortcomings or other topics which are personal. Give students a feeling of importance in the group, and give each student an opportunity to assume responsibility. Reprimand students when they need to be reprimanded, but do it judiciously, and usually privately. Criticisms should be constructive. Most learners will make errors, but when correcting them do not destroy their enthusiasm or arrest all hope for improvement.

Be willing to listen to grievances. No teacher is above reproach, no organization is infallible. Teachers can learn from students and should be willing to consider their comments and complaints. These may range from comments on instructional materials to teaching methodology or the conduct of the department. Remember that many points of view are worthwhile, and sometimes students will notice things which the instructor has overlooked.

Many of the devices which are part of good organization and management will bring about the rapport which is the end result of a good teacher-student relationship. Some of the devices follow:

1. Honor system. The problem of handling the out-of-room pass can be solved with the honor system. Here is an excellent opportunity to instill responsibility with trust. The honor system can work only as well as the class uses or abuses it.
2. Rotation of shop duties. The assignment of foremen, tool attendants, and those responsible for housekeeping, safety, maintenance, and other departmental chores should be on a rotation basis. The fact that some students are better or worse in the performance of these duties is no excuse for depriving them of the opportunity to learn the duties each assignment entails. Trust is developed by putting youngsters in positions of trust. This is an excellent way to develop student responsibility and leadership. Orderliness is learned by being taught orderly procedures. Shop duties must be defined, explained, assigned, and checked.
3. Visual aids. These can be built by students. Students should be recognized for their contributions by having their names put on the object or device that they have constructed.
4. Suggestions. Teachers should ask their classes for suggestions from time to time. Very often, teachers will face problems of selecting jobs, purchasing materials, entering competitions, building instructional aids, and many other teaching problems. The teacher should try confronting the class with these problems for its consideration and solution. Together, they can find a solution, which by virtue of having been a cooperative effort, will make the solution more binding to the class.
5. The progress chart. The use of a progress chart is important as an instrument of objectivity in arriving at grades. Students will feel

that the progress they make is recorded objectively and that they truly have earned their grades.
6. Other school duties. From time to time teachers have the opportunity of recommending a student for one of the various service squads. The fact that a member of a class is chosen often serves as a strong motivating force for higher standards of conduct and efficiency. One of the authors appointed the members of the auditorium squad from his shop group for a number of years. They established a fine record for reliability and efficiency. As a result the individual boys in the class aspired to duplicate the standards of the squad so as to become eligible also.
7. Group situations. The teacher must be alert to changing patterns and situations. He must be in close contact constantly with his students in order to act wisely and properly in dealing with different groups. He must avoid cliques and promote group spirit. He must make the best use of extra assignments and duties to promote discipline and *esprit de corps*. Sometimes, temporary solutions resolve more or less serious personal problems.
8. Citizenship. Organizational procedures should be based on the democratic concept of self-government and sharing of responsibilities and duties. The shop group that disciplines itself will be well on the way to habits of good citizenship. Citizenship does not stop here, however, for teachers should see to it that students in their classes take part in school activities and school organizations. Students should be encouraged to take part in fund drives, clubs, teams, and other activities.
9. Home contacts. Teachers should find ways and means to establish contact with parents and guardians other than through the report card. Many schools conduct open house, open school days, or other opportunities for adults to visit the school. These occasions present excellent opportunities to meet relatives of students. If such opportunities do not present themselves, teachers should encourage students to invite their parents.
10. Tone of voice. The old adage "It is not what you say but how you say it" still holds true, especially when dealing with students. Tone of voice is often the key to an attitude. Sincerity radiates from your voice just as impatience does. Adolescents particularly are sensitive to scorn, insinuation, disgust, and ridicule. The tone of voice should be well-modulated, pleasant, and reflect the effort of the teacher to reach his students.

At the beginning of this text, teaching was defined as helping others to learn. The characteristics and qualities which have been discussed in this section are in keeping with that concept. It is quite apparent that a teacher should be a person who likes people. People can be influenced and taught, but it is much easier for the teacher who, because of a combination of personality factors, likes people and likes to see his efforts reflected in the growth of young learners.

The teacher of occupational skills should keep abreast of developments in his specialized area. He should attend trade shows and exhibitions, subscribe to magazines and periodicals, and generally keep himself informed. He should display pride of craftsmanship and show expert knowledge of the requirements of the occupational area he teaches. He should be loyal to his religious beliefs, at the same time respecting those of his students. He should be loyal to our country and the principles in which we believe. Democracy must be implemented in the school or it cannot be respected outside of the school. Above all, teachers must cultivate an open mind and encourage the same attitude in their students. Again, variety enters the picture and, again, the benefits of variety will assert themselves. Films, field trips, visitors, guest speakers, special reports, assembly programs, special lessons, special jobs and projects all help achieve the goals for which we strive in teaching. It is the combination of all these things which will make the teacher successful.

Summary

"Teachers should work closely with counselors and should be examples to their students."

Counseling is a profession that requires special training and preparation. Teachers of occupational skills, because of the informality of shops and laboratories, can exert a positive influence upon their students. They can become part of a guidance team by understanding the guidance process and by contributing their own occupational knowledge and experiences as further resources for counseling.

Teachers of occupational skills should constantly learn about job requirements, opportunities, and trends in their occupational areas. They should cooperate with guidance counselors in programs to assist students in learning about careers. Occupational information can become part of the curriculum. They should know how to interpret standardized scores and how to use scores as a basis for instruction. They must respect the confidentiality of information about students. Record-keeping must be accurate, since school records are used many times during a student's school career.

Teachers should be examples to their students. They can help students develop good attitudes toward educational and vocational goals and show them the means to attain their goals. Teachers can earn respect for many positive values by observing such traits as punctuality, honesty, integrity, fairness, firmness, organization, and preparation. Healthy relationships between teacher and student make for an atmosphere of trust. In such an atmosphere, discipline problems decrease and student learning increases.

Questions and Projects

1. Write an information sheet describing job and promotional opportunities in your field.
2. Develop a flow chart that shows job progress and advancement in your occupational area.
3. Develop a lesson plan for teaching "Facts About the Job of . . ." (insert your occupational title).
4. You are asked to assist the guidance counselor in your school to develop a questionnaire to be used in selecting students for your occupational course. List some physical factors, abilities, and aptitudes you feel are necessary in making a good course choice.
5. Review the cumulative record card used in your school. List sections or entries that are either unclear or of special interest to you and consult with the guidance counselor at your school about your findings.
6. Make a survey of your occupational field, with an emphasis on:
    a. Job opportunities in industry.
    b. Need for further education.
    c. Opportunities for self-employment.
    d. Apprenticeship credit for course completion.
    e. Job opportunities in government.
    f. Requirements for teaching the occupation.
    g. Long-range career aspects.
    h. Licensing requirements for employment, if they apply.
    i. Job opportunities in fields related to the occupation.
    j. Job trends and the effects of automation.
7. Make a list of work attitudes that you would like to inculcate in your students.
8. Describe how you would seek to accomplish your goals listed in answer to question 3.
9. List several group activities that will help to develop each of the following:
    a. Independent thinking.
    b. Cooperative work.
    c. Creative work.
    d. Citizenship.
    e. Service.

15

Other Roles and Responsibilities of Teachers

STARTING THE NEW JOB

The first real test the new teacher faces comes when he starts his initial assignment. There is seldom a transitional period of internship because the teacher of occupational subjects usually goes from a program of teacher training or industry directly into shop, class, or laboratory teaching. For most people the experience is a very difficult one. The many details of school administrative procedures for which a teacher is responsible increase the burden of orientation to the new situation.

The authors recognize this fact and have developed a series of suggested points of reference for the new teacher to use in getting started. Since schools and systems differ, the suggestions given can serve only within a general framework to minimize the task for all teachers.

The two main divisions of personnel contacts in any school consist of the teaching staff and the student body. The new teacher must acquaint himself with his duties, responsibilities, and relationships to each group. It is rather difficult to draw a sharp line of demarcation between these relationships because the school's purposes and goals are directed toward the needs of the student; therefore, there is overlapping. The two divisions are used to clarify the explanation of the suggestions as the school administration conceives them.

Responsibilities Relating to Teacher Personnel

The new teacher should do the following things at the time of his first contact with the school organization:

1. Present any necessary documents and certificates to the chief clerk. At the same time request an opportunity to meet the principal and his assistant.
2. Request a copy of the teacher's handbook or bulletins which contain explanations of procedures and routine duties expected of you.
3. Ask for a copy of your teaching schedule. This probably will be given to you by the department head.
4. Ask for keys to rooms, shops, laboratories, and lockers you expect to use. Some schools will ask for a small deposit for the keys.
5. Ask for the rollbook, cards, and other records pertaining to the daily administration of your classes. Study the books and records, and become familiar with both the format and the manner of recording data.
6. Obtain a copy of the rules, regulations, and bell signals for:
    a. Fire alarms and drills.
    b. Air raid shelter drills.
    c. Return to home room.
    d. Other signals and means of interschool communications.
7. Ask for a plan of the building which will help you learn the layout and location of rooms and facilities. Some schools have mimeographed copies of the building plan.
8. Study the bulletins which give information about:
    a. Assembly schedules and procedures.
    b. Passing bell schedules.
    c. Your time schedule.
    d. Where and how to check in and out of school.
    e. Student time schedules.
9. Ask for the location and use of your letter box.
10. Locate the teachers' bulletin boards and learn how they are used.

11. Inquire about your personal clothing locker.
12. Determine the accommodations for teachers' lunch periods.
13. Become familiar with the facilities for use during your unassigned periods to prepare instructional material and supplementary teaching tasks.
14. Check on parking facilities and parking rules.
15. Do not overlook elementary details. Come prepared with your own pen, pencil, and other minor accessories. It would be rather embarrassing for a new teacher to have to ask for these simple pieces of equipment.
16. Tour the building in your free time and become familiar with the offices, the facilities, and the general *modus operandi* of the school plant. Do not overlook the custodian—his services will be valuable and you will have occasion to call on him many times in the course of your employment at the school.
17. Confer with the department head about the work of the department and your place in the organization.
18. Become acquainted with the senior teachers—they can be a source of inspiration and help to you.
19. Meet the members of the faculty from the various departments. They will aid you in appreciating the relationships of the various departments and help you develop an overview of the school.

Meeting Your Classes

The teacher's first meeting with his class has a great influence on his future success or failure. Consequently the first session should be well-planned in accordance with the suggestions offered. Planning in advance with an understanding of the procedures to be followed will help the teacher become more confident and well-poised. A program for the first meeting might consist of the following:

1. Introduce yourself to the class in a pleasant manner. Write your name on the blackboard in a clear, legible hand.
2. Have all the students take seats and check attendance. If the rollbook is not ready the first day, have students write their names on a prepared sheet to be checked against the rollbook later.
3. Check and sign program cards. If the class is your official class, you will probably distribute the new program cards.
4. Decide on the type of seating plan you will use before you meet the class. Make provision for the students with seeing or hearing difficulties in your planning. Assign seats. Keep the students together; leave vacant seats in the rear.
5. Review bell signals with the class. Check on exits and stairways for fire drills and shelter drills. Assign monitorial duties such as shutting off lights and closing doors.

6. Discuss other phases of class management such as:
    a. Attendance.
    b. Punctuality.
    c. Room passes.
    d. Housekeeping.
    e. Student responsibility for school property.
7. Discuss topics that might be assigned by the guidance officer or other administrative official.
8. If you are an official class teacher, be prepared to discuss the importance and seriousness of electing capable class officers. Be ready to assist your class in conducting these elections.
9. Conduct an informal discussion with your students concerning their work, future plans, interests, etc. Start learning all you can about the students as soon as possible. Your interest in your students will result in respect for you.
10. Tell your students something about your background, especially your educational and occupational experience. It will help the students know you and respect your occupational ability and authority.
11. Prepare in advance so you can leave your class "on their toes" instead of the class having you "on your heels."

Becoming Familiar with Your Shop or Classroom

1. Visit the shop or other facilities where you will work before you meet students. Become familiar with the following:
    a. Location and type of fire extinguishers.
    b. Door and stairway locations.
    c. Washbasins and lockers.
    d. Tool and supplies storage facilities.
    e. Material and equipment facilities.
    f. Machinery—type, location, and condition.
    g. Department bulletin boards.
    h. Visual aids that may be available.
    i. Files, lockers, and similar facilities.
    j. First-aid kit location and contents.
    k. General condition of shop, laboratory, or room.
    l. Shop library—contents and condition.
2. Confer with your department chairman and learn about:
    a. First-aid procedures and follow-up accident reports.
    b. Safety tests—copies and filing of tests.
    c. Your copy of the course outline.
    d. Procedure for obtaining custodial services, room repairs, etc.
    e. Requisitioning of supplies.
    f. Textbooks being used.
    g. Methods of keeping materials inventory.
    h. Procedure for obtaining films and other visual aids.
    i. Types and quantity of projectors and other aids.

ASSEMBLY PROGRAMS

Teachers in occupational education can make many unique contributions to the rest of the student body through assembly programs. By displaying their students' projects, they can become part of the cultural life of the school. They can add to the value of guidance programs by describing careers in their individual occupational fields. Assembly programs can be instructional and at the same time fill a guidance function.

There are two broad types of assembly program assignments. One is easy, and the other requires more work. An easy assembly program assignment is one for which the teacher calls in an outside agency to present a film while he introduces the program and expresses thanks at the conclusion. The difficult one is the type of program presented by the students under the guidance and direction of the teacher. It requires planning, script, scenery, and props. It is hard work and takes a lot of time. A number of hazards are involved. The star may become ill on the day of the program, the props may fail, the students may forget their lines, and it is quite probable that students will not enunciate effectively. No program will mean as much to the students, live as long in their memories, nor have the stimulation as the actual experience of participation in this type of assembly program.

In highlighting the value of student participation and opportunity for ingenuity on the part of teacher and student, we have tended to discredit the so-called "easy" type of program. The picture is not an entirely accurate one, since there are many excellent programs that only outside agencies can present. Our plea is against the use of that type of program entirely to the exclusion of the type in which students participate.

It is important to recognize the purpose of assembly programs. Since each program should teach something, it would be rather untenable to defend a program of pure entertainment. School assembly programs can be entertaining, pleasant, and gay, but they should not be presented for the sole purpose of entertainment. It would be a waste of time and would only serve to inculcate values that schools are constantly combating. Assembly programs are an extension of a teaching session. It is very often a form of guidance and includes many classes rather than one group. A good program should have a central theme or aim. Sometimes the administration or assembly coordinator will assign a title, such as "Red Cross Drive," "The Meaning of UNESCO," "Student Organization Rally," or the title may be left open. When arranging an assembly program, it is wise to use the following type of checklist.

ASSEMBLY CHECKLIST

DAY and DATE _____ TIME _____ LOCATION _____

Groups in attendance (By class) _____

Standing of groups: (*Seniors, Juniors, Sophomores, Freshmen*)

General nature of other programs during term:

_____

_____

Topics that may motivate the student:

1. Current interest or events.
2. Occupational guidance.
3. Community interest.
4. Consumer value.
5. Safety program.
6. Relation to other subjects.
7. Opportunities in Armed Forces.
8. Further education in occupation.
9. Dealing with the public.
10. Proper dress.
11. Social graces.
12. Citizenship.

Estimate of time:

Marching in, salute to the flag, messages _____

Introduction of program _____

Program _____

Credits for assistance _____

Introduction of cast _____

Closing, school song, etc. _____

    Planning for a good assembly program calls for a careful breakdown of many factors. The checklist has been kept simple because it is meant to be only a guide. Each instructor can elaborate according to his individual needs. The development of such a checking device is very helpful and can be especially valuable at a later date when filed as a record of the programs presented.

    Teachers should vary their assembly presentations if they hope to develop and retain interest. Keeping accurate records will help in planning future programs and in making each one a little easier to present and more effective in results than its predecessor. Teachers should consult with their supervisors and senior teachers when confronted with the problem of presenting an assembly program. The experience of associates can be a very valuable source of reference and can save a lot of time and wasted motion.

Planning the Program

The job of actually planning the program can proceed when the aims and purposes are established. If the program includes the services of students, it is necessary to discuss the program with the students who will best profit by the experience and do the program justice. Stimulating youngsters, or for that matter any group, is necessary if the members of the group are expected to put forth their best efforts. Students often have fine ideas about programs, especially if they have already been in programs under the direction of other teachers.

Planning an assembly program is similar to planning a lesson. Establish the aim and then develop the presentation, which may be a skit, a playlet, a series of tableaus, or other type of presentation.

Refer, if necessary, to colleagues in the dramatics department for advice on staging, projection, coaching, and prompting. Make a list of the materials needed. Provide for building props, coloring posters, or painting other materials. Pick the best student for each part and remember to have an understudy. Find something for each student to do. You will need stagehands, electricians, property men, and perhaps ushers. Staging an assembly program provides a rare opportunity for recruiting students into activities that are valuable for them.

Provide for a good, unusual beginning or introduction. Develop an attention-getter by use of a line, a prop, a sound, an incident, an unusual display, lighting effects, or any other device that will motivate interest. Develop the body of the presentation to include the theme by explanation or application of the message. Relate the message to the members of the audience and their needs. Conclude with a summary finish by emphasizing the main point.

Teachers must bear in mind that they are displaying their talents in an auditorium. They are, in a sense, selling their occupation, themselves, and their students. Assembly programs are a wonderful opportunity for showing the school what students in a specific department can do. Directing such a program calls for the best possible planning and the best possible presentation. Be alert for constructive criticism from colleagues; make note of weaknesses and shortcomings, just as notes should be taken of strengths and talents. The evaluation should be a continuing process that results in growth and improvement. The first assembly program is difficult, much as the first lesson or the first job, but the succeeding ones will be much easier.

There are many types of programs which are almost impossible for the average teacher to produce or the school to support. They may be difficult because of size, cost, or necessary form of presentation. If a proposed program seems to offer exceptional promise and value, yet the cost becomes a prohibitive factor, teachers sometimes solicit the aid of parent-teacher groups, chambers of commerce, service clubs, and other community groups. Teachers should refrain from initiating programs that are too costly or require too much outside assistance until after they have had considerable experience in handling such projects.

There is another interesting type of program which can be presented. Many business concerns have developed school service divisions or public relations departments whose express purpose is to present programs to large groups dealing with either products, services, or research facilities of the company. The material they present is usually up-to-date and often beyond the ability of schools to present properly. The speakers are people who know how to present their material with the use of attractive visual aids or working models to help explain and clarify various points as the topic is developed. There is a threefold value to this type of program:

1. Students can see and hear about the latest inventions and advances, or learn specialized information about industrial processes or social problems. Such programs should not be restricted to technical or occupational areas. Teachers should be concerned with the overall aspects of education, as well as technological progress.
2. It is also an excellent way for instructors to keep up with current developments. Outside agencies appreciate the opportunity to reach the school population with their special messages.
3. This type of program helps bring school and community closer together. It provides an opportunity to develop respect and understanding for each other's needs and problems.

Teachers should send letters to local industrial concerns asking for information on the type of educational services they offer. Some have none, while many offer literature, films, and provide speakers or complete programs. Inquiries of this type should be made on school stationery, as they incur no obligation. Each inquiry should be phrased in good English, be clear and understandable, and stated in language that avoids embarrassment to anyone or any company which does not have available the services described. All such contacts with the public tend to influence the teacher's professional standing.

The following discussion of the classroom speaker suggests some of the techniques that teachers should observe and develop when dealing with outside people and agencies.

THE CLASSROOM SPEAKER

Emphasis has already been made on the use of a variety of methods to become an outstanding teacher. An application of this idea is the use of speakers representing the occupational interests of the class. Instructors of vocational subjects naturally have connections in the occupational field. These connections might be with owners or managers of businesses, supply houses, manufacturers, contractors, salesmen, inspectors, employment managers, and skilled craftsmen. These people are active in their vocational pursuits, and therefore are aware of the latest trends and innovations. They bring realism and the latest information into the shop and classroom. They should be requested to visit the school shop, and in that way get a clear picture of the work being done. Many of these people are impressed by what they see, and consequently leave with a heightened respect for practical arts and technical education. It is not often that you can bring the mountain to Mahomet, so bring Mahomet to the mountain.

Never contact a guest speaker and request him to appear on the following day. Make the invitation a written one and send it sufficiently in advance to give the guest ample time to prepare his material. A speaker's presentation should fit approximately the work of the school at that particular time. The letter of invitation should include the following information:

1. A brief description of the class, the school grades represented, and the range of interests of the group.
2. A topic with an alternate. The speaker wants his talk to be successful, and unless he is an extraordinarily able guesser, he will be rather puzzled concerning a topic of interest to the students.
3. How much time he will have for his presentation. Request that he allow a five- or ten-minute question-and-answer period following his talk.
4. An offer to help with any visual aids, projectors, extension cords, tables, tools, equipment, or other material that he may wish to use in his presentation.
5. The time, day, and place of the meeting. Give simple instructions, if necessary, on how to reach the school. It is customary to have all visitors report to the office to sign a guest book. It is good practice to observe these amenities. The shop monitor might be sent to the office

a few minutes early to greet the guest and conduct him to the meeting room.
6. Your school and your home phone numbers so the guest can reach you if necessary.

There are some other preparations that should be made which do not belong in the letter of invitation:

1. Invite your supervisor or principal because he might like to attend the meeting and meet your guest. His presence reinforces the value of the session and aids considerably in emphasizing the importance attached to the visit. If the pressure of business interferes with the principal's attendance, the instructor should realize the situation and not resent the absence.
2. If the topic under discussion is a very important one, the instructor might ask another class with similar interests to join his class for the meeting. Cooperation of this kind among teachers is highly desirable and results in fine *esprit de corps*.
3. The members of the group should be prepared for the visit. Instructors should discuss with the students the guest's purpose in coming and briefly orient them on the topic to be presented. They should be prepared to recognize the highlights and even make minor notes as they listen. These notes may be the basis of a follow-up discussion the next day.
4. The instructor should introduce the speaker quickly, courteously, and competently. Once the speaker has the floor, the instructor should become unobtrusive. He should make mental or written notes of pivotal points that can be used for further discussion at a later time.
5. Be prepared for a closing to the program. Either the instructor or one of the students can thank the guest. An expression of appreciation on school stationery, signed by the class officers, might be sent to the speaker.
6. Regardless of the expression of thanks by the students, teachers should always follow visits with a commendatory note and expression of appreciation. In some cases a copy might be sent to the guest's superior. A copy should be kept in the teacher's personal files and another copy sent to the supervisor, principal, or director.

Guest speakers present a change of voice and a change of pace. Students enjoy these experiences because in change there is rest. They learn much when hearing men and women from the field. Furthermore, job contacts may be established and the youngsters realize this. In the meantime the teacher grows in stature and prestige by these outside associations.

THE TEACHER AS A GUEST SPEAKER

It seems reasonable to expect teachers to be good public speakers. Teachers talk a great deal. In fact students would probably agree that teachers usually talk too much. Oddly enough, many teachers break out into a cold sweat at the thought of addressing a group outside the shop or classroom. Public speaking is an art just as teaching itself is an art, and a good public speaker is not necessarily a good teacher nor is a good teacher necessarily a good public speaker.

Teachers do have quite a head start on most people, however, when it comes to speaking to groups. The skills they have acquired over the years in planning and organizing lesson presentations are the same skills they will draw upon for speaking in public. The experience of addressing groups is an invaluable one. It develops assurance, confidence, poise, and of course helps in developing a truly professional personality. Teachers have many opportunities to give talks. If they will think in terms of talks rather than speeches, they will be on their way to successful speaking.

Topic and Content

Selecting a topic and content does not differ from the problem of selecting what to teach. The topic and content will depend on the aim and purpose of the talk. Furthermore, it depends on the audience to which the talk will be delivered and the time at which it will be given.

1. The delivery, method, and enthusiasm.
2. The simplicity of presentation.
3. The connection of thoughts and ideas.
4. Relation of material to the interests and needs of the audience.
5. Accuracy of facts and statistics.
6. Evidences of forethought and planning.

Audiences unconsciously react to speakers positively or negatively, although they may not be skilled speakers themselves. A touch of humor goes a long way in speaking. The right touch at the right time, in the right amount, will help insure the success of a talk.

An invitation to speak to service clubs such as Rotary, Kiwanis, Lions, parent-teacher groups, trade groups, church groups, youth groups, or at faculty and department meetings and other professional meetings, all present opportunities to develop and improve

TEACHING OCCUPATIONAL SKILLS 252

skill in speaking. Most invitations to speak are written invitations. If extended orally, ask that the invitation be confirmed by letter. Check for date, place, and time. Discuss probable topics with the person who issued the invitation. Decide whether or not you want to use a visual or auditory aid. Unless a specific time limit is stated, plan on 20 to 30 minutes. Unless the topic is an unusual one and the audience is exceptional, 20 or 30 minutes are sufficient to make important points, deliver a message, and keep an audience in good humor. Above all, do not be pedantic. Forget the classroom. The same rules of planning and organization may apply, but the atmosphere is not the same. Be simple; use good, plain English and present your material in logical sequence. Talk to your audience, not at them. Maintain eye contact, be relaxed, and maintain a pleasant manner.

If a technical talk is delivered, check all the facts and figures. Be accurate. Do not present opinion for fact. Give credit to sources and references. There may be reporters present; therefore, do not include remarks which cannot be supported or which you would not want

Occupational teachers should have students set up displays of their work.

widely distributed. If the reporting is to be done by an amateur, a summary of the talk might be prepared for that person.

"Selling" Your Shop

Whether or not the instructor realizes the effect, every presentation of a program helps "sell" his subject or shop. Sometimes he is called upon to give a program for an outside group. This type of program might be offered for educational and vocational guidance at the elementary or junior high school level. It may be presented at the request of a lay group for the purpose of learning more about the school and its curriculum.

A well-balanced and nicely paced program given by the members of a shop class can be most absorbing and effective. Here again, as in all the programs where students participate, the learning value is great. Real meaning is given to such phrases as preparing for life experiences, developing future leaders, instilling good ideals of citizenship, and the many other phrases which describe the values that should be taught during the period of adolescence.

What To Include

It is far better to do some small thing well than to attempt something big and fail. In developing any program, select a small part of the occupation to present. The presentation might be centered around a concept, a principle, or a job of the occupation. It might be developed around job opportunities, the history of the occupation, consumer education, or the technical aspect of the occupation. Whatever area the instructor chooses, he should remember the advice he received in preparing a lesson: develop a single-purpose air. Multipurpose presentations are vague, confusing, and might very well lose the support and acceptance of the audience.

Student demonstrations must be as carefully and completely planned as teacher demonstrations. They must be well-done and performed smoothly and safely. Visual aids, equipment, and material in good working condition should be used. Everything should be tested beforehand and the program rehearsed.

If the program is to be presented outside the school, then the instructor should make provisions for transportation of material and/or students to the place where the program is to take place. Parent consent slips might be obtained to assure the willingness of parents and guardians to permit students to take part in the program. Instructors should acquaint themselves with the school policy and procedure regarding leaving the school building or traveling with students during school hours.

OTHER SCHOOL DUTIES

Most secondary schools are large institutions and require a comprehensive organization to function properly. The educational staff of any school consists of four main divisions:

1. Administrative staff.
2. Supervisory staff.
3. Teaching personnel.
4. Student personnel.

Each division operates in a definite area, with responsibilities and duties of its own. There is a great deal of overlapping, however, and many administrative and supervisory duties are assumed by members of the teaching staff. Just as the administration may call on teachers to assist in administrative duties, teachers often request students to work with them in the discharge of many of their simpler duties. A wise instructor will look on the assignment to an administrative post as an opportunity to learn more about the school organization. It can be the beginning of a program of advancement within the profession or, at the very least, a means of becoming a more capable teacher. Assignments to guidance posts, attendance, cafeteria, course construction, program committees, class counselor, student organization counseling, or club advisor should be valued for their worth in professional growth.

Teachers should serve on teacher interest committees and other professional groups. They should assist in the conduct of fund drives and community appeals. Such duties are often rotated so that no one teacher becomes overloaded with work of this type. In many cases teachers ask for assignments that are of particular interest to them.

There are many services that instructors of occupations can provide which are of value to the school and assistance to the students. High morale can be generated among the members of a staff if teachers display enthusiasm for their school, their shop, and their students. It has been pointed out that students can profit by helping develop and construct visual aids and props for programs. This same spirit of cooperation and enthusiasm can be carried over to the formation of student service squads such as:

1. Visual aids squads.
2. Auditorium squads.
3. Repair squads.
4. Poster and display squads
5. Various marshal squads for:
   a. Special events.
   b. Ushering.
   c. Hall and stairway traffic.
   d. Cafeteria supervision.

Typical situations, which offer teachers the opportunity to develop moral and ethical values in students, have been presented here. Teachers of occupational subjects should be just as much concerned with character and personality training as their academic colleagues. Students at the secondary level, and often at college level, are adolescents who register as boys and girls and leave as young men and women. Teachers who neglect character and personality are doing a disservice to their students.

MANAGEMENT AND ORGANIZATION

Three areas pertinent to the training of occupational instructors are:

1. Occupational analysis.
2. Shop and laboratory management and organization.
3. Methods of teaching industrial and technical subjects.

Although this text is concerned with the techniques of teaching, it should be stressed that the best methods of teaching when applied in a poorly organized shop, based on an inadequate analysis of occupational content, will terminate in poor teaching. A corollary statement would be that teachers can only become capable and truly professional teachers when they apply the principles of careful occupational analysis as well as good organization and management. Teachers who are orderly in their thinking and performance are usually good teachers.

Although not sufficient for effective teaching when taken by itself, orderliness counts for a great deal. One of the long-recognized precepts of the teaching profession is that good teachers teach by example. Carelessness, slovenliness, indecision, monotonous repetition of presentation, lack of enthusiasm and ideas are all stultifying to learners. Teachers who are guilty of these shortcomings might keep their jobs, but will fool no one, particularly their students. Teachers cannot demand respect by virtue of their positions; they must earn it. They can merit respect very easily, with a program of effectively presented material and constant self-improvement.

Teaching is a vital profession. Teaching occupational skills in this age of industrialization and mechanization is more important than ever before. We read that every engineer must be supplemented by a team of about ten technicians, and they in turn by a team of approximately 40 mechanics. It must be obvious to any thinking person that programs in the industrial arts, and vocational and technical education on the secondary level, must be supported and encouraged. Teachers in these areas must possess a very high degree of mechanical skill, as well as expert skills in the art of teaching.

Teaching should be pleasant and rewarding if the techniques and suggestions made in this and other texts are used. Enjoy teaching, strive to improve, and, above all, keep an open mind. Learn and experiment with teaching devices which are ethically, morally, and legally sound. New ideas, new methods, and new concepts are needed as never before in the field of education. Perhaps you can be the discoverer of something new, something better.

Summary

"The successful teacher never fails to keep informed of social and technological advances."

Each instructor should determine for himself the kind of teacher he wants to be. He can grow and become a better teacher with each succeeding experience. He can implement the skills in organization and planning which he learned during his training courses by accepting assignments in school which might be outside his immediate shop or laboratory duties. Each assignment should be accepted as an opportunity to become a better teacher, help students, and learn the school organization in all its phases.

Assembly programs are stimulating and important. Teachers are asked to present assembly programs either in their fields of interest or in an area of general interest assigned by the school administration. Assembly programs offer exceptional opportunities for training students in values, skills, and talents not readily apparent in the shop or laboratory situation. The principles of planning and organization apply to assembly programs, as well as to other teaching ventures.

Guest speakers and visitors provide valuable experiences for students. Teachers should make use of these devices and learn how to prepare for them. Teachers themselves are often asked to speak before other groups. These invitations are opportunities which they should accept to improve themselves. Public speaking is an art that teachers should cultivate. Speaking before groups gives the teacher the chance to "sell" himself, his occupational area, and his school. He should plan his talk carefully and completely and do the best possible job in terms of his audience and his profession.

There are many opportunities for teachers and students to learn cooperatively. Teachers should recognize the value of squads, clubs, and other school assignments which help the teacher train his students in developing good attitudes. The skill with which teachers analyze occupational content and develop a good system of shop management and organization will influence greatly their success in teaching these values. Teachers must be examples of what is correct and good in both their personal conduct and professional spirit.

Questions and Projects

1. List five values of good assembly programs.
2. Make a list of at least five themes or ideas that an assembly program in your occupational area might seek to convey.
3. The local chamber of commerce has asked your school to place a display from five occupational areas in a show window on Main Street. Each display will remain in the window for two weeks. You have been asked to prepare an exhibit in your area. Make up a project sheet that describes your ideas, the materials needed, the message you hope to convey, and other incidentals which you feel are important. Include key sketches if necessary. The window is 14 feet wide and 7 feet deep.
4. Write a letter of inquiry to a manufacturer asking about educational services available, with a special request for a speaker to participate in an assembly program.
5. Write a letter of invitation to an expert in your field of interest to address your class.
6. Develop an outline for a ten-minute talk on your occupational area to be delivered to a group of younger high school students who are potential students in your shop.
7. There are many good, simple texts in the library concerned with public speaking. Read one and submit a report on its contents. Include the highlights.
8. Teachers are often assigned to administrative or supervisory duties on a part-time basis. Show how each of the following assignments can help you become a better teacher:
    a. Attendance coordinator.
    b. Guidance counselor.
    c. Grade advisor.
    d. Program committee.

  e. Cafeteria supervisor.
  f. Club advisor.
  g. Student organization advisor.
  h. P.T.A. representative.
9. Make a list of approximately ten values or attitudes you feel should be instilled in your students. Describe how each of these may be developed.

Bibliography

BORDEN, RICHARD C., *Public Speaking as Listeners Like It.* New York: Harper & Row, 1935.
CENCI, LOUIS, *Skill Training for the Job.* New York: Pitman, 1966.
FARWELL, GAIL F., and PETERS, HERMAN J., *Guidance, A Developmental Approach.* Chicago: Rand McNally, 1959.
HAAS, KENNETH B., and PACKER, H. G., *Preparation and Use of Audio-Visual Aids.* Englewood Cliffs, N. J.: Prentice-Hall, 1955.
HIGHET, GILBERT, *Art of Teaching.* New York: Knopf, 1950.
HOFFMAN, BANESH, *The Tyranny of Testing.* New York: (Crowell-Collier) Macmillan, 1962.
LEIGHBODY, GERALD, and KIDD, DONALD, *Methods of Teaching Shop and Related Subjects.* Albany, N. Y.: Delmar Publishers, 1955.
MATHEWSON, ROBERT H., *Guidance Policy and Practice.* New York: Harper & Row, 1962.
MICHAELS, W. M., and KARNES, M. R., *Measuring Educational Achievement.* New York: McGraw-Hill, 1950.
ROSE, HOMER C., *The Instructor and His Job.* Chicago: American Technical Society, 1961.
SANDS, LESTER B., *Audio-Visual Procedures in Teaching.* New York: Ronald, 1956.
SILVIUS, G. HAROLD, and CURRY, ESTELLE H., *Teaching Multiple Activities*

in Industrial Education. Bloomington, Ill.: (McKnight & McKnight) Taplinger, 1956.

STATON, THOMAS F., *How to Instruct Successfully.* New York: McGraw-Hill, 1960.

TYLER, LEONA E., *The Work of the Counselor.* New York: Appleton-Century-Crofts, 1961.

WRENN, C. GILBERT, *The Counselor in a Changing World.* Washington, D.C.: American Personnel and Guidance Association, 1962.

VENN, GRANT, *Man, Education, and Work.* Washington, D.C.: American Council on Education, 1964.

ZERAN, FRANKLIN R., and RICCIO, ANTHONY C., *Organization and Administration of Guidance Services.* Chicago: Rand McNally, 1962.

Index

Action, part of learning process, 13, 47
Administrative and supervisory duties, 254–255
Adolescence, 231
  development process, 34
  emotional differences, 37–38
  sense of belonging, 40
Advanced students, 101
Advanced theory classes, 30
Aims and objectives
  lesson plans, 46, 51, 54, 56
  occupational analysis, 18–19
Analyzing occupations; *see* Occupational analysis
Antipoverty programs, occupational education, 3
Applications, lessons, 47, 51, 55
  sample lesson, 119–120
Apprenticeship training, 5, 28, 30
Armed Forces training films, 137
Assembly programs, 245–249, 256
  arranged by business concerns, 248
  checklist for, 246
  evaluation of, 247–248
  guest speakers, 249–250
  by outside agencies, 245–248
  planning, 246–249, 256
  purpose of, 245
  staging, 247
  student participation, 245
  on vocational guidance, 23
Assignments, 55
  kinds of, 53
  sample lesson, 120
  sheets, 181–182
    writing, 191–193
  treatment in lesson plans, 48, 53, 55
Attitudes and values, teaching, 236
Auto mechanics, instruction sheets for, 187
Automation, 9, 228–229

Basedow, Johann, 9
Beauty culture
  instruction sheets, 188, 190
  occupational analysis, 23
Blueprints, 207
Books and textbooks, 101–102; *see also* Reference sources
  illustrations in, 206
  procedures used in listing references, 193
  reference sources, 206
  teaching aids, 144

Cabinetmaking, instruction sheets, 190
Carpentry, instruction sheets, 190, 192
  jobs in, 24–25
  occupational analysis, 22
Cartoons, 144
Chalkboards, 122–126
  care of, 125, 131
  demonstrations and, 83–84, 95
  equipment for, 124, 131–132
  as motivating device, 124
  pounce patterns, 125, 133
  substitutes for, 126, 131
  techniques for, 124–126
  use of, 122–126, 131, 143
Character training, 8, 38, 236
Charts and graphs, 126–128, 132, 144
  construction of, 126
  mounting and storing, 128
  types of, 127–128
  use of opaque projectors, 139
Citizenship training, 8, 238
Classes; *see also* Students
  first meeting with, 236, 243–244
  homogeneous and heterogeneous, 32
  intellectual level of, 11
  organization and management, 40
  physical differences, 34–35
  size of, 99
Classroom speakers, 249–250
Cleanliness and hygiene, 34
Comenius, John, 9
Communications
  between teacher and students, 122, 133
  use of senses, 12–15

Index

Community colleges, 34
  occupational education, 4
Completion-type tests, 161–162
  advantages, 161
  construction of, 161–162
Consumer education, 8, 128
Cooperation, developing, 4, 39, 98, 101
Counseling, 227; *see also* Guidance
Counselors, 227–228
  relationship with staff, 231–232
Courses of study
  aims and objectives, 29
  occupational analysis for, 17–30
  organizing teachable content, 27–30
    for effective learning, 27–28
    students' requirements and, 29
    trade analysis or inventory, 27
  revising, 29
  sample lessons, 107–116
    critique of, 116-121
  specialized training, 30
Craftsman, The, 184
Creativity, 8
Cultural differences, 36–37
Cultural influences, 10
Curiosity, learning and, 10

Democratic atmosphere for learning, 4
Demonstrations, 35, 39, 81–85
  aims and objectives, 83
  art of demonstrating, 81–82
  art of explaining, 85–88, 95
  attention-getting function, 82
  chalkboards used with, 83–84
  checking lesson plans before, 57
  complexity of, 82
  definition, 81
  with enthusiasm and poise, 89–90
  flexibility, 89
  followed by information, 82–83
  for groups or individuals, 82
  hanging a door, 24–25
  illustrations and, 83–84
  material and equipment for, 83, 94–95
  for motivating students, 82
  need for, 82
  operation sheets used with, 188
  operation-type lessons, 84, 94, 188
  planning, 82–83
  by students, 51, 253
  suggestions for improving, 83–85
  teacher's manner, 83–84, 86, 89–90
  timing, 83
  use of films and filmstrips, 84
  visual means of teaching, 94

Diagrams and illustrations
  commercially published, 206
  instruction sheets 181, 186, 193, 205–206
Dictionary of Occupational Titles, 228
Directions, following, 184–185
Discipline problems, 38, 237
Dressmaking
  instruction sheets for, 188, 190, 192
  rating factors, 215
Duplicating techniques, 207–208
  blueprints, 207
  instruction sheets, 193, 195–196, 207–208
  mimeographing, 207
  offset process, 208
  tests and quizzes, 175
  use of color, 208

Education, definition of, 7–8
Educational Film Guide, 143
Electrical installations
  instruction sheets, 191, 192
  occupational analysis, 21–22
Electrical skills, 9, 86
Electronic skills, 9
Emotional differences, 37–38
Enrichment programs, 101
Environmental differences, 35–36
Environmental influences, on students, 4, 10, 41
Essay type of questions, 155, 164–166, 177
Evaluation
  of lessons, 60–64
  of students, 212–226; *see also* Grades and grading
  progress charts, 223–224
Examinations, 171–172, 177; *see also* Tests and testing
Excursions; *see* Field trips
Exhibits, 144
Experiences
  learning from, 10–11, 57, 69
  providing, 40
Experiments, 40
Explanations, 85–88, 95
  aim and purpose of, 85–86
  art of explaining, 85–88, 95
  easy to follow, 85
  examples of, 86–88
Fast learners, special help for, 33
Field trips, 145–147, 149
  follow-up, 147
  for learning occupation, 145
  motivational value, 145

parent consent slips, 253
  participation in, 146-147
  preparation for, 145-146
  value of, 145, 147
Files and filing
  examinations, 173
  instruction sheets, 208
  lesson plans, 64, 65
Films and filmstrips, 39, 136-138, 141-143
  card file of, 143
  for demonstrations, 84
  Educational Film Guide, 143
  previewing, 137
  projectors, 141-143
  purpose of using, 138
  records used with, 143
  screens for, 141, 142
  selection of, 137
  slide films, 137-139
  sources of, 143
  storage of, 139-141
  suggestions for using, 137, 142-144, 149
  training films, 137

Grades and grading
  composite grades, 214
  criticism of, 212, 213-214
  dual rating plans, 214-215
  final grades, 222
  notebooks, 221-222, 225
  other factors, 220
  performance tests, 154
  personal conferences and, 215
  progress charts, 223-224
  quizzes and tests, 222, 225
  rating factors, 219
  rating scale, 217-219
  rating student characteristics, 215-221
  rating students' work, 215, 216
  reasons for, 213
  record of progress, 213
  symbols and gradations, 214, 216
  types of ratings, 213-220
Group teaching, 82, 99-102, 104, 238
  advanced students, 101
  advantages, 98
  checking and testing progress, 99
  class size, 99
  control of groups, 99-100
  enrichment programs, 101
  individual differences and, 98-99
  major factors, 99-100
  provisions for fast and slow learners,
    95-100, 101, 104-105
  use of notebooks, 102-104
Guest speakers, 249-250, 256
  teacher as, 251-254
Guidance, 31-32, 227-241
  changing world of work, 227-228
  evaluating students, 230, 232-233
  information on vocations, 230-231
  need for, 228-229
  personal relationships in, 231-233, 239-240
  with students, 231
  personality traits, 233-235
  personnel, 11
  process of, 229-231
  relationships with professional counselors, 231
  respect for confidentialities, 231
  staff relationships, 231-232
  student aptitudes and abilities, 230
  training and retraining programs, 228
  use of student records, 232-233
  by vocational teachers, 229-233, 239

Health programs, 11, 35
Hearing, learning through, 82
  sense of, 12-13
Herbart, Johann, 45
Heritage, biological, 35-36
  influence of environment, 35-36
Home contacts, 238; *see also* Parents
Honor system, 237

Illustrations and diagrams, 144
  demonstrations, 83-84
  instruction sheets, 181, 186, 193, 205-206
Imagination, 8, 14, 57
Imitation, learning by, 14, 39
Indexing and filing
  examinations, 173
  instruction sheets, 208
  lesson plans, 48, 50, 64, 65
Individual differences, 32-38, 236
  cultural differences, 36-37
  emotional differences, 35-38
  handling, 38-40
  mental differences, 32-33
  physical differences, 34-35
Individual instruction, 98-99, 101, 104
  advantages, 98
Industrial arts, 3-4
  goals, 8
  occupational analysis, 23
  occupational education and, 3-4

Index

Industrial organizations
  assembly programs presented by, 248
  models used by, 135
Information sheets, 181
  writing, 190–191
Information-type lessons, 43–47, 85
  aims, 46–47
  area covered by, 43–44
  definition, 43
  flexibility, 89
  source material for, 44
  theory and basic fundamentals, 43
  versus operation-type lessons, 56–60, 88–91
Ingenuity, 8
Instruction; *see* Teaching
Instruction sheets, 39, 144, 180–210
  aid in learning, 209
  assignment sheets, 181–182
  care of, 209–210
  characteristics of, 182
  developing, 181, 183, 186
  diagrams and illustrations, 181, 186, 193, 205–206
  disadvantages, 182–184
  duplicating techniques, 193, 196–198, 207–208
  experiment sheets, 182
  function of, 180–181
  indexing and filing, 208–209
  information sheets, 181, 190–191
  job sheets, 181, 183, 186–188
  layouts, 188, 193, 199-202
  operation sheets, 181, 188–190
  outline form, 181
  physical make-up, 193-202
  preparation of, 181–183
  project sheets, 182
  reading directions, 184–185, 186
  requirements of learners, 180–181
  step-by-step instructions, 181
  to supplement teacher, 181, 210
  types of, 181–182
  use of, 51, 208–210
  value of, 182–185, 209
  as visual aids, 202–206
  work sheets, 182
  working from, 104
  writing, 181–183, 186
Instructional aids; *see* Teaching aids
I.Q. (intelligence quotient), 32–33

Job costs and material estimates, 180
Job sheets, 181, 183, 186–188
  developing, 186–188
Jobs, 40
  and ability of students, 28
  analyzing, 28
  carpentry, 24–25
  definition, 24
Junior colleges, 34

Key phrases and notes, in lesson plans, 48, 51
Key questions, 47, 50, 119

Learning process, 7–16
  action, 13, 47
  atmosphere for, 4, 235
  differences in rate of learning, 33
  experience as basis of, 57, 69, 79
  imagination, 14
  imitation, 14
  importance of five senses, 12–15
  memory and recall, 14, 71–72, 79
  learning how to learn, 5
  observation, 13–14, 39, 57, 82
  principles, 9–12
    learning by doing, 9–11
  psychological principles, 5, 9–16
  reasoning, 14
  repetition, 14
  unit of learning, 44
  ways in which students learn, 13–14
Lectures and lecturing, 91–95
  disadvantages, 91–92
  illustrations, 92
  organizational techniques, 91–93
  preparing, 92–93
  to provide supplementary information, 92
  shop talks, 92–93, 95
  use of, 91–92
Lesson plans, 48–53
  aims, 46, 51, 54, 56
  application, 47, 51, 55, 119–120
  assignments, 48, 53, 55, 120
  benefits for teachers, 60
  checklist for, 53–56
  developing from occupational analysis, 26–30
  divisions, 46–48
  for effective lessons, 107
  flexibility, 50, 65
  headings and numbering of, 48
  improving and revising, 50, 65
  indexing and filing, 48, 50, 64
  key phrases and notes, 47, 48, 50–51, 119
  motivation, 47, 51–54, 118–120
  outline form, 116
  presentations, 47, 51, 54–55, 118–119

references listed, 48, 53, 55, 120
safety precautions in, 51
sample, 57–59, 107–116
  application, 119–120
  assignment, 120
  critique of, 116–121
  instructional aids, 120–121
  key questions, 119
  motivation, 118, 119–120
  presentation, 118-119
  references, 120
  summary, 120
student preparation, 47, 51, 54
summary, 47–48, 55, 120
teacher preparation, 47, 51, 54
tests based on, 166–169
topics, 46, 50, 54
use of instructional sheets, 51
use of teaching aids, 51
writing, 50–53
  in outline form, 51, 116
Lessons
  aims and objectives, 83, 89, 116, 118
  characteristics of, 44–45
    adapted to needs of students, 45
    beginnings, 45
    introduction of new material, 44
    presentations, 45
    reasonable in scope, 44
    standards of performance, 45
    unit of learning, 44
  checking and testing for progress, 46; see also Grades and grading
  definition, 24
  developing from occupational analysis, 24–25
  evaluation of, 60–64
    range of content, 61
  flexibility, 89
  information-type, 43–47, 65, 85, 89
    aims, 46–47
    area covered by, 43–44
    definition, 43
    flexibility, 89
    source material for, 44
    theory and basic fundamentals, 43
    versus operation-type lessons, 56–60, 88–91
  main parts, 46
  meaning of, 44
  operation-type lessons, 43–44, 65
    area covered by, 44
    flexibility of, 89
    for showing manual skills, 43, 89
    source material, 44
    use of demonstrations, 84–85, 94
    versus information-type lessons, 56–80, 88–91
  organizing teaching content from occupational analysis, 26–30
  plans; see Lesson plans
  presentations, 89–90, 94, 107
  references used in developing, 46
  sample, 107–116
    aim of lesson, 116, 118
    critique of, 116–121
  teacher planning, 45–48
    Herbartian steps, 45
  teaching points, 43, 65
  types of, 42–45
  unit of learning, 44
  use of key questions, 47, 50, 119

Machine shops, 86
  instruction sheets, 187, 190, 192
  occupational analysis, 22
Machine skills, 9
Magazines, trade, 131
Manpower Development and Training, 3
Manual skills, 17
  analysis of, 19–23
  operation-type lessons, 43–44, 65, 89
  teaching, 8–9
Manuals, work, 144
Marks; see Grades and grading
Matching-type tests, 163–164
Mathematics, teaching, 10, 33
Mechanical drawing, rating factors, 215
Memory and recall, 14, 71–72, 79
Mental differences, 32–33
Mimeographing material, 207
Mock-ups, 135, 144, 147, 149
Models, 134–136, 144
  commercial, 135
  construction of, 135
  cutaways, 144
  miniaturization, 134–135
  types of, 134–135
  used in teaching, 134–137, 144
  working mock-ups, 135, 144, 147, 149
Moral values, teaching, 236
Morale, developing, 4
Motion pictures, 137, 144; see also Films and filmstrips
Motivation of students, 14–15, 236
  demonstrations used for, 82
  drives common to all, 52–53
  lesson plans, 47, 51–54, 118–120
Multiple choice tests, 158–160
  construction of, 158–160

Index

Notebooks, 102–104, 105
  creativity in keeping, 103
  distributed material for, 103, 209
  evaluating, 221–222, 225
  form, 103
  indexing notes, 103
  instruction in note-taking, 104
  instruction sheets kept in, 209
  reasons for taking notes, 102
  use of, 105
  value of, 102, 103–104

Observation, learning by, 13–14, 39, 57, 82
Occupational analysis, 17–30
  according to divisions of occupations, 22–23
  advance planning, 18
  aims and objectives, 18–19
  benefits for teachers, 18–19
  breakdown of occupation, 25–26
  carpentry, 22
  cosmetology, 23
  for developing courses of study, 17–30
  for developing lessons, 24–25
  electrical field, 23
  electrical installations, 21–22
  industrial arts, 23
  listing requirements, 19–20
  machine shops, 22
  organizing teachable content, 26, 27–30
    principles of, 27
    students' learning requirements, 27
  pipefitting, 21
  plumbing, 22
  printing, 22
  sources of reference material for, 23–24
  for teachable content, 19–23, 26, 27–30
  technique for, 18
  woodworking, 20-21
Occupational education, 3
  growth of field, 3
  on secondary level, 3–4
Occupational skills
  demonstrating, 81–85
  practicing, 81
Offset process, for duplicating material, 208
Opaque projections, 137, 139, 144
Operation sheets, 181, 118–190
  writing, 188–190
Operation-type lessons, 43–44, 65
  aims, 46
  area covered by, 44
  flexibility, 89
  to show manual skills, 43, 89
  source material for, 44
  use of demonstrations, 84–85, 94
  versus information lessons, 56–60, 88–91
Operations, definition, 24
Overhead projectors, 139–141

Parents
  consent slips, 253
  discussions with, 231–232
  home contacts, 238
  interviews with, 153
Parsons, Frank, 227–228
Part-time work experiences, 10, 36
Past experiences, learning from, 57, 69, 79
Peer groups, 36
Performance
  standards of, 45, 236
  tests, 152, 153–154
Pestalozzi, Johann, 9
Physical differences, 35
Pictures and slides, 128
Pipefitting, occupational analysis, 21
Plumbing
  instructional sheets, 190, 192
  occupational analysis, 22
Popular Mechanics, 184
Posters, 128
Pounce patterns, 125, 144
Practicing occupational skills, 81
Presentations
  in lesson plans, 47, 51, 54–55
  method of, 119
  sample lessons, 118–119
  variety in, 56
Printing
  instruction sheets, 187, 190
  occupational analysis, 22
  rating factors, 215
Problem sheets, 116, 119–120
Problem-solving, 33
Progress charts, 223–224, 237–238
  benefits of, 223
  construction of, 224
  use of, 224
Projectors, 139–143
  filmstrips, 141–143
  opaque, 137, 139
  overhead, 139–141
Projects, 40
Psychology, educational, 5, 32–40

Public speaking, 93, 99–100, 251–254, 256–257
  eye contact, 252
  habits and mannerisms, 93–94
  presentations, 253–254
  techniques for delivering talk, 93–94
  topic and content, 251–253
  use of humor, 251
  use of visual aids, 250, 252

Questions and questioning
  for attracting students' attention, 71, 76–77
  to check progress of lesson, 78
  competence in forming questions, 70, 73
  developing skill in asking, 70, 73, 79
  double questions, 74
  guessing answers, 72–74, 77
  integrated into lesson, 70, 77–79
  key questions in lesson plans, 47, 50, 119
  memory questions, 71–72, 79
    characteristics of, 71
    examples of, 72
  oral questions, 70
  planning, 77
    to create interest, 78
    key questions, 77, 79
  in quizzes and examinations, 70
  reasons for, 70–71
  responses to, 73–74
    guessing answers, 72–74, 77
    improper or undesirable, 73–74
    vague answers, 74
  to summarize lessons, 78
  technique for questioning, 73–79
    allowing time for answer, 75–76
    calling on specific student, 75
    care in framing, 70, 73
    checklist for, 78–79
    encouraging questions from students, 77
    key words, 77, 79
    language and grammar, 73
    questions related to student's ability, 76
    requiring complete answers, 77
    requiring individual not group answers, 77
    scatter questions, 75
    specific aim of question, 73–74
    stimulating class before calling on student, 75
  on tests; see Tests and testing
  thought-provoking 71, 72, 79
  challenge of, 72
  characteristics of, 72
  timing, 70, 77–79
  tone of voice for asking, 75
  types of, 71–73
  use of, 78
Quizzes, 167, 169, 177; see also Tests and testing

Rating performance, 212–226; see also Grades and grading
Reading
  difficulties, 154, 185
  individual differences, 33
Reasoning, 14, 57
Recall and memory, 14, 57, 71–72, 79
  questions to stimulate, 71
Records, student, 232–233, 239
  cumulative, 33
Reference sources, 101–102, 131, 144
  listed in lesson plans, 48, 53, 55
  for occupational analysis, 23–24
  procedure used in listing references, 193
  sample lesson, 120
Repetition, 14, 57
Report writing, 104
Reproducing material; see Duplicating technique
Resistors, lesson plan on, 108–116
  RETMA color code, 109–112
Rousseau, Jean Jacques, 9

Safety precautions, 27, 83, 88
  demonstrations, 83, 88
  detecting danger signs, 13
  in lesson plans, 51
Science courses, 10
Secondary school level, occupational education, 3–4
Senses, importance in learning, 12–15
Sheet metal, instruction sheets, 190, 192
Shoe repair, instruction sheets, 188
Shop experience, 25
Shop programs
  care of instruction sheets, 209–210
  management and organization, 255–257
  rotation of duties, 237
Shop talks, 92–93, 95
  delivering, 93
  technique for preparing, 92–93
Shop teaching; see Teaching
Short-answer type tests, 160–161
Sight, learning through, 12–13, 82, 94

Index

Skill training
  operation-type lessons, 43, 89
  repetition, 101
Slide films, 137, 138–139
  overhead projectors, 140–141
Slow learners, special help for, 30, 33
Smell, learning through sense of, 12–13
Social attitudes of students, 36–37
Speakers, guest, 249–250, 256
  letters of invitation, 249–250
Staff, educational, 11, 243, 254–255
  relationship with, 231–232
Students
  backgrounds of, 69, 91
  challenging, 33
  competency of, 33
  demonstrations by, 253
  developing potential, 32
  individual differences, 32–38; see also Individual differences
  paths open to, 5
  preparation for lessons, 47, 51, 54
  psychological needs, 5, 32–40
  questions for inattentive, 71, 76–77
  rating characteristics, 215–221
  records, 232–233
  service squads, 254–255
  social attitudes, 36–37
  suggestions made by, 237
  underprivileged, 36
  understanding, 31–41
  visual aids developed by, 135–136
Success, achieving, 33
Summary, in lesson plans, 47–48, 55
  sample lessons, 120
Supervisors, courses for, 28
Swedish Sloyd System, 9

Taste, learning through sense of, 12–13
Teachers of occupation skills, 3
  accuracy of judgment, 14
  activities, 4
  administrative and supervisory duties, 254–255
  appearance, 14, 109
  art of explaining, 84–88, 95
  assembly programs, 245–249
  characteristics and qualities, 233–239
  developing students' abilities, 4
  effective, 4
    occupational or subject mastery, 4
    teaching personality, 4, 14, 100, 233–235
  enthusiam and poise, 89–90, 100
  example to students, 239–240, 257
  first meeting with class, 236, 243–244
  flexibility, 89–90, 95
  functions, 38
  as guest speakers, 251–254
  guidance function, 227–241
  habits and mannerisms, 93–94
  helping others to learn, 7–16
  importance of humor, 37
  influence on students, 8, 239–240, 257
  insight and understanding, 37–38
  loyalty of, 239
  management and organization, 255–256
  manner, 83, 86, 93–94
  molding human character, 9, 38
  need for tolerance, 34–35
  new teachers, 3–4, 37–38, 241–244
    becoming familiar with shop or classroom, 244
    first meeting with class, 236, 243–244
    organizing teaching content of occupations, 27–30
  performance of, 14, 90–91
  personality traits, 4, 14, 100, 233–235
  preparation for lessons, 47, 51, 54
  professional preparation, 82, 239
  public speaking by, 89–94, 99–100
  qualifications, 235–239
  qualities students admire, 234–239
  reference library, 101–102
  relationship with counselors, 231–232
  relationship with staff members, 11, 243, 254–255
  relationship with students, 4, 8–16, 31–41, 235–239
  resource personnel, 3
  responsibility of, 14–15, 31, 85, 241–260
  suggestions made by students, 237
  tone of voice, 75, 238
  understanding students, 31–41
  use of simple language, 86, 95
Teaching
  according to planned sequence, 82, 86
  art of explaining, 85–88
  attitudes and value, 236
  characteristics of good teaching performance, 90–91
  creative, 121
  demonstrations, 81–85
  effective, 4, 31
  environment for, 4, 235
  group and individual instruction, 97–106
  importance of, 255–256

information lessons versus operation lessons, 56–60, 88–91
inspiring, 121
learning process, 9–12
lecturing and telling, 91–94
methods and techniques, 4–5, 7, 121
  variety of, 38–39
occupational skills, 4
organizing teachable contents, 27–30
  for effective learning, 27–28
  students' requirements, 27
  trade analysis or inventory, 27
preparation for life's experiences, 5, 8
social and technological advances, 256
step-by-step instructions, 181
training youth for gainful employment, 8
variety in, 38–39, 147
Teaching aids, 26, 91, 133–150
  advantages of, 143–149
  construction of, 132, 143
  instruction sheets, 180–210
  lesson plans and, 51
  sample lessons, 120–121
  suggested aids for specific purposes, 143–144
Teaching content of occupations, 17–30
  organizing, 27–30
  student learning requirements and, 27
Teaching points, 65, 83
Teams of students, 35, 39, 40
Tests and testing, 151–178
  completion-type, 161–162
  duplicating methods, 175
  essay type of questions, 155, 164–166, 177
    advantages, 164, 166
    criticism of, 164–166
  examinations, 171–172, 177
  factual evaluation of, 152, 164–166
  functions, 152–153, 176
  guessing answers, 155–156
  indexing and numbering, 173, 175
  instructions for taking tests, 173–174, 178
  intelligence tests, 32–33
  matching-type, 163–164
  to measure students' progress, 152
  multiple choice questions, 158–160
  objective, 155, 164, 177
  oral, 154
  performance tests, 152, 153–154
  planning, 154–155, 174–176
  practical tests, 153–154

preparation of, 166–167
  based on lesson plan, 166–167
  outline of material to be covered, 173
  using variety of types, 172–173
pretests, 166
purpose of, 152–153, 173
questions, 70; see also Questions and questioning
quizzes, 167, 169, 177
results, 153, 232
reviewing with class, 173, 175, 178
scoring, 173, 175, 177–178
  partial credit, 173
short-answer type, 160–161
subjective, 164, 177
timing, 173, 175
true-false tests, 156–157
types of, 153–156
written, 154–156, 177
Tone of voice, 238
  for asking questions, 75
Tools and equipment, 10
Topics, lesson plans, 46, 50, 54
Touch, sense of, 12–13
Trade and technical training, 8–9
  goals, 8–9
Trade analysis or inventory, 27–30
Trade extension programs, 28
Trade schools, 8–9
  occupational education, 3
  unit trade school, 3
Travel experiences, 10
True-false tests, 156–157

Underprivileged students, 36
United States Department of Labor, 228
Upward mobility, 36

Values, teaching, 236
Visual aids; see also Teaching aids to add variety to teaching, 147
  advantages, 144
  chalkboards, 122–126
    care of, 125, 131
    demonstrations and, 83–84, 95
    equipment for, 124, 131–132
    motivating device, 124
    pounce patterns, 125, 133
    substitutes for, 126, 131
    techniques for, 124–126
    use of, 122–126, 131, 143
  characteristics of, 129–130
  charts and graphs, 126–128, 131–132, 144

Index

construction of, 126
mounting and storing, 128
types of, 127–128
use of opaque projectors, 139
construction of, 116, 121
developing, 39, 135–136
field trips, 145–147, 149
  follow-up, 147
  for learning occupation, 145
  motivational value, 145
  parent consent slips, 253
  participation in, 146–147
  preparation for, 145–146
  value of, 145, 147
films and filmstrips, 39, 136–138, 141–143
  card file of, 143
  for demonstrations, 84
  Educational Film Guide, 143
  previewing, 137
  projectors, 141–143
  purpose of using, 138
  records used with, 143
  screens for, 141, 142
  selection of, 137, 143
  slide films, 137, 138–139
  sources of, 143
  storage, 139, 140–141
  suggestions for using, 137, 142–144, 149
  training films, 137
function of, 128–129
impact on memory, 133
instruction sheets, 39, 144, 180–210
  aid in learning, 209
  assignment sheets, 181–182
  care of, 209–210
  characteristics of, 182
  developing, 181, 183, 186
  diagrams and illustrations, 181, 186, 193, 205–206
  disadvantages, 182–184
  duplicating techniques, 193, 196–198, 207–208
  experiment sheets, 182
  function of, 180–181
  indexing and filing, 208
  information sheets, 181, 190–191
  job sheets, 181, 183, 186–188
  layouts, 188, 193, 199–202
  numbering system, 208–209
  operation sheets, 181, 188–190
  outline form, 181
  physical make-up, 193–202
  preparation of, 181–183
  project sheets, 182
  reading directions, 184–185, 186
  requirements of learner, 180–181
  to supplement teacher, 181, 210
  types of, 181–182
  use of, 51, 208–210
  values of, 182–185, 209
  work sheets, 182
  writing, 181–183, 186
models, 134–136, 144
  commercial, 135
  construction of, 135
  cutaways, 144
  miniaturization, 134–135
  types of, 134–135
  use in teaching, 134–137, 144
  working mock-ups, 135, 144, 147, 149
motivational value, 135
opaque projectors, 137, 139
overhead projectors, 139–141
posters and pictures, 128, 131
slides, 137, 138–139
suggested aids for specific purposes, 143–144, 148
use of, 130–131, 148
vital aid to learning, 133–134
Vocational education, 3; *see also* Occupational education
Vocational guidance, 3; *see also* Guidance
  counseling function, 227–228
  lectures, 92
von Fellenburg, Philipp, 9

Woodworking
  instruction sheets, 190
  occupational analysis, 20–21
Work experiences, 40
Work manuals, 144